Eat, Pray, #FML

GABRIELLE STONE

Eat, Pray, #FML
Copyright © 2019 by Gabrielle Stone

This is a work of creative nonfiction. While all the stories in this book are true, some names and identifying details have been changed to protect the privacy of the people involved.

Cover Design Copyright © 2019 by Gabrielle Stone
All rights reserved.
Cover Design by Murphy Rae, www.murphyrae.net
Cover Photography by Johanna Siegmann
Back cover photography by Jonathan Stoddard -
Booked It Photography
Edited by Ink Deep Editing
Formatting by Elaine York, Allusion Graphics, LLC
www.allusiongraphics.com

ISBN-13: 978-1-7339637-0-1

Come play online!

@eatprayfml
@gabriellestone

www.EatPrayFML.com

Eat, Pray, #FML

Table Of Contents

To the ones who loved me,
broke me, lost me, and healed me.
You're all the reason I found myself;
and for that—I thank you.

Buckle Up...

It all started with a kiss. One seemingly harmless simple fucking kiss. More specifically, a kiss in the fourth picture of a photo booth that five of us were crammed into. Well...technically it had really all started six years earlier, with a different kiss that happened coincidentally to Prince's song "Kiss."

But for you to understand the monumental life path that this kiss sent me on, I'll have to take you back to the beginning. Well, not the actual beginning, cause who the fuck has time for that? But back a little bit, to the first love, the artificial marriage, the unfathomable deceit, the seemingly insurmountable heartache, and the mind-boggling revelation—all of which led me on the life-altering journey I so appropriately call *Eat. Pray. Fuck My Life.*

Fuck Your Past

(Just because it was your "story" doesn't mean it has to define you.)

Hello, world.

My name is Gabrielle. I'm an actress born and raised in Los Angeles, twenty-eight years old. I love to dance, and I curse like a fucking sailor. It's something I need to work on...but not in this book. Twenty-eight sounds so young, doesn't it? It is. Regardless, anyone who knows me will tell you I've lived a lot of damn life in these twenty-eight years. It's almost daunting to think about. Shit, if all this happened in my first quarter century, what the hell is coming in the next two?

My mother is an actress who has been in the industry for over forty-five years. She's also a five-time author and world-renowned healer. She too curses like a sailor...admittedly, not nearly as bad as me.

My father was also a well-known actor and director, and a former Hollywood playboy—until he met my mother. They were each other's great love. Movie fairy tale, soulmates, so-perfect-it-makes-you-puke kind of love. They got married and tried for six years to get pregnant with me. Yeah, I know...dramatic from the start. What can I say? I know how to make an entrance.

I had an incredible childhood. Even when my parents were struggling financially, I never knew it. My mom was superwoman. We celebrated everything. Any excuse to have a party. If one of my parents booked a job, the other wouldn't take one. If someone had to work out of town for more than a week, the whole family went to go visit. I got to go to some incredible places at such a young age—South Africa, New Zealand, Brazil. Life in my family was quite...blissful.

On October 20th, 1995, that all came to a screeching halt. It was one month before my seventh birthday. Mom was in New Zealand shooting a movie called *The Frighteners*, and my nanny Kristen and I had just returned home from a three-week visit there. I woke up and ran from my room past the kitchen where Kristen was cooking breakfast. I burst into my parents' room to jump into bed with Dad for some morning cartoon time. He was nowhere to be found. I walked around the bed to the large master bath. The door was open and there, lying on the floor, was my daddy. I raced into the kitchen.

"Kristen, Kristen! Daddy passed out." I remember seeing her face drop before she dashed toward the bedroom. I ran to my room and turned on the TV, thinking he had just fainted and would be fine. Shortly after, I heard the sirens.

I will never forget Kristen coming into my room, sitting on my bed, and saying, "Honey, Daddy didn't pass out. Daddy died."

He had suffered a fatal heart attack. My mom was on the first flight home. Over the next week, she got everything in order. We had a memorial, or as we called it, a celebration of life. I will forever be grateful to her director at the time, Peter Jackson, who told my mom to go home and take care of me and let him know when she could finish filming. When she went back only a week later, Kristen and I went too. I will never forget Michael J. Fox spending his breaks playing four square with me. He will never know what an impact he had on my life. The whole crew took such incredible care of us—and my mom finished the damn movie like a fucking champion. This was the first real example I'd gotten of how to handle the things that would erupt into my life. It was then, at the ripe age of six, I developed the belief I would carry throughout my life—when I love someone, they die.

* * * * *

Holy shit. I'd done it. I had graduated from high school. It was 2007, and I was finally eighteen and so freaking stoked on life. I couldn't wait for the summer! I had just moved into the condo where I'd be living while I went to college. *On my own.* The next phase. I had been with my boyfriend for just about three years—my high school sweetheart. He was the ultimate bad boy with just enough sweetness to be the first big puppy love of my life. His name was Jake Carter, and the year before he had moved down to San Diego for college. He had a pierced lip, tattoos, and an incredibly sexy BMW. At the end of July, I spent a long weekend with Jake, his brother, and his dad in San Diego before my first semester of college started. It was a perfect end to a perfect summer. Until it wasn't.

On August 3rd, 2007, my cell phone rang at 7 a.m. It was a girl I had been best friends with in early high school, but we'd had a bad falling out. Although we had kind of patched things up, we definitely weren't friends. Why the hell was she calling me at 7 a.m.?

"Hello?" I mumbled, half-asleep.

"Gaby?" she said in a manic and unsettled tone.

"Yeah?" I waited.

"Jake is dead."

I immediately hung up the phone. I didn't burst into tears. I didn't even register what she had said. I picked up the phone and dialed Jake's dad.

"Hello," he answered.

"Tell me it isn't true," I said. His tears on the other end were all the response I needed. There I sat in my new condo, ready for a new chapter at eighteen years old, when the painfully familiar wound was ripped wide open. When I love someone, they die.

Fuck
Mistakes

(If you learn from them, they were worth making.)

Okay! Sorry for that heavy little intro. Important and imperative to understanding all that is to follow, but *Oy vey*, am I right? Let's skip forward a few years, shall we? Those that know me are rolling their eyes and thinking, "Oh that's convenient, Gabrielle. Skip the crazy years of experimental debauchery and ridiculous, reckless decision-making." YEP. Don't mind if I fucking do. And to my exes who fall into this part of the timeline, you're welcome.

This next part is the real beginning of what my friends and I refer to as "the Netflix show that is Gabrielle's life." So buckle up—here's where the completely normal fairy tale turned into a big fucking mess.

* * * * *

I had met the man of my dreams, or so I thought. He had swept me off my feet and taken me to Maui where he proposed to me with a picture-perfect ring under a waterfall. If that isn't romance, I don't know what is. Daniel seemed to be the answer to everyone's prayers, even my friends and family. I had a record of dating men who needed to be "fixed," and Daniel was the epitome of a well-put-together man. He had a great job coaching sports, he was driven and determined, passionate about life, and knew what he wanted. My mother had even said after meeting him only twice, "That's the guy she's going to marry." And I did. On September 4th, 2015, we had an absolutely gorgeous wedding filled with everything any little girl could dream her wedding day would be. The wedding was followed by a beautiful honeymoon at the incredible St. Regis Bora Bora that finished with wine tasting through Napa. After that, we nested in a beautiful three-bedroom house we rented. Life was good.

Things began to change when Daniel and I had been together for five years and married for about a year and seven months. Our relationship had its issues as all do but, for the most part, things were good. He was working to build his sports empire while I was focused on my career. The biggest issue Daniel and I had was his huge lack of support around my career. He was definitely more than a little jealous and would have awful fits whenever I was on set, especially if I had any kissing scenes. This led to many fights, lots of tears, and hours of counseling. To be clear, I had always said I didn't know if I could ever date an actor. It's difficult to see your significant other be intimate with another person, even if it is acting. But Daniel had known from the beginning that this was my career. Even so, I jumped through hoops to do things that he said helped him feel better, things he said he needed, even when it affected my work. It was really difficult for me to have the joy stripped from something I was passionate about by the one person who was supposed to be cheering me on. Alas, every time I said "no more," I was met with tears, apologies, and empty promises that I would accept. I would forgive him because when things were good with us, they were really good, and we were happy. Or so I convinced myself.

From the beginning, Daniel showered me with things: presents, shopping sprees, amazing dinners, incredible trips. He truly made me feel like his princess, so much so that I lost a lot of perspective on the issues that were beginning to develop. Looking back on it now, it was never healthy and it was never done with the right intentions. His gifts and money became a Band-Aid for things and whenever he did something wrong, that was his answer for it.

I guess you could say our marriage unraveled like a sweater. One tiny thread and then a whole mess of string. We women notice tiny strings that dangle and when we do, you better believe we fucking pull that shit until we see what's at the end. Before you continue reading, let me state: I do not believe women should be crazy and dig through their men's personal things. I had *never*, in the five years Daniel and I had been together, felt the need to do so. I trusted him completely, to a fault as it turned out. But I will tell you to trust your intuition if you feel something is truly wrong. Unfortunately, this next chapter will demonstrate not only that I missed my calling as a private detective, but that sometimes women aren't fucking crazy—men can just be fucking dogs.

Fuck
Marriage

(If it is to the wrong person.)

Things had been...well, for lack of better words, things had been fucking awful. It was June 2017, and I had been pretty miserable since December. Miserable in my marriage, that is. Professionally, I had been receiving more attention than I ever had before, and I was on cloud nine. I had been feeling so much love and support and excitement from everyone in my life. Everyone except my husband. By this time, I had received huge awards at three big festivals. Daniel didn't attend any of them. He was always either out of town for work, which I understood, or couldn't get out of coaching because they had an important tournament coming up. He wouldn't even seem that excited when I would call to tell him I'd won. It was just...strange.

It was no secret between us that we had been unhappy; we just couldn't seem to figure out why. Let me clarify that: *I* couldn't seem to figure out why. We had started going to counseling, even doing healing sessions with my mom to try and get back on track. Looking back on it now, I don't see why he even bothered spending the time or money on it. I worked my ass off to try and make things better. I put effort and energy into adopting every exercise or suggestion our therapist gave us. Daniel, on the other hand, was doing nothing.

Daniel and I were very open with each other, often looking at each other's social media pages and scrolling through each other's pictures when we were bored. It was never done secretively. It was just something we would do occasionally if we were hanging around doing nothing. Lately, though, weird things had been making me feel strangely uneasy. One day he was in the shower with the door open, and we were talking while I sat on our bed watching videos on his Snapchat. The name "Laurel" popped up.

"Who's Laurel?" I asked casually.

"Uh...who?" he replied as he got out of the shower to dry off.

"Laurel...On Snapchat," I continued.

"Oh...um...I think it's this girl I went to college with," he replied, clearly acting as if he had to think of who it could be. I decided to let it go. Although I had never heard of her, he did go to school in another state way before we met. I didn't think too much of it at first. Then one day, the first little string appeared.

I was arriving home a few days after this incident, and my gut was screaming at me. Call it intuition, but I felt like I needed to go through his phone. However, I'm an adult and this was my husband, so I wasn't going to be sneaky. His assistant was over, working in the office, so I asked him if we could speak in the backyard.

"It's probably just my old insecurities coming up, but I would really appreciate it if I could look through your phone," I said honestly, feeling bad that I was even having to ask.

"Uh...Okay. I guess if you feel like you have to. Can I sit here while you do?" His tone was defensive, and his body immediately tensed up.

"If you need to, sure," I said. I began to look through his text messages and emails, not finding anything out of the ordinary. Then a Snapchat from Laurel came in. I opened it and it was a picture of her with foils in her hair at a hair salon. *Weird*, I thought.

"Why would she be sending you this?" I asked calmly.

"It's probably just one she's sending out to her entire friend list," he answered.

Okay, fine. I know that's part of the social app. Then another Snapchat came through, this time text.

Laurel: So how's the marriage going?

My stomach dropped. My hand involuntarily started shaking. I turned the screen to face my husband and gave him a look to let him know that I was waiting for an explanation. He immediately snatched the phone out of my hand.

"You need to respond saying, 'What do you mean?' right now, Daniel," I said, trying to keep my composure. He quickly typed out:

Daniel: Good, I'm sitting with her right now.

That was the guilty confirmation I had been hoping to not receive. Just then, there was a knock at the door. It was one of the other coaches and a player stopping by. Now I had a house with three people in it during a situation that needed to be addressed right away. I walked into our bedroom and shut the door. A few minutes later Daniel walked in.

"Why are you being crazy?" he said, trying to keep his voice down but with an accusatory and defensive tone, nonetheless.

"Are you kidding?" I scoffed. I reached my hand out. "Give me your phone." He rolled his eyes and handed me his phone. I opened his Snapchat and went to the message that had come in.

It said, "Laurel has unfriended you."

Awesome. Just keeps getting better.

"Wanna explain why she just happened to unfriend you so quickly after that?" I asked.

"I have no idea! We're literally just friends, and she helped me through my college breakup. We've never hooked up or anything. I don't know why she'd just unadd me," he defended.

"So why would you act like you had to think about who this person was when I asked you a few days ago, if you've clearly been talking to her?"

"I just didn't want to explain it. I don't know!" he said.

Really? Men. By this time, the tension in the conversation had escalated. I was furious and he was in full-on defense mode. I knew whoever was in the house was hearing us argue.

"Get everyone out of my house, right now," I said.

"Don't be ridiculous, I—"

"NOW!" I yelled. He left the bedroom and somehow convinced everyone that they needed to go. Once everyone was gone, he came into the kitchen to find me.

"This is insane. I will give you her number and you can call her. There is nothing going on. She's just a friend," he said.

"Great. Send me her number," I replied calmly.

"Fine."

"No. Right now." I waited. He screenshotted her number and texted it to me. "Why is she asking how our marriage is, Daniel?" I asked.

"Because I didn't have anyone to talk to about how tough things have been with us lately, and she helped me through my college break up!" he yelled. I laughed.

"And out of all your friends, your brother, your parents, my mother, all the sports moms you're so close with...you think a twenty-something blonde chick is the correct person to discuss your marriage problems with? To discuss *my* personal business with? Are you stupid?" My voice became more intense.

"I have to go coach, I'm going to be late," he said.

"I don't want you to come home tonight. I need some space," I responded.

"Okay. This just sucks. Now instead of working on our problems we're gonna be all focused on this bullshit," he said in frustration.

"You bet your fucking ass we will," I said. He grabbed his stuff and left for work. I called my mom in tears. First. Fucking. String.

Fuck Cheaters

(There's no explanation needed here.)

Daniel spent the next four days at his co-worker's house, or so he told me. We had very little communication during that time. The one person I did have communication with? *Laurel.* What? You really think I was going to decide if I wanted to leave my husband without talking to the woman in question? Please. Daniel and I had a therapy appointment scheduled on Monday and after filling our therapist in on our current situation, I decided to text Laurel.

> Me: Hi, Laurel, this is Gabrielle, Daniel's wife. I'm sorry to bother you, and I'm sure this is as awkward for you as it is for me. I would really appreciate if you have time for a quick phone call with me, just woman to woman, so I can assess what I'm going to do moving forward.

Of course, I received a text back, not a phone call, because who actually talks on the phone anymore? Eye roll. She responded, explaining to me that when Daniel had written her about sitting right next to me, she'd panicked and deleted him in fear of me thinking that something was going on between them. I asked her questions to see if she could verify things that Daniel had told me, and she willingly obliged. Some questions were completely made up just to see if her answers were good enough. It was weird. I genuinely believed her. And my gut didn't say not to.

That weekend I happened to have a life reading scheduled with a well-known medium/psychic, which my mom had gifted me for Christmas. Such appropriate timing, no? I wouldn't say I'm skeptical of these types of things, but I do hold people who claim to have these abilities to a very high standard.

She was a beautiful woman in her mid-thirties with a really sweet energy. I went in with an open mind, knowing how much bullshit was currently swarming around in my life. I also went in without my wedding ring and kept my hands tucked into my sweatshirt.

This woman proceeded to tell me everything that was currently happening in my life, without me saying a word about myself. She knew I was newly married, just under two years, and that there were recent fidelity questions arising in our marriage. She stated the woman in question didn't live close, out of the state most likely. She even knew that my husband was an athlete who needed to have his ego stroked. She told me the relationship was salvageable but only if I decided I wanted it to be, because while he wasn't necessarily lying, he had convinced himself that he wasn't doing anything wrong. The amount of seemingly correct information was astonishing.

Then she hit me with something really interesting. "I don't see that you and your husband have necessarily completed your souls' journey together. Souls come together to learn and grow from each other. However, I do see that there is another soulmate for you and that connection is much stronger."

Wow, I thought.

She told me she saw me having a daughter by the time I was thirty-three, and different things in the realm of my career.

"You have a lot of moving pieces right now. The next six to seven months are going to be really rocky for you. It will feel like a roller coaster and like a really stressful time in your life. Try and stay grounded and keep balanced because it's going to feel very draining." This stuck with me. If only I had known how damn right she was.

She also kept telling me that I needed to be writing.

"I need you writing. I really need you to be writing," she kept repeating throughout. I have to admit, I didn't feel any inspiration to be writing at the moment. I left the session feeling a ton of different emotions.

Later that day, Daniel and I met at therapy. After a lot of apologizing and discussing why it was such a poor decision to bring that specific person into such a private problem, we both agreed that we were going to work as hard as we could to get back to a good place. For me, it was deciding that I was going to stay. After being unhappy for some time, I couldn't say this situation didn't make me want to leave. It did. The four days he was out of the house I genuinely thought about leaving him. I didn't want to be with someone I couldn't trust, and I certainly wouldn't put up with lying and shady behavior. Leaving was a very real option for me. But in the end, I had made a commitment and I wanted to do everything I could to try and see it through. Maybe a part of me just wasn't ready to give up and disappoint so many people. For whatever reason, I decided to accept the apology and put everything I had into helping us find our way back. That decision, however, would be very short-lived.

* * * * *

Over the next three weeks, I worked. I mean I *really* worked. Everything our therapist suggested, I did. I flipped a switch and made sure I was doing everything in my power to get us back to a place of love and happiness. Daniel would soon be leaving for a two-week period to coach his girls' team at the Junior Olympics in Orlando, Florida, and was then going straight to Columbus, Ohio, to coach a boys' team I was close with. I had always gone to this particular tournament to cheer them all on, and this year Daniel was being very... *strange* about it all. He would say he wasn't sure if he could afford to get my plane ticket this year, even though he was in the midst of transitioning to a new company where he would be making twice as much money. It all just didn't seem right, but I figured it was just because of how off things had been with the two of us. The weekend before he was going to be leaving, the boys had a tournament in Anaheim.

Wanting to make sure I was there to be supportive, I drove down late Saturday night after one of my films had screened. Daniel had been there since Friday. When I arrived, we went to a fun dinner with a few of the parents and other coaches, then went back and had sex in our hotel room. I was finally feeling like maybe all the work I was doing was actually helping us get somewhere.

The night before Daniel was leaving for Orlando, I was doing laundry while he was packing. I went to put a bunch of folded socks in his sock drawer and pulled it open to find his phone sitting in it. *That's odd*, I thought.

"Why is your phone in your sock drawer?" I said as I picked it up. Without me pressing anything, a text message notification appeared. From someone named...*Laurel*. With a heart emoji in the contact name. Daniel swiftly came over to the dresser from the bathroom and snatched his phone out of my hand and stuffed it into his pocket.

"I'm not fucking doing this shit with you again!" He immediately went from zero to one hundred. He looked like a teenager who'd gotten called into the principal's office. His breathing quickened, he started to tremble, and I could literally see his heart pounding in his chest.

"Let me see your phone, Daniel," I said as calmly as ever while I placed my hand out.

"You're insane! What is wrong with you? I'm not doing this again!" He continued to panic.

"Let me see your phone, Daniel," I repeated, not losing my calm demeanor.

"This is ridiculous. I can't believe you're doing this." His panic turned to anger.

"Let me see your phone, Daniel." I smiled. He stormed into the bathroom and immediately locked the door. I stood frozen for the next forty-five seconds, just waiting. When he finally emerged, he walked straight over to me and handed me his phone.

"Look, my phone's fucked up. It won't even work right now, take it," he said handing over his phone. God, did he even realize how freaking ridiculous he sounded? Way to make yourself look even *more* guilty, dude. I turned his phone back on, and there was, of course, no message from Laurel nor a contact to be found.

"I'm not stupid, Daniel. I saw her name when I picked up the phone," I said.

"Look through my damn phone then!" He was full-on yelling at this point. He stepped toward me, which made me back up toward the wall between our bed and dresser. I wasn't physically scared, but my defense mechanism kicked in big time. I handle intense emotions in one of two ways: either I will yell louder and overpower the person I'm combating with, or I will cry. Most of the time, I don't want to go psycho and be that person. But the emotion has to get out somehow, so usually I choose to do that with tears. This was not that time.

"I can't believe you're doing this the night before I leave!" he screamed. "What, do you want my fucking phone records? I'll get them for you!" He raised his voice even louder. My husband should have known after five years that he would not outfight me. He will agree to that even now.

"DO YOU THINK I'M FUCKING STUPID, DANIEL? I'M NOT GOING TO LET YOU BACK ME UP AND CORNER ME JUST BE-CAUSE YOU GOT CAUGHT LOOKING LIKE A FUCKING IDIOT!" I screamed a full octave louder than his previous attack. He reached for me to try and hug me.

"DON'T FUCKING TOUCH ME!" I said as I quickly pulled away from him.

"I'm sorry, let's just talk about it. Come here, please," he said in a much calmer tone. Mine did not lower to match his.

"BACK THE FUCK AWAY FROM ME, RIGHT NOW!" I yelled at him. After a few moments of trying to initiate a hug and failing, he finally backed away, opening the cage he had cornered me into.

"I'm sorry. I'm leaving tomorrow, and I don't want our last night to be like this. What do you want? I'll get you my phone records. Please." It was so interesting how he went from anger and defensive-ness to pleading. It was like two different people were in my house, and they had swapped out mid-conversation.

"I'm keeping your phone tonight," I said blatantly.

"Okay. Fine. Whatever you want to do," he replied.

"Good," I said as I walked past him to finish the laundry. "You'll also give me all your social media passwords before you leave this house," I added.

"Okay. Done," he said. What a big mistake that would be. He continued to pack and would randomly say things, as if everything was suddenly okay. I would either not respond or give a very short, very not-okay answer. Then, of course, a Snapchat came through on his phone.

I opened it. It was from one of the female coaches that worked for him named Heather. It was a mirror photo of her slightly heavy figure in her underwear and a sweatshirt being pulled halfway up to show her stomach. Written on the message was something sports related that mentioned partying in Orlando. Oh, it just keeps getting better, doesn't it?

"Wanna explain this?" I asked with a sarcastic curiosity as I flipped his phone toward him to replay the Snap. He peered in as if he was very focused on reading the message. He read it under his breath to himself.

"Okay...so?" he asked. That response had to be for lack of having time to come up with an actual excuse. So? So, this random chick who works with you is sending a married man a half-naked and—no offense—poorly executed photo at 11:30 p.m.? Well, darling, that isn't a good enough answer for your wife.

I looked over at him with angry tears in my eyes and said, "Why can't you just tell me what is going on? Whatever it is, we can work through it. You must be exhausted by this. What is going on?" His eyes welled up with tears.

"You won't freak out?" he asked. What a stupid question.

"No," I said. What a stupid answer.

"She just flirts with me all the time and likes to party, so she wants to go out when we're in Florida, but that's it. It's nothing like that. She knows I'm married, obviously, and, I mean, look at her, come on," he said with a panic. I sat there for a moment, taking this all in. Surprisingly, I didn't feel like I wanted to smack him across the face or even yell. I felt sad. Because part of me knew he was lying, and I felt bad that he had the audacity to make a comment about her being ugly when he was so clearly having some type of interaction with her. Guys can be so goddamned shallow.

By the end of this, I was so done. I didn't even want him in our room, much less our bed. He was supposed to leave for the airport at 3 a.m., which was in a few hours. I could handle a few hours. He climbed into bed and clung onto me like I was the last life raft on the *Titanic.* I lay there, as stiff as Jack was when Rose let him sink, and waited for his alarm to go off. It seemed like forever. When his alarm finally went off, he got up and came over to kiss me goodbye.

"Text me your passwords for Snap and Instagram. Or don't come home," I said softly.

"I'll do it right when I get in the car. I love you," he said, and I held my breath until I heard the front door shut. I didn't sleep the rest of the night. Second. Fucking. String.

* * * * *

It was Wednesday, June 28th. The night before, I had attended an industry party with a good friend of mine. I had confided in him that I was 95 percent sure I was going to leave Daniel after all the things that had gone down. I had also said, "I don't think he's done anything physically. I don't think he has the balls to." Well...I had vastly misjudged the size of his balls. And that lingering 5 percent? It was about to get blown the fuck out.

I was at home in our office, and Daniel had left his email signed in and opened on his giant iMac. I still, to this day, do not know his email password. I didn't even go digging at first. I was in the office getting things out of the closet when I heard a ding come from the computer. An email had come in. Curious, I looked at the computer to see an Uber receipt. The receipt showed that Daniel had gone from where he was coaching in Florida all the way to Miami. Odd. Why would he take an hour-long Uber out to Miami? No...something was not right.

That was the only thing I needed. I immediately felt it in my gut. I began to look through his emails. Nothing. Then I went to the deleted ones...and there it was. A hotel receipt from the Four Seasons for $898.49. The Four Seasons that we had been to so many times together. It was no more than two miles from our house. A water-fall view room, drinks at the bar, dinner, and a couple's massage. On April 19th, 2017. The reservation name read "Andrew Mader." Interesting. But who the hell was he there with? Well...this is where I tell you how I missed my calling as a private detective.

I picked up the phone and called the Four Seasons Spa.

"Hi, my husband and I came in for a couple's massage a while back, and I'm trying to do our taxes. He's in the industry so we usually book under a fake name, but I was hoping you could tell me which names we used when we were there?" I said in an overly cheery voice while shaking on the inside.

"Of course! Let me pull up the reservation..." Really? It's too easy. To any cheating men that may be reading this or any employees of the Four Seasons—get your shit together.

"Yes, I have it right here...Andrew Mader and Laurel Dorando."

"Awesome, thank you!" Click. Boom. At first, I immediately thought, *Motherfucker. This whole time it was Laurel.* Then I paused. She lives out of state where he went to college. This made no sense whatsoever. Plus, that wasn't Laurel's last name.

See, guys, the thing about social media is that it has single-handedly made every human on it ridiculously accessible. I typed in the name on Instagram. It was *not* the Laurel from Snapchat. A very blonde, very not clothed, and very young girl popped up on my screen. I began to look at her recent photos. What do you know? She just so happened to be in Miami.

It didn't stop there. The email digging located numerous hotel room receipts, dinners, shopping sprees, and massage treatments. Even replicas of dates that Daniel had taken me on. Dinner at Fogo De Chao and a night at the Beverly Hills Hotel. A $500.00 shopping spree at Naimie's, a professional makeup store. But the worst part? Looking at the dates of all of the receipts. The night I was winning my best actress award and Daniel just couldn't take work off? He was boning her in a hotel room in Calabasas that our wedding guests stayed at. The Tuesday night I went to see my friend in a show at the Pantages with my mom? He was getting a couple's massage at the Four Seasons before he came home and slept with me. The night he said he had to go to Anaheim to handle sports tournament stuff, even though I was at home sick with an awful stomachache? He was spending the night with her, having dinner and drinks. Don't worry, he still FaceTimed me that night to say goodnight. The Friday before the big Anaheim tournament (remember, the one I drove down to on Saturday to support them at? Where we went to dinner with all the parents and then went back and had sex in the hotel room?) Ya...he was at a hotel having sex with her in Beverly Hills. And trust me when I say, Daniel has never been one for condoms. The blatant evidence dated back to March. Which meant it had been going on as early as January/February, if not earlier. Six months. It had been happening for *six months*. The gym class he had been going to multiple times a week? It wasn't Orange Theory Fitness like he told me. It was Barry's Bootcamp where Laurel worked. It was blow after blow. And just like that, the 5 percent was incinerated. I was getting a divorce. However, not before I made sure I had all the proof in the world. And, oh, did I get everything. And I mean *everything*.

After finding her on all social media platforms and a very amateur modeling profile site, I learned that Laurel was at the ripe age of nineteen. One of my best friends, Jess, came over to stay with me for the rest of the time that Daniel would be out of town. We made a fake Snapchat account, added Laurel, and began watching the next forty-eight hours of their trip. She and an equally trashy blonde friend were gallivanting around Miami with my husband. A lavish hotel, dinner at Nobu, shots and drinks, even though she was clearly underage. She was very careful to keep Daniel's face out of any of her snaps. Not careful enough, however—at their sushi dinner we could hear him talking in the background. She snapped a picture of his arm with his distinctive white watch. Of course, by this time we were following her friend as well and watching all of her snaps. It was only a matter of time. Then, boom. Daniel's face popped up in the corner of one of her friend's videos. Meanwhile, every Uber he took was coming in on his email so I knew everywhere he was going. Even his credit card receipts were coming in. At this point it was literally too easy.

But that wasn't all I found. There were subscriptions to secret Snapchat porn accounts where you paid $30.00 a month to get nude photos and videos from random girls. The list went on.

My mom and I began the process of finding a lawyer. It was probably the worst week and a half of my life. I had debilitating anxiety from not being able to tell anyone other than my mom and a few girlfriends what was going on. I was waiting, not able to say anything in fear Daniel would catch wind that I knew. I was so ready for him to come home so I could hand him papers and be done. The waiting while watching all of this unfold right in front of me was insane and surreal. And not one damn person saw it coming.

When Daniel flew to Ohio I breathed a sigh of relief. At least I knew he was with all the boys and families I knew, and I didn't have to check social media and emails 24/7. Or so I thought. After I signed with a lawyer, I began to pack all the things I would be taking with me from our home. It was now just a waiting game.

He had stupidly left his car parked at my mother's house before he Ubered to the airport. I, of course, had a spare key. After all I had found, I figured I might as well look in the car, right? There, sitting in his back seat, was an iPhone box. I picked it up and opened it. Inside was a number on a little yellow Post-it. Interesting. I went inside and called it from a blocked number. Someone answered and there was silence on the other end for a good fifteen seconds before they hung up. But I knew very well who it was. To be sure, I went to the computer and typed the phone number into Google. Anyone want to take a guess what name popped up? Andrew Mader. The same name that was on the hotel receipts. It all started to make sense. Remember the initial fight before he left for his trip? When I was putting socks away and found his phone with a text from Laurel? Well...that was his *second* phone. The second phone he took into the bathroom where he swapped it with his original phone that he brought back out and handed to me. Well played, you fucking sociopath. Well played.

I had all the evidence I needed and more. I would later find out through the grapevine (all his "friends" who were so quick to call and tell me things) that his family thought my mother and I had hired a private investigator to uncover all the information about the affair. No, sweetheart, the woman you married is just *actually* fucking smart. What did I say? I missed my calling as a private detective. He still to this day has no idea how much proof I have of his sloppy mess.

The next few days, I knew the boys were playing in the big tournament. After a few days of relaxing on the social media stalking, for whatever reason, I logged into the fake Snapchat account and looked at Laurel's story. Ohio? *Ohio*. She was in fucking Ohio. That was the last straw. He had taken her to Ohio, where his father was, where all the kids I had been so close to were playing, where all the parents who went to our wedding were—the place I had been with that group for the past four years. Cherry on the cake? They flew home first class together. She took a picture of just their hands holding, of course, because she couldn't show his face...just yet.

Daniel arrived home on July 4th. He hung out with Laurel and her friends in Calabasas where she lived with her parents. We had met with my lawyer, the papers were filed, and now it was just a matter of getting him served.

We planned to have the process server come to my mom's house and, when Daniel came to get his car, we would hand him the divorce papers. Great. Still wrestling with this awful anxiety and intense betrayal and rage after finding out he'd brought her to Ohio, I went to my girlfriend's house to try and have some sort of Fourth of July. Admittedly, a small dose of prescribed Xanax had become necessary for me in the morning and at night. It was really the only way I could make it through my days while I was holding on to all of this. After all, my life had literally changed overnight. The rug had been pulled out from under me, and I had fallen *flat* on my fucking ass. Luckily, I have enough padding down there. That night I came home to my mom's and she gave me an Ambien for a good night's sleep. Even with that, I slept one hour that night.

At 5:30 a.m. I finally gave up on trying to fall asleep and went to the kitchen to make some tea. Daniel's car was gone. He had come in the middle of the night to pick it up. All the while he still hadn't even let me, his wife, know that he was back in town. Now how were we going to serve him the papers? Shit.

Fortunately, Daniel made it quite easy for me. A few hours later that day he texted me and asked if I would be home later on so we could *chat*.

Um, no, motherfucker, you've been home for three days, staying at your girlfriend's parents' house.

Still, I wanted to make sure everything appeared normal. My only goal at this point was handing him the damn divorce papers.

> Me: Glad you're home...I have an event tonight, but I could do like 3ish?

I got a response confirming. That was it. It was happening. The anxiety I felt that day was literally indescribable. So many variables I couldn't control: when Daniel would actually show up, if the process server would be there...it was unreal. I stood in the home that we had only been in eight months. I looked at the bare walls where our wedding pictures had hung, thinking about all the memories we had created. It was all about to be done. And I was ready for that. I couldn't just stand around. I needed to do something...anything. So I sat down and wrote the following:

> An open letter to the nineteen-year-old Instagram model who slept with my husband.
>
> As I looked around at what was our home—our wedding pictures hanging on the walls, memories that we had created over the past five years—I realized that I had been living with a stranger. The man I had married was not the man I was living with. Far from it. For months, my husband had been cheating on me. Never in a million years did I think the person who vowed to keep my heart safe until death do us part would so carelessly and blatantly disrespect our marriage, my body, or my trust. The intricate web of lies and deceit that were weaved, the sociopath that so many of us loved and thought we knew. He seamlessly

transitioned from a marriage to a relationship without missing a beat.

To my soon-to-be ex-husband I want to say this: Thank you. Thank you for not waiting until we had children. Thank you for being so careless that I was able to find everything. Thank you for showing me your true character after five years and not ten. Thank you for making your mother feel shame and mine feel pride. Thank you for giving me the ability to choose myself. To know that I am enough. And that you did not deserve me. Thank you for showing me how strong I am. Because I will come out the other end of this so much stronger than before.

To the nineteen-year-old who knew he was married: I get it. He showered you with the same exact gifts, spa days, restaurants, and hotels he showered me with. Lack of originality, to say the least. I hope that one day when I have a daughter, she knows the difference between right and wrong. I will raise her to treat people with respect, and to respect herself and her body. I'm so sorry no one was capable of giving you that. But mostly, I want to say I forgive you. I forgive you for falling for the lies of the person I fell for. I forgive you for knowing that he was married. And I hope that, one day, you will realize that you don't need to exploit yourself on the internet to earn love. Just as I hope he realizes he doesn't need to buy people's love. In the end, all that really matters is knowing who you are and being true to yourself. You've both shown me that I am strong, resilient, and true. I hope you can both learn to have those qualities one day.

To my friends, family, and mother: I do not know what I would do without my incredible support system.

Thank you for being there for me through one of the most shocking and devastating times of my life. Daniel, thank you for setting me free so that I can one day find a person who sees how wonderful I am and will love me fearlessly and fully in a way you were never capable of. You, in the darkest way, gave me the best gift of my life: A second chance to find someone who truly values me and makes me feel like I am the only woman in the world... I can say without a doubt, this was the tragic end to an incredible new beginning.

* * * * *

At 2:30 p.m. his BMW pulled into the driveway. Luckily, I had told the process server to be there early in case he showed up before 3 p.m. Daniel stepped out of the car and opened the mailbox. I watched from the guest room window as the process server ran up to him and handed him the papers.

"Are you Daniel?" he asked him.

"Uh, yeah," he replied.

"Here you go," the process server said as he handed him the papers and began to walk away. Daniel stared down at the papers.

"What's your name? Who are you?" he called out after him.

"Doesn't matter, bro." And he was off to his car. Just then, I walked out the front door.

"I know everything. But if you still want to come in and talk, that's fine," I said.

"Yeah, of course I do," Daniel responded. Little did he know I had just viewed a Snap of him and Laurel at Barry's Bootcamp. He was still in the same workout outfit.

"Just so you know, there are four different people that know I'm here right now and are waiting for me to call when I leave," I said calmly.

"Jesus, I'm not a psychopath," he responded. I laughed as I headed into the house and he followed behind me.

"Leave the door open," I said. He did so. I sat on the couch and he sat across from me on the love seat. The next fifteen minutes were filled with more bullshit and more lies, and none of it surprised me in the least. He told me he did love me and how he hoped I would have an amazing life and accomplish all my dreams. He told me that he had never wanted this to happen and how sorry he was that we couldn't make it work, that we were just too young. Never once did he admit to or mention Laurel.

"Nice shorts," I said, smiling and nodding toward the Barry's Bootcamp logo. He quickly continued talking.

"So, do you just want to, like...figure out what you want to take, and we can sort through everything?" he said. Um, no sweetheart, this isn't the end of a playdate, it's the end of a marriage. A legally binding marriage. For being a business major, he sure was really naive.

"You can talk to my lawyer about that," I responded. "Damn."

"What?" he asked.

"I'm a great actress. But you're a really good liar," I said.

"I don't think so," he said. Wow, naive and stupid.

"You know what's so sad? If you would have just come to me and said, 'We can't make this work and I want a divorce,' I would have said, 'Okay, let's be friends, I don't want anything from you.'" And I meant it. But he and I both knew now that was not the case.

"I don't want to make this any harder on you..." he said. I laughed. Now looking back on it, he knew that the only one who would be dealing with hard karma would be himself. "Just please, Gabrielle, whatever you do, don't come after my new sports deal. It's the way I give back to the kids, and it's my passion." I literally swallowed the bile coming up my throat.

"Then say it," I said.

"Say what?" he asked.

"Say it," I repeated.

"Say *what*?"

"Say it." Again, I was calm.

"What, that I've been in another relationship?" he finally said. And that was all he would say about it, having no idea the amount I knew. I smiled, stood up, and grabbed my keys.

"Goodbye," I said. I walked out the front door.

Driving away from our home that day, I felt a huge weight lift off my shoulders. I felt like I could finally breathe again, because I knew I hadn't just dodged a bullet—I had dodged an army of fucking snipers. As I drove to my mother's house, I thought about what a big blessing in disguise this really was. I decided that I, the girl who was *never* single, was going to say *fuck men* and be by her damn self for once. Best-laid plans, Gabrielle, best-laid plans...

Fuck
Love

(It will break your heart...do it anyway.)

Well, I guess it's about that time—time to introduce you to the other main character of this ridiculous adventure. The person who came into my life and shook things the fuck up. There I was, two weeks fresh off handing Daniel divorce papers, saying fuck all men, I am focusing on myself and being single for at least a year...Enter Javier.

Technically, he didn't enter. Javier and I had met six years earlier, literally a month and a half before Daniel and I met. He was seven years older than me, Latin from Argentina, could speak five languages fluently, danced like nobody's business, and, like me, was an actor. We had gone on two dates that involved a lot of dancing and a lot of making out. On our first date, we were in the middle of a circle on the dance floor (literally like out of one of the *Step Up* movies) dancing to Prince. Of course, being mister Rico Suave, he danced over to me and kissed me right on the lyric "kiss." There was definitely passion and chemistry there, but he was fresh off a bad breakup and I was a baby at the time, so it was never anything more than casual. *Casual.* Oh, how I fucking hate that word. Any of my girlfriends will tell you, "Gabrielle can't do casual." To be fair, I'm aware that I'm really bad at it. However, this ONE time, six years ago, with Javier, I had successfully done casual. So naturally, when I saw his Instagram pop up on my popular page, I thought...following him can't hurt, right?

Literally a few minutes after I hit the follow button, I received a message from him.

> Javier: Gabrielle. Where the hell have you been for the last six years?

Dude. You have no idea. We chatted about bullshit for a little bit, and he asked if I wanted to go dancing that weekend. I thought about it...for like two seconds. Yes, I want to go dancing. Yes, I want to go casually make out with this sexy Latin man while dancing. Because I'm single and focusing on myself and this is the one person I can be casual with.

We decided to go to the beach that week to catch up on the past six years since a club isn't the best place to do so. He pulled up on his motorcycle looking older but just as sexy as I remembered. We spent the day on the beach drinking mate (an Argentinian tea), laughing, and catching up on life. I, of course, told him the insane story of Daniel. He looked dumbfounded when I told him about the affair.

"What an absolute idiot," he said. "And that's mental kidnapping. I mean a nineteen-year-old? Jesus."

After I was done giving him the details on my life, he told me about what had been going on with him. He had just come back from shooting in Canada for six months and was heading off to Argentina to visit family in a week. *PERFECT,* I thought. It is literally impossible to not be casual with this human.

Then he opened up to me about the event that had really changed his life. A little over a year before, his younger brother had taken his own life after struggling with depression for years. His name was Christopher. This had affected Javier profoundly, and you could see the pain on his face when he spoke about it. He had so much love for Chris and it was so obvious what a connection they must have had. It was heartbreaking. He told me it had been difficult for a long time but, after his time in Canada, he felt like he had come a long way toward making peace with it all.

After getting some sun, we headed up to the pier to grab lunch. We continued to talk and laugh while we ate. Everything was just really…easy. He walked me to my car and we hugged goodbye. It was a strangely long hug that lingered a little more than I was expecting.

"I'll see you on Friday," he said and smiled.

"Sounds good," I replied. And so I went home, not thinking too terribly much about everything. It was pretty perfect…he was leaving for three weeks in Argentina, and we had been able to be casual all those years before. Fat fucking chance, Gabrielle.

* * * * *

Friday night came and we had made plans to meet a few of his friends at a salsa club. I pulled up to where his truck was parked and hopped out of my car.

His jaw dropped. "Oh my God," he said, "you look absolutely gorgeous." We got into his truck and there was this strange electricity between us that we were both trying to ignore. Once we got to the club, we danced a little and laughed while we waited for his friends to get there. Luckily, I grew up as a dancer and know how to dance, because it was Latin night, and I was most definitely the only white girl in the building. Something about dancing with the right person makes things get really intense really fast. There's a different type of sensual connection you get from dance that you can't get from having a conversation over dinner. It was really apparent between the two of us.

Once his friends came, we all headed over to the main dance floor. I chatted with his friend Manny, who was really sweet. All of a sudden, I felt Javier squeeze my hand. I looked at his face and he looked like he was stuck between panic and anger.

"What's wrong?" I immediately asked.

"That guy over there…" He pointed out someone across the bar.

"What about him?" I asked.

"He was one of my best friends. When my brother died, I didn't hear from him at all. He just disappeared. I have a lot of anger toward him." I could literally feel him shaking as he spoke. I gently put my hands on each side of his face and pulled his gaze into mine.

"Hey. You're fine. You're with me," I said. He looked at me like suddenly all the fear and anger that was building up just...went away. Looking back now, it was kind of a strange thing for me to have said on what was more or less our first date. Something about Javier's energy just made me want to take care of him, especially in that moment. I think that was the moment where he realized that whatever was happening with me was...different.

After dancing for a while, we all decided to cram into the club's photobooth to take a picture. It was seriously squished in there but we somehow managed to fit all five of us in there. The countdown went and we snapped funny photos, changing positions each time. On the last one, Javier grabbed my face and kissed me. And *that*, my friends, was the beginning of the downfall of casual.

A half hour, some more dancing, and a lot of making out later, he looked at me.

"What are you doing August 19th?" he asked.

"Um...I don't know, why?" I replied.

"I want you to come to my friend's wedding with me." Well, that went from casual to 100 real fucking quick. I don't know if it was the kissing or if we just stopped fighting what had been happening since the beach, but it was as if every intense emotion just started flooding out of both of us. I looked at him and smiled. I could see a bunch of thoughts rushing through his head as I stood there with his arms around me.

"What?" I asked.

"Shit," he said, "I fucking like you." I laughed. "Like I'm gonna date you."

"Yeah, we're fucked aren't we," I responded.

"Yeah, we are," he agreed, and then he kissed me.

When the night was over, we rode back to where my car was.

"I want to spend the night with you," he said.

"I do too." And I did. "If we spend the night together, we are not having sex," I stated. I don't know why I felt the need to say this. Maybe it was because I knew how we'd been dancing, and I didn't trust myself to spend the night with him and not let that happen. He laughed.

"I promise," he said. "That's not even why I want to stay with you. I just don't want to leave you." It was such an accurate statement. I didn't want to leave him either. Even if we were just talking or lying together, something about being with him felt really right. We laughed as we discussed the fact that both of us were currently staying at our parents' houses. Obviously, I had just moved home after filing for divorce, and he was only in town for a few weeks between shooting in Canada and heading to Argentina. After making the decision to go to a hotel, at twenty-eight and thirty-five years old, we both texted our moms to tell them we wouldn't be home.

That night, we talked until the sun came up. I had never felt so comfortable with someone so fast. At one point, he turned to me and said, "I really feel like my brother and your dad brought us together." My heart melted. As I lay on his chest with his arm around me, we talked about a million things, laughing about how I had been banking on him being my casual option.

"You have me rethinking everything right now," he said. "I have a month in Italy booked in September and now I don't know…"

"I would never tell you to not go travel," I said.

"No, I know. I'm saying I want you to come with me," he replied. I laughed because the whole situation was so ridiculous. There I was, lying in bed in a random hotel room with a guy I met six years ago, who was supposed to be a fun casual night out, discussing how intensely we felt about each other and whether I should run off to Italy with him for a month. Oh, my life. After two hours of sleep, we took a horrendous but hysterical picture in the bathroom mirror to remember this crazy first night. We made plans to get dinner Sunday night and said our goodbyes, and I headed home, trying to wrap my head around what the hell had just happened.

Before I had even made it home, we were texting back and forth. He sent me the god-awful picture we took in the hotel room.

Me: Such a perfect representation of this morning.

Javier: You beautiful gorgeous woman. Thanks for fucking up both our lives!

Me: I still maintain that this was all put into motion by youuuu. But either way, you're welcome.

Javier: I'd rather blame your pops and my brother. That way we don't have to take any responsibility.

Me: Fair enough…I'm sure it's a party up there with those two.

I was slightly hesitant about the possibility that all these insane feelings were actually…happening. So I made a conscious effort not to be the one saying crazy things right away or verbalizing all these feelings just yet. However, Javier was the opposite. He sent the other photo we had taken earlier that morning.

Me: That one's even better.

Javier: I love this one.
Javier: Get used to this face.

Me: Ya, I'm missing it already.

Javier: Fuck! I miss you too. Damn, Gab! We are for sure screwed.

Me: Eventually we'll move past the denial phase.

We talked all day and all night, into the bachelor party he was at, where he FaceTimed me and had me wave to all his friends.

Javier: I feel like a kid flirting in middle school, and it's the best I've felt in a long long time.

Me: What can I say, it's the youngster in me.

Javier: I actually miss you a lot!! This is nuts.

Me: I miss you too. And it's only been like…5 hours lol.

Javier: I know, boo. I've been telling my friends about you. I can't shut up.

Me: Oh I would loooove to be a fly on the wall…they're probably all like, wait, what? Lol.

Javier: They are happy for me. They can tell I'm elated. I'm showing them your pictures too haha. Sorry, boo!

Me: Stopppp! Of me looking like a dead lion this morning?!

My hair was exceptionally untamed after dancing and our night in the hotel room.

Javier: You are beyond stunning. You're fucking gorgeous! Sexy as hell!

Me: That is so far from sexy. You're blinded by whatever we're both experiencing lol.

Javier: Hahaha not at all! I'm seeing more clearly than I ever have.
Javier: I'm so glad you met my friends last night. They loved you.

Me: Aww. Well I had a blast with them…I hope they weren't thrown off by the ridiculous story that is my life right now.

Javier: Our group has stories that will blow your mind. We accept everyone for who they are, and we look at the funny and positive in everything.

Me: I know, it's just a lot. I'm aware how ridiculous the whole timeline and situation itself is…I say as I stomp my feet and say, "I'm gonna be by myself for a year."

Javier: Hahaha. I always believed that one does what makes them feel good and if I feel like talking to you every day and seeing you, I'm gonna do it. There's no rules in love. It happens when you least expect it, clearly.

And there it was, in an actual text message. He had just flat out mentioned what I had been fighting for the last twenty-four hours. Was this even possible? I mean I had been *married* and had never once felt what I was experiencing now. It was...crazy. We would stop talking for a half hour or so while he hung with all the guys at the bachelor party, but it wouldn't be long before I'd hear my phone go off, which would immediately bring a smile to my face.

Javier: I know I talk a lot but being with you last night and waking up next to you this morning has been one of the best moments I've ever experienced. I've never felt so comfortable with someone before, I swear.

Me: Honestly, last night was something I've never experienced before either. And really special.

Javier: It really was, and I'm so so so so excited for what's coming next for us.

Me: This is crazy. Where did you even come from lol.

Javier: I ask you the same.

Me: That answer would be learning lots of life lessons teaching me exactly what I do and don't want.

Javier: And that's exactly how I feel. I've never felt this secure and fearless about being with someone. Power couple in the making baby!!!!

Me: In the last 24 hours…absolutely insane. My mom is gonna fall over lol.

Javier: Hahaha, poor mom! Mine already asked me when she gets to meet you.

Me: Stopppp.
Me: "Son, when do I get to meet the white girl you stayed in a hotel with night one?" LOL.

Javier: Noooo, I told her the real story. The whole truth and how it made us feel.

Okay, if we weren't in serious territory before, now we most definitely were. It was so mind-blowing to me that I was even having all these feelings, but the fact that the person on the other end was vocalizing it all in such a fearless way made it feel very intense. Whatever we were in…was real. Again, casual to 100 real fucking fast, am I right?

The way we talked was already like we had skipped the new-relationship wave and had been together for weeks. It was crazy, but amazing. Later that night, after I went to dinner, he texted me a photo with "Gabrielle Stone" under it.

Javier: Hahahaha, this was for my sister!!! She's demanding pictures.
Javier: Sorry, boo hahaha.
Javier: You just caught me talking about you to my sister. She's dying to meet you.

Me: Oh my God, babe, I look so ridiculous in that picture.

Javier: Oh, I'm sure she's already stalking your Instagram.

Me: HAHAHAHAHA.

Here I was thinking that this was the safe casual bet because he was leaving in a few days for three weeks. But the intense emotions from the first twenty-four hours would only continue over the next three days.

Sunday night came and we met to get dinner. We were smitten with each other and definitely the annoying couple who couldn't keep their hands off one another. In the middle of eating, he brought up Italy again.

"So, I'm serious. I want you to come to Italy with me." He was going to visit a group of friends in Sicily that had been begging him to come for a long time, and he was planning on traveling around before since he had never been to Europe. "I've been putting off doing Europe for so long because I've always wanted to do it with a woman but never had the right person to go with." I laughed but began to seriously think about the proposition. Europe had been on my dream list for quite some time and after the divorce, I had even said I was going to go next summer.

"When do you leave?" I asked.

"September 4th," he responded.

"You're fucking kidding me," I said. September 4th would have been my two-year wedding anniversary. A sign from the universe? Possibly. "When are you coming back?" I continued.

"October 4th," he said. October 4th is my dad's birthday. Jesus Christ. OKAY UNIVERSE, I hear you. He was really insistent on wanting me to go, and it was all very romantic and appealing.

"Let me check what it would cost and see," I said.

"I'll pay for it. It'll be an early birthday present," he said.

"Absolutely not," I quickly responded. "I mean, that's very sweet, but no. Let me see where I'm at and figure it out." If anything had stuck with me from my divorce, it wasn't to keep your heart guarded or take things slow—it was that I did not want people paying for things. Daniel had definitely left a mark on me as far as how I viewed people and money. Never again did I want to be dependent on a man, nor distracted from issues by shiny gifts or luxurious getaways. I wanted to take care of myself. And on that note, I paid for dinner.

After dinner, we headed to a little café for dessert. We talked about past relationships and why they hadn't worked, typical stuff like that.

"I've never been in love," he told me. It was pretty mind-boggling to me that a thirty-five-year-old who has had plenty of relationships had never been in love.

"How is that possible?" I asked, genuinely curious.

"I don't know. I want to be a husband and a father, so the second I don't see that possibility with someone, I don't want to be with them anymore." Fair answer. "So I sent that picture of us from yesterday morning to my family in Argentina and they're all freaking out." He laughed.

"Javier!" I tried to seem upset as I giggled. He pulled out his phone and showed me the message to a rather large group chat of the photo we had taken in the hotel bathroom with the text "Meet my lady, Gabrielle." It was insane how sure he was of me. Talking to his mother about me, sending this to his family...it was like he had never been more sure of anything before. It was so incredible to feel that type of confidence from a man.

That night after I said goodbye and drove home, I knew that whatever this was that I had found myself in, it was going to be something big. Just when I got home...

Javier: Sleep well, beautiful...Thanks for tonight. Your company is priceless. See you tomorrow.

We decided to go camping the next day, and I was excited to spend a romantic night on the beach. Javier was like Bear Grylls from *Man vs. Wild*. When he camps, he takes a hammock and a spear gun to hunt and just walks into the wilderness. Luckily, his mother had made sure to tell him that if he wanted to keep me around, he needed to at least bring wet wipes and silverware.

When I pulled up to the campsite, he had already set everything up—rocks lined up as a walkway that led to a tent with a flower outside, a full spread of blankets with pillows, chairs, and snacks, and a little speaker for music. I was pretty impressed and it was adorable how excited he was. We took photos on his Polaroid camera and some on our phones. Those pictures are still some of the most genuinely happy photos I think I've ever taken. I sent one to my mom and he sent them to his family. We took a long walk on the beach and talked about a variety of things. After all, we were still technically getting to know each other.

"I want to post a picture of you. I want everyone to know I'm taken," he said. What?! I thought...*that is the opposite of what most men want to do right away on social media.* Here was this man who was so ready to scream about me from the rooftops. It was refreshing and romantic, and it made me feel like the center of his universe. I was blown away, but most of all I was absolutely smitten. We both knew I couldn't be open on social media just yet with all the things up in the air around the divorce, but he had managed to capture a picture of me running on the beach where you couldn't quite see my face.

He posted it with the following caption: "And suddenly...out of nowhere...unexpectedly...you show up and turn my life upside down...in the best way possible." What an accurate fucking statement that was.

We opened a bottle of wine, and he insisted I sit down as he made dinner. As I watched him build a fire from scratch and cook, all I could think about was that Daniel would have called Uber Eats five minutes into being here. It was so sexy that a man was able to do all of this. After we had dinner, he FaceTimed his mom for me to say hi. I could already tell what an incredible energy she had just from looking at her through the phone. Once the sun set, we sat in the chairs by the fire and talked.

"What are the moments that impacted your life the most?" I asked. He was so open with me. We talked a lot about his work, his family, and mostly his brother, Chris. At one point, I saw tears starting to come to his eyes. I grabbed his hand and he looked over at me.

"It's okay. I got you," I said to him. And I did. We were so connected so fast for whatever reason. I felt this instant protectiveness toward him, like I didn't want to let anything hurt him. It was indescribable what was happening.

We had such deep conversations that night that really allowed us to see each other's souls. There were no façades or masks or anything but our authentic selves being shown to each other. If only we humans could do that with everyone, what a different world we would live in, huh?

The next morning when we woke up on the beach, I rolled over and looked at him still sleeping next to me. I just knew. I was in love with this man. It was a particularly big revelation for me because I had never felt like this for my husband—or really for anyone. Sure, I had *loved* people in the past...but this was incredibly different. Did that mean I had never *really* been in love before? It should have been absolutely terrifying, but it *wasn't*. I could see it when he looked at me. I could feel it when I was with him. However it happened, within the span of four days, we had fallen in love. So, I decided...hell yes. I'm going to Italy.

* * * * *

The next three weeks were grueling. Well, not really, but three weeks is a long-ass time to be apart when you just so recently became obsessed with one another. However, it was probably the best thing for us. We talked all day every day, texting and FaceTiming. Now let me clarify: I was very aware of the fact that all of this was happening ridiculously fast and so soon after I had found out my husband had been cheating on me for six months and I had filed for divorce. But I must say, after I finally handed Daniel the papers I was...fine. I knew in my heart that it was a huge blessing and that I was lucky to have had him do something that made it so easy for me to walk away. You know how you look back on past relationships and feel like it was a lifetime ago? I felt that way the minute I drove away from the house. The two weeks before I went to the beach with Javier, I was in a really good place. Even my mom and friends were surprised how okay I was. I'm emotionally aware enough to know that if I had been in a depressed and awful state when Javier came into the picture, it wouldn't have been healthy at all. But Javier and I talked openly about Daniel and all the legal bullshit that was swarming around my life, and I wasn't going to fight the universe or my feelings.

Me: Babe. I never want you to question whether or not I have unresolved feelings with this whole divorce thing. I'm sure a lot of people looking in on your side that care about you are wondering that. And I don't ever want you to think twice about it. I will always be open and honest with you about how I'm feeling, and I can promise you that chapter is closed.

Javier: I have not doubted that for one second, love. I would not have given us a thought if I felt that was possible. I 100 percent feel that you're in a different place. And I appreciate you saying that. I will always be honest with you, as well.

He would also constantly joke that he needed to write a letter to both Daniel and Laurel thanking them for all that had happened because it had led me to him. It genuinely seemed that everything was happening exactly how the universe intended it to. And Jesus, did we plan. We had events for my work, his friend's wedding in Santa Barbara, a trip to Las Vegas for a film festival I was in, plans to meet the family, all leading up to a one-month trip to Italy.

It hadn't been lost on me how insane this all was. I mean I had literally handed my soon-to-be ex-husband divorce papers less than a month ago and here I was, head over heels in love with a man who was the complete opposite of the one I'd married. Of course, my mom and all my friends were more than freaked out to see how intense this was and how fast it was all moving. No one wanted to see me get hurt again after having gone through such a violating situation with Daniel. My mother was especially worried. Daniel had fooled everyone, including her. He was the last person any of us thought would ever be capable of doing something so devious and hurtful. My mother's opinion mattered immensely to me. But let me tell you, I was ready to say fuck everyone—I will move to Hawaii and live in a tent with this man, have his babies, and not give two shits about what anyone has to say. Yep. It was at that level.

All my mother saw was her little girl rushing into a love affair with a sexy Latin man. When he dropped me off after our forty-eight hours of camping bliss, she had pulled him aside.

"Do not hurt her. She's fragile," she said to him.

"Your daughter is not fragile. She's the strongest woman I've ever met," Javier replied.

"Then you don't know my daughter," she told him. She, and all of my friends, were worried. Nevertheless, they all were trying to be supportive as they saw how insanely happy I was. Admittedly, a few times I had heard the psychic medium's voice in the back of my head: "The next six to seven months are going to be really rocky for you." But, I mean…come on, not *everything* she said had to be exactly true, right? Whatever, psychic medium lady, I'm happier than I could have ever imagined I would be.

Javier: My body is craving your body when I sleep. It's crazy.
Javier: Like I actually miss sleeping next to you. As much as I need mate.

Me: Aw baby. And you said you hate cuddling. Lol.

Javier: I swear I did.

Me: I love sleeping with you. I feel safe.

Javier: I'm glad. I got you.

Me: I know you do.

Javier: I'm just thinking about our camping, and it makes me feel really good. I can't believe I get to be with you. I feel super lucky.

Even with all the amazingness we were experiencing, there were still the legal issues looming over me. Was I even allowed to leave the country for a month? I had a call into my lawyer and was waiting to hear the verdict. One day my friend sent me a photo that Laurel had posted of her and Daniel. On Mother's Day. *Which was in May.* Javier asked if I was okay.

I was. I was just ready for it all to be done. The legal stuff…everything. When I saw the photo, I truly felt nothing. I was so emotionally disconnected from the relationship already.

Then finally, I got the answer from my lawyer I had been hoping for. I could go to Europe. Thank God.

Even things with his family were happening while he was away. His sister, Sophia and I had started following each other on Instagram. She had commented on one of my posts saying, "Can't wait to meet you!" and I had sent it to Javier.

Me: She's so cute. I love her.

Javier: She's amazing. And if she wants to meet you, it's a big deal for her.

Me: Aww. Your family is probably like whatttt is going on.

Javier: Not at all, they just ask about you every day.

Me: Tell me again the places we're going so I have it written down.

Javier: Florence, Venice, Rome, Amalfi, Positano, Cinque Terre, Pompeii, San Vito Lo Capo.

Me: So like heaven basically.

Javier: Yes.

Me: I wouldn't wanna go with anyone else.

Javier: Me neither.

We had so much planned that we were looking forward to. I couldn't believe I had actually booked a plane ticket and we were going to Italy.

Javier: I can't keep up with all the shit we have planned but let me tell you something from the heart...the fact that you're so into everything and willing to try things and explore makes me soooooo fucking happy!!

Me: Of course…what is life without adventure, boo? And I couldn't be happier that I'm doing it with you.

Javier: We are lucky people.

Me: Good God what is happening? How is it possible that I have all these feelings and YOU AREN'T EVEN HERE? Lol.

Javier: Yeah I can't understand it but I won't try to. I just let it happen cause I love it. No need to analyze it.

Me: Fair enough.

Those three weeks until Javier was finally home went by painfully slow. The day he got back, I went over to his house. He had brought me back presents from Argentina: a bathing suit for Italy, my own mate cup, and a shirt with a symbol of his city in Argentina with my last name printed on the back. We were ridiculously happy. I met his mother Ana that day, and we had dinner and talked for hours. I felt instantly comfortable with her, a feeling that was so refreshing after coming out of Daniel's toxic family dynamic. She made me feel like I had been part of her life for years, and we instantly bonded in the few short hours we were there that night.

That weekend we headed up to Santa Barbara for the wedding. Believe it or not, I had kept my word to myself and had been waiting to sleep with Javier until we had been together for a little while. His being out of the country for three weeks had helped because, let's be real, there's no way that shit would have happened if we had been together every night. There's only so much I can do. And the night we got to Santa Barbara was the night I couldn't—or just flat out didn't want to—wait anymore. I'm not going to give all the details, but let's just say that the last (and important) piece of the puzzle was mind-blowingly perfect, and definitely worth the wait. For both of us.

At the wedding, I was introduced to all of his friends as his girlfriend. We had an incredible time and danced the night away as we always do. I could tell that some of his friends from college were surprised in an excited way to see that he had someone he cared about so much. One of the girls even pulled me aside during the night and told me she had never seen him like this. It wasn't the first time I had heard that. His mother and his sister, who I had begun talking to and had become very fond of, were both quick to tell me that this was definitely different. Lying in bed that night, Javier looked over at me.

"We need nicknames for each other," he said.

"You can't just decide on a nickname. It has to just come." I laughed.

"How about Plum?" he offered.

"What? What the hell does Plum even have to do with me?"

"I like it. Aw, Plum!" he teased.

"I absolutely hate it. It's a big round purple thing. I veto that," I said. And so became our new nicknames: Veto and Plum. Eye roll.

The following week we went to REI to pick out a backpack for me for the trip. I've camped and traveled my fair share, but I normally travel with, you know, actual luggage. Fitting a month's worth of stuff into a large backpack seemed pretty daunting to me.

"You guys going on a honeymoon?" a sweet older lady asked. We both laughed.

"This is the trip to decide if there will be a honeymoon," he replied with a chuckle. We frequently got mistaken for a newlywed couple or people who had been together much longer than a month. We were making plans far down the road and it felt totally normal to us.

Then came Las Vegas, and we were in a constant state of happiness. Everything with us was so ridiculously passionate. Seriously, you guys, every time we had sex it was like a freaking performance that deserved a standing O (no pun intended). I had nothing to complain about. If anything, I was trying to hold back from telling him I was in love with him because all of this was happening so fast. One night, we were in our hotel room in Vegas and had just finished... performing in the bathtub. I was lying with my head on his chest and had to force my mouth shut because I just wanted to tell him. I let out a big sigh.

"What?" he asked, stroking my head.

"Nothing..." I said. He wrapped me in his arms and squeezed me tightly. I felt like I was exactly where I was supposed to be, that this was where so many painful situations and hard decisions had led me. I was so incredibly content in that moment, I could have stayed there forever. In a month and a half, we had gone from a casual thought to a full-on serious relationship. And in a week we were jetting off to Italy to have what would obviously be one of the most romantic and passionate months of my life. But if anyone can tell you, it's me—so very much can happen in a week.

Fuck
Everything Happens For A Reason

(It definitely does...that doesn't make it any easier.)

The day we returned home from Vegas, something had shifted with Javier. He seemed down and not quite himself. I figured he was just as tired as I was and didn't really think much of it. Unfortunately, that was not the case. The following day he called me and said he needed to talk. I could hear in his voice that something was really...*wrong*. He explained to me that the last night in Vegas, he'd had a dream about his brother. It was powerful enough to really change his mood for the rest of the day. The feeling that had surfaced from it was grief, and it wasn't going away. I immediately felt what I will refer to as "the surge" in my chest. The surge had become an unfortunate yet familiar feeling over the past two months. It was the tightening of my chest, the bad feeling in the pit of my stomach, the instinct that something wasn't okay. I felt it when I found the first hotel receipt of Daniel's. I felt it when I found out Laurel was in Ohio. And I felt it right then when Javier called. I have experienced my fair share of grief and dealt with close deaths in my life, so I deeply sympathized with what he was experiencing. We stayed on the phone for a while, and I offered any guidance and love that I could think of. He told me he was going to book an appointment with a therapist he had seen a few times. He kept repeating how frustrated he was that he was feeling this way.

"Everything is so new with us. It should be all happy and amazing like it has been. I don't want to feel like this," he said.

"That's completely irrelevant. We haven't done anything normal in this relationship. Why would you be worried that this isn't the right time? I'm right here and it's fine, we'll get through it," I replied. After talking for a while, he let me know that he wasn't going to meet with his friends that night like he had planned and instead would pick me up after my event that night. We hung up and I immediately texted his sister, Sophia, whom I had grown close to over the last few weeks, even though we hadn't actually met.

Me: Just got off the phone with Javier. I know he spoke to you earlier about how he's feeling. I'm just worried about him. But he's taking steps to handle his feelings differently, which is good. My heart hurts for him. For your whole family.

Sophia: I encouraged him to feel it all and share it with you, and show you. But everyone has their own process, and he is sad and hurting, so I will just support him.

Me: He did. I'm glad you encouraged him to. I told him he shouldn't be worried about not being in the "right" state because there is no "right," and none of it will make me feel any differently about him or us. I just want to be there for him.

Sophia: I cannot wait to meet you! Also...Javi is soooo stubborn! Haha. So the fact that he is actually doing things differently is so amazing. It means a lot. He is a creature of habit and knows the current habit is bad for him. I am going to push the shit out of him in the most loving sisterly way! He will not stay in this for long. I will not allow my brother to not enjoy and love his life due to guilt. Not going to happen.

Hearing he was handling things differently and seeing that he was sharing it all with me gave me a small bit of comfort.

That night he picked me up from my event. As he wrapped his arms around me I could feel it. *Fear.* I could literally feel how scared he was about his emotions, what they all meant, and what was to come of them. We drove back to the Airbnb he had rented for the time between Argentina and Italy. On the way, he said that he felt disconnected from the world and didn't understand why he was still here and his brother wasn't. I offered as much sound advice as I could and gave all the support I had. Tears rolled down his face as he tried to explain what was going on inside of him. It was heartbreaking to see him in so much pain and feeling so helpless. He explained that he had stuffed a lot of unresolved emotions down, and everything he was experiencing with me had opened it all up. We talked for three hours, and I finally looked at him and asked, "Are you sure you want me to go to Italy with you?"

"Yes. Of course," he answered. My heart breathed a sigh of relief. Still, part of me felt that these emotions were going to last more than a day or two. And that part of me was right.

The next day we met his parents at the beach. We spent the day relaxing, and although I could see he was still not himself, he was definitely better than the day before. I absolutely adored his mother, and I could tell she adored me. We sat and talked as Javier and his dad ran around with the dogs. We just clicked. I shared with her that I was worried about what he was going through, and she opened up to me about how difficult it had been for the whole family since losing Chris. We talked about our trip to Italy and how excited I was to finally go to Europe. She kept reiterating how Javier had never been like this with anyone and how happy she was to see him finally find someone like me.

That night we went out with his friend Manny, whom I had met the first night we went dancing. Javier seemed to be getting back to a more balanced state, which made me happy. At one point, he went to the bathroom, and Manny and I were left at the bar talking.

"I'm worried about him," I admitted.

"I know. But he'll be okay and get through it. I've never seen him as happy as he has been with you," he said. We came home that night and made love before falling asleep in each other's arms. That whole day was a moment of hope that I tried to hold onto.

The following day, those hopes dwindled. That afternoon for two hours I sat with him, cried with him, and talked about things in my past that I had never shared with anyone. I tried to help him see that there is a light at the end of the awful tunnel of grief. His feelings were so overwhelming, he was on the verge of having a panic attack. He kept repeating that he had been so happy this past month and was so frustrated these feelings were coming *now*. At the time I didn't understand why he kept bringing this up. Now, looking back on it, I know that it went much deeper than that.

However, it was during this conversation that I had my first giant revelation of this journey.

"I'm scared to death if I love anyone as much as I loved my brother, they'll die," he said. I was so proud of him for being able to recognize and admit that, and I knew that belief all too well.

"I totally get that. I've dealt with that belief my entire life," I explained. "I loved my dad and he died. I loved Jake and he died. So I married someone I wasn't fully in love with because it was *safe*."

Holy. Fucking. Shit. I literally stopped mid-conversation. How had I never seen that before? It all made *so* much sense.

We talked for what seemed like forever. At one point, he mentioned the trip.

"What if this feeling doesn't go away, and it ruins our trip, and you're miserable with me?" he asked.

"What part of I'm not going anywhere do you not understand?" I responded. "If we have to have these talks every day to help you heal then that's the type of trip it will be. We're either going to go and come back wildly happy and in love or come back best of friends. Either way, stop feeling like it's not okay." I put my arms around him. It was so crazy to see this strong man weep in my arms. It was like his feelings for me were being forced aside by his fear. As if his fear was so intense, it was making him want to throw in the towel just to protect himself.

After we had both calmed down, we met Manny and some of his friends at the beach. His spirit seemed to come back a bit being with the guys. I stretched out on the beach, closed my eyes, and tried to quiet the million thoughts that were going on in my head. Later that night, when I hugged him goodbye, he looked at me and said, "Thank you, Gabs. For everything. You've been incredible."

* * * * *

The following week he went to see a therapist. We continued to talk about things. He would call and share things with me that clearly made it sound like he was breaking up with me but then would assure me that he wasn't, that he was just trying to be completely honest and tell me how he was feeling.

"I'm not running," he would say. I decided to order him a journal in hopes that he would benefit from writing some of his feelings down. It was a beautiful leather journal that I had personalized with the nickname he and his brother shared with each other. On the back, it had his last name and the symbol for his city in Argentina. On the inside, I wrote a long letter to his brother, Chris. It was deeply honest and very personal. It was one of the most thoughtful gifts I've ever given someone. I could tell he loved it.

On Friday, September 1st, it all came to a head. He had spent the day with his dad, and I was trying to give him as much space as possible, but the past week he had been completely different. We went from talking all day every day to checking in once or twice. He knew it, I knew it. I was just hoping it would somehow go back to normal.

That night he called me and said that he would pick me up Sunday morning. We would stay over at his parents' house and spend some time with them, and then his dad would take us to the airport on Monday. We talked for a few minutes about packing and trip details. The moment I hung up, I felt the surge. It was undeniable. Something was wrong. I picked up my phone and texted him.

> Me: Look. I'm doing my best to tell myself everything is fine, but in my chest and my heart I just know it isn't.

He immediately called me. That three-hour phone call was nothing short of heartbreaking. We talked about his grief, how frustrated he was that it was all happening now, and that he didn't know how to handle it all.

"I don't feel anything for my parents, I don't feel anything for my sister, I don't feel anything for you." Boom, there was the surge again.

It hit me like a fucking freight train. In that moment, I knew exactly where the conversation was heading. Finally, after many tears from both of us, I asked him.

"Do you feel anything for me right now besides friendship?" He paused for what felt like a lifetime.

"No," he said through tears. I don't think I have ever felt more hurt by such a simple word. How was this happening right now? How was this even possible? We both stayed on the phone crying because neither of us knew how to get off.

"I fucking hate that we're having this conversation over the phone." I cried.

"Do you want me to come over? I'll drive over right now," he said. He knew he was killing me and just wanted to make it better. I eventually managed to wrap my head around the situation enough to tell him that he needed to take the night to think and make a choice. He needed to decide if he wanted to go on this trip alone or go together as friends. Then I would figure out if my heart could even handle that possibility, and ultimately we would settle on what to do. We decided that he would come over the following evening, and we would discuss it all in person. After lingering for another twenty minutes on the phone just listening to each other cry, we finally hung up. I. Fucking. Lost it.

I cannot remember the last time I cried with that much pain underneath it. Even when I found out about Daniel cheating on me, the one big cry I had was motivated by anger and betrayal. This cry was just pure, deep pain because I knew what the answer was going to be. My mom came in and I saw her heart break right in front of me. Only her heartbreak was full of anger and rage for her little girl, and mine with sadness and grief. To be fair, my mother and every one of my friends had every right to hate him in that moment. Because no matter what he was dealing with, it was unbelievable that he would convince me to go on a grand Italian adventure with him and then bail on it two days before our flight left, after I had just gone through a horrendous divorce. That night, I cried myself to sleep, trying to find an answer as to what the fuck had just happened to my seemingly perfect fairy tale.

* * * * *

The next day we had a life celebration planned for my uncle, who had been given a few months to live. He had been battling cancer for quite a while, and it had come back full force. Putting on a smile for all the people who were there and answering questions about this incredible trip I was about to go on was literally the hardest acting I've ever done. My anxiety the whole day was through the roof. When it was finally that time, Javier picked me up and we sat in his truck up the street.

"I feel like I have to go on this trip by myself." I nodded. Deep down I had known that would be the answer. "But Gabs, I need you to know I'm not running. You literally have changed my life, and I can't tell you how much I care about you. I want you in my life always, that I am really sure of."

It was all so confusing. He only felt friendship feelings toward me yet he wanted me in his life forever. How had everything he'd been feeling just disappeared overnight? There were a million un-answered questions. So, I had a decision to make—either stay home and be heartbroken or go travel Europe for a month by myself. And staying home heartbroken? Fuck. That.

The one big fear I'd had since I was a little girl was being alone. Ever since my dad died, I'd always needed someone around me. I would always have at least one friend over or be at someone's house on a playdate. When I got older, I lived with roommates and would have all my friends over all the time. Even when I found out about Daniel, Jess slept at my house every night until everything had set-tled. I had never really been alone with myself or truly gotten to know myself, and the universe had just delivered a clear way to make me fi-nally go face that shit head on. When I told him I was still going to go, his face lit up. I think part of him was relieved that I had something I needed to go fix and heal too, and that I wasn't going to be stuck at home crying. And part of him was just genuinely proud of me. We talked and laughed about the different things I could possibly do on this adventure.

I don't really know how to explain it. Even with all the tears both of us cried, all the heartache we were both feeling, and the gravity of the situation, we were still able to laugh and be totally connected. I would soon come to learn that this would be a recurring theme with us. No matter what was going on, when we were together or communicating, we were always good. We decided that we would possibly meet up at the end of the trip, depending on how he was feeling and how my heart was doing, and then fly back on the same plane. He dropped me off at home, and we decided that he and his dad would pick me up on Monday to go to the airport.

"How are you feeling, Gabs?" he asked.

"Like I'm about to go on a journey of eat, pray, fuck my life." We both laughed.

We hugged goodbye and I went inside. I was expecting to burst into tears the moment I walked in. Instead, I felt sort of...*okay*. It was then that I made the decision. *You are going on this trip, Gabrielle. You are going to face your fears, be a badass, and fucking come out the other end a better human. Now...where the hell do you want to go?*

Fuck
Fear

(When you face it...it will change you.)

oly shit. It was September 4th. I had slept maybe three hours the previous night. Two years ago on this day, I'd had a dream wedding with someone I *thought* I would most definitely still be married to. Now it was the day I would face a lot of fucking fear. In forty-eight hours, I'd gone from being over-the-moon excited about taking a romantic vacation with my boyfriend to being single and venturing off for a month abroad by myself. Yeah...holy shit.

The only planning I had done was to contact one of my best friends, Emma, who lived in London, and make arrangements to stay with her for the first five days of my trip. She had moved two years ago with her boyfriend and had welcomed me, no questions asked. Those who know me know I plan...a *lot*. Even for weekend nights out I plan ahead. So for me to take a month-long trip with no plans in place? Well...it was insane.

The other hard thing that I had done in the past forty-eight hours was to tell all my friends and family, who were expecting me to be jetting off with Javier, that I was actually going alone. Needless to say, more than a few of them were extremely upset. Most of them were heartbroken for me, which I could understand. I mean, fuck, I was heartbroken for myself. Even so, for whatever reason, I felt this innate need to protect Javier. I found myself defending him and trying to make people understand where he was coming from. I was extremely protective about how people viewed him. Maybe it was because I knew what we had both experienced in the month and a half together. Or maybe it was because I had seen how much it broke his heart, too, when he'd made the decision. Either way, I fiercely defended him to anyone who saw what he did as a cop-out.

I had spoken to his sister, Sophia, and his mom since all of this had gone down. Sophia was already abroad on her own trip and would still find time to check in on me. His mom was just as heartbroken as I was. None of us could truly comprehend how such immense feelings had just...*disappeared*. His mom had shared with me that it was her hope he would be able to heal and find his way back to me, and that deep down she believed I would be the mother of her grandchildren. Jesus. Talk about unintentionally pouring salt in a giant gaping wound. She also had offered to stay in touch with me while I was on my trip if it was something that I wanted. Javier and I had also kept in frequent touch over the previous forty-eight hours, and he had let me know that he had a gift for me that I could take on the trip. He would bring it to me Monday.

I was all packed and as ready as I was going to be. My mom gave me a hug goodbye, and we stood together and cried. My mom has always been my best friend and my "person." I think part of her didn't want me to go, but the part of her that was overwhelmingly proud of me outweighed that. She left before Javier arrived to pick me up. There was no way she could see him that day. For fifteen minutes I sat in my house by myself, not sure whether I was going to have a panic attack, burst into tears, or start laughing at how ridiculous my life had been the last two months. I was so *not* ready for this.

I had come across an image online that simply said, "You Can." I set it as the background on my phone as a constant reminder that I could do this...even if I didn't fully believe I could just yet.

When Javier arrived, he came in to give me my gift. It was a little stuffed animal that he had kept since he was a baby. The sentimental value of it was tremendous. I sat on my bed next to him, holding it for a few moments.

"I can't take this," I finally said.

"Okay," he said understandingly.

"It really means a lot to me. Thank you. I just can't take it." I fought to hold back tears.

"I totally get it. You ready?" he asked, standing up.

"No?" I laughed. We grabbed the giant backpack that he and I had picked out and headed to the car.

Once we were at the airport, everything was yet again surprisingly...normal. It was like nothing monumentally bad had happened, we just weren't holding hands and kissing all the time. We talked about where I thought I might go, what I thought the trip might bring. We had a few hours to kill before the flight, so we grabbed some wine and food at one of the restaurants. I decided that it was time to finally announce on social media about the divorce. I was tired of having to explain it to people every time someone new heard something. And shit, if I was going to go on this journey, I wanted it to be with a clean slate. So, I had Javier snap a picture of me with my ridiculously heavy backpack on (I was extremely proud of how much shit I had been able to fit in that thing) and wrote the following:

"This has been long overdue. This year has been one of the most personally challenging years of my life. Earlier this year I found out my husband was having an affair for six months. I filed for divorce and left. Navigating the disrespect and the betrayal was by far the most difficult part of healing. My mother, my friends, and my family have once again proven to be an unwavering force. I do not know what I would have done without them. I can now truthfully say it was one of the best things that could have happened to me. Everyone around me was adamant that I be by myself, don't rush into anything, focus on my career. The universe had a different plan in mind. I have always preached that it is better to have loved fully, with everything inside of you, and be heartbroken a dozen times, then to live with walls around your heart and never love at all. I met someone who changed my life. And I know that I changed his. Someone who will be in my life forever. I will forever be grateful for the day it happened, and all the days after. Since my father died when I was a little girl, my biggest fear has been to be alone. I'm choosing to share these incredibly personal things so that someone, anyone, can know that it's possible. That you are not alone. And that you are enough. So today, on what would have been my two-year wedding anniversary, I will go alone. To learn how to be by myself. How to be okay with myself. And how to love myself. And I am absolutely terrified... 'It takes a lot of courage to release the familiar and seemingly secure, to embrace the new. But there is no real security in what is no longer meaningful. There is more security in the adventurous and exciting, for in movement there is life and in change there is power.' Peace out USA. See you on the other side."

Boom. Posted. It was now out for everyone to see, to know, and I felt a huge weight lift off my shoulders. I wasn't sharing it for anyone but myself, and it felt so damn good. In the two hours before our flight, I received literally hundreds of messages. People thanking me for my bravery, telling me that seeing it helped them get through their day, connecting with things that I said, and most of all asking me to please keep sharing my journey. So that is what I decided to do.

While we waited and drank the rest of our wine, I pulled out an envelope. I had walked into a store the day before my trip to pick up some last-minute things and found the perfect card to give to Javier. On the back of the envelope, I had written "To open if you ever feel scared or alone." He smiled and stuck it in the journal I had bought him.

We boarded the plane and settled in for what was going to be a ten-hour flight to London. Javier would head on to Rome, as we had planned, and I would catch an Uber to Emma's house. On three hours' sleep, I figured I would pass right out, especially with the Ambien I had with me. No such luck. I maybe slept two hours, none of which was good sleep. I watched *Moulin Rouge,* a personal favorite of mine, and chatted with the people next to me about where they thought I should go. Javier slept most of the way. The ridiculousness of this situation was not lost on me. I was sitting right next to my now ex-boyfriend, on a ten-hour plane ride to a city we were supposed to be traveling through together. And yet somehow, everything was totally normal between us. When we were getting close to our descent, Javier looked over at me.

"So we'll be meeting up in Amalfi before we head back," he stated.

"I mean maybe...we'll see," I said.

"Gabs, we're both going to be there. It's not like I'm just gonna wave at you from across the street." We laughed. The plane touched down and we grabbed our things. While we were waiting in line to exit, he put his arm around me. I could sense he was nervous. I was too.

He walked me to where the customs line was and we hugged.

"Please let me know when you get your bag and when you get to Emma's," he said sternly.

"I will."

"Be safe, okay?" he added.

"You too," I said. We hugged again, and then we quickly kissed. I turned around and started walking and didn't let my feet stop. I didn't look back. I knew that if I didn't keep going, I might not make it to baggage claim. Once I got through customs and got my bag, I hopped in an Uber to Emma's. It's amazing how handy Uber can be all over the world. Javier and I texted until his flight to Rome took off. Surprisingly, I wasn't as much of a mess as I was expecting to be after saying goodbye to him. I felt strangely liberated that I had decided to take this crazy leap of faith all by myself.

Javier: Gabs, have a great journey, stay safe and, anything you need, please call me.

Me: Ditto, boo. Proud of you. See you soon. Let me know when you get to the hotel.

Javier: Will do. Text me when you get to your friend's please.

Me: Will do.

Javier: I'm about to board. See you on the other side, Plum.

Me: Fly safe, Veto.

Pulling up to Emma's and seeing her come outside was such a

relief. It was like having a piece of home across the world. It was so good to see her and her boyfriend, Mark, and we immediately started catching up on everything. I don't know if I would have been able to do this trip without Emma. Having a comforting place to start when everything had fallen apart only a few days before was so invaluable to me. She had been such a big support system for me over the last seventy-two hours, and I was grateful to have one of my friends there by my side. We went out for dinner and a beer at a London pub and laughed and chatted for a few hours. When we got back to their apartment, Javier FaceTimed me. He had made it to Rome and was all settled in. We said goodnight, and I got ready for bed. Since Emma and Mark were both working the next two days, I would be on my own exploring the city. I again heard the psychic medium's words in my head. "The next six to seven months are going to be really rocky for you." Shit. That had been in June. Was it really going to be another four months of...*this*? I didn't know how much more I could handle after the last three. I plopped down, sure I would pass the fuck out after how little sleep I had gotten the past two nights. Apparently, there is such a thing as reverse jet lag. Surprise, Gabrielle. You'll only be getting a solid two hours tonight. Sleep tight!

Fuck
Reactions

(It's about finding out what causes them.)

R ecently, I've realized that in order to truly get in touch with your feelings, you have to be willing to authentically meet yourself where you are. It is only then you give yourself the permission and the opportunity to deal with and understand the feelings you're experiencing. So, I committed to allowing myself to meet...well...myself, exactly where I was every day on this journey. *So* much easier said than done. Why? Because that means sometimes you have to sit in the shit. Figuratively. And more often than not, that is super fucking uncomfortable.

DAY ONE.

I would like to say I woke up with a serious pep in my step. But the jet lag was too real, and I had been up writing at 2 a.m. after two hours of sleep. Once Emma and Mark got up for work and the bright light had poured through my window, I figured I would get up and power through day one. Admittedly, I was slightly concerned that I would fall over and die halfway through the day from lack of sleep, but I actually felt really...good. Hell yes. I'm a fucking badass. I got ready while singing along to some feel-good Spotify station, and then it was time—time to go explore by myself. I walked the ten minutes to the train station, used Emma's oyster card, and hopped on the train to

Waterloo station. The twenty-five-minute train ride was peaceful. I pulled out the first of three books I had packed for the trip, Paulo Coelho's *The Alchemist*. Seriously, ten people had told me this book changed their life and got them through, and at this point, I would have eaten one of those gross concoctions on *Fear Factor* and had sex with an elephant if it meant making everything better. I'm not a huge reader. Being an actress, I read a bunch of scripts so my brain never thinks, "Oh, let's cuddle up and read more!" But whatever, I'm committed (insert eye roll here). I read until I arrived at the station.

The second I stepped into the open city I felt this overwhelming sense of...*freedom*. I felt liberated, if only because I'd managed to get from Emma's to the city. I walked through a beautiful park to get to the London Eye, a giant Ferris wheel that gives you a 360-degree bird's-eye view of the city. I bought my ticket and walked up to the entrance, where there was a photo station everyone passed through before entering. A young couple was in line right in front of me.

"Beso!" The photographer prompted them to kiss, which they did—a small reminder that I wasn't standing there with Javier.

"Next!" The photographer snapped me out of my thoughts. I walked forward. "Just one?" he asked. Yes, dude, clearly, but thank you for reinforcing the awkward embarrassment. I smiled for the photo that I would not be purchasing. I stepped onto the giant fish-eye cart with about fifteen other people, all couples and one family. As I looked out and admired the view, I suddenly became very aware that I was the only one by myself. I took photos of the incredible views of London. There was something strangely poetic about being high above the world below, literally forced to have a new perspective. Something about being that high and seeing so much makes you feel so small. To be honest, one of the reasons I don't ever sit and ponder "what's really out there" and the science of the universe is because it makes me realize how small and insignificant we are in the world. It's quite overwhelming.

You need to get a picture up here, Gabrielle, I said to myself. I wouldn't consider myself shy at all. I'm pretty outgoing and usually the energetic spunky one in the group. So why did I suddenly feel like I couldn't ask one of these fifteen people to snap a photo of me? Was it because I was embarrassed that I was alone? Was I worried other people would judge me for being alone? How fucking superficial of a thought is that? *Grow a pair and get over it, Gabrielle*, I told myself. I asked one of the couples and the man, of course, obliged—and voila, my first solo pic.

Stepping off the Eye, I had a rush of excitement. I could literally go anywhere, do anything. No plans, no one else to come to a decision with. And so I began to walk, in my power, with myself.

About two minutes in, I glanced to my left and saw a stand that said (I kid you not) "Argentine Empanadas." I literally laughed out loud. Here, in the middle of fucking London, the first thing I run into is a random fucking ARGENTINE empanada stand. So, of course, I bought one.

As I walked across the massive bridge, enjoying this insanely delicious chicken empanada, I looked up at Big Ben. *Time.* What a strange thing time is. We always feel like there is not enough time. Except when we're bored, or excited, or nervous, then there is too much of it. Do we ever get to a place where we feel there is exactly the right amount of time? Oh, I don't have an answer for you. I genuinely want to know. In movies, they always say, "If it's meant for us to be together in the future, our paths shall cross, and we will find each other." What the fuck is that? What if I don't want to wait, to let days, months, years go by? You can't just get all that time back you know.

I continued to stroll around the busy city streets. There was so much to take in, so many incredible buildings surrounding me. I felt like I was walking on a Hollywood film lot. It didn't even seem real.

Then I stopped dead in my tracks. The busy streets kept hustling around me, but I couldn't move. There, before me, was Westminster Abbey. I cannot explain it, but I felt a deep emotional pull toward this massive structure. Although I had no idea what it was, I knew I had to go in. I walked through the garden gate entrance and strolled along, not taking my eyes down from this...*place*. I stopped at the giant entrance. What on earth was making me feel so pulled? I saw a woman nearby and asked her to take a photo of me.

"Smile!" she said. But I turned around, my back facing her, and looked upwards. I knew whatever I was about to experience inside was going to be...impactful. I wanted this moment to be represented how it was—me, looking up, in pure awe. I walked inside and bought a ticket. I had to remind myself to breathe. A woman directed me to where you could get headphones to listen to a guided tour. I walked directly past it and began to take in the emotional beauty of where I was. Indescribable architecture. Breathtaking stained glass. Looking back on it now, it was as if something or someone was guiding my body through this place. I walked directly to a big altar with candles. It was a prayer space. The sign explained that guests could light a candle and write a prayer on one of the cards, and a priest would deliver them the same day. I wish I could say I thought about giving this prayer to my incredible mother or my deserving friends. I did not take even a moment to contemplate. I picked up a card and wrote:

> Dear God,
> Please help the Alvarez family find peace around the death of Chris. Please help Javier let go of the guilt, grief, and suffering. Fill them with light and love. Thank you.

I took it to the altar, lit a candle, and read what I had written. As I placed it in the box, tears filled my eyes. Part of me just wanted to scoop up all the grief this family was feeling and take on the burden of it myself.

As I continued to walk around the Abbey, my soul felt so much. It was quite indescribable, to be honest. Then, I heard a priest's voice come over a loudspeaker. He said that we would all have a moment of silence and pray together for the world. I stopped where I was, closed my eyes, and listened to his words. Tears began to stream down my cheeks. I cried for Javier. For his family. For my mother. For my father. For myself. For the world.

I sat down with my journal, turned to the last page, and wrote what I had just experienced.

Walking out of Westminster Abbey, I felt like I had just had a spiritual experience. Something about the space and how it made me feel was so profound. But I didn't feel sad. I felt moved. And *alive*.

I stumbled into a coffee shop and ordered a coconut latté. I sat by the window and wrote my mom a postcard I had grabbed at the Abbey gift shop. I sent a picture of the journal page I had written to Javier's mom, Ana.

Me: I didn't share this with Javier but felt compelled to share it with you for some reason.

Ana: Thank you for sharing this with me. It means a lot.

After resting my feet for a bit, I continued to walk through the streets of London, this time heading off to see Buckingham Palace. It was about a mile and a half walk, and I'm proud to say I found my way there all by myself. I can't say this place had any type of incredible effect on me, but it was definitely stunning. There were beautiful chandeliers, grand staircases, and hundreds of gifts for the queen from around the world. The sculptures looked as if they had real souls inside them. You could feel the history walking through it. I think the gardens were my favorite, with beautiful ponds lined with all different kinds of trees. Willows hung over into the calm water. It felt like one of the few places in the world that still had complete stillness and peace.

I exited the palace onto a completely different street than where I had entered. I picked left and started walking. Right away I passed a random sign someone had written and stuck on a street container. It read, "The path of most resistance is paved with lessons. –Notes to strangers." Yeah, no fucking kidding.

I strolled up and down streets, guessing which way would lead me back. After about an hour, I considered giving up (and by giving up I mean calling an Uber). Just as my brain was about to say, *You're fucking lost, Gabrielle*, I looked across the street to see...what? The same coffee shop where I had written my postcard! Ha! Take that, brain. I fucking rule.

I popped into the shop, grabbed a snack, and connected to Wi-Fi. It's amazing how connected you can still be anywhere in the world. I posted the photo of me outside Westminster Abbey. A few minutes later, text messages from Javier came through, commenting on my Instagram story.

Javier: Holy crap with your view!
Javier: And the empanada??!! WTF.

Me: I have had the most unbelievable day.

Javier: I'm so happy for you.

Me: I've been by myself the whole day. And it's been fucking amazing.

Javier: Until I bothered you.

Me: Correct.
Me: Kidding, lol.
Me: But I started my book.

Javier: Same.

Me: Same? As in book?

Javier: Not a book but a journal, which I've never had in my life.

Me: Good.
Me: Only good will come from doing that.

And then it happened. Twenty-two photos came through. Twenty-two photos of the Spanish Steps, the streets of Rome, the Coliseum, and last but not least, of Javier, standing center frame, flashing his swoon-worthy smile. I. Fucking. Lost it.

This was the surge times twenty. My chest tightened, my stomach sank, and my heart hurt. Fuck, did my heart hurt. Why? Because right in front of my face were pictures of the trip that *I* was supposed to be on. The romantic streets that *we* were supposed to be strolling down. The steps that he was meant to be kissing *me* on. Only I was in London. Before my brain realized my fingers were typing, I wrote:

Me: Wow.

I grabbed my bag and walked back to the train, trying to figure out what the fuck just happened.

God dammit, Gabrielle. What is wrong with you? You've been *fine*. You've been *more* than fine. You spent four hours at the airport and a ten-hour plane ride with him, *and* said goodbye, and you were fine. You've been empowered and ass-kicking all day. What. The. Fuck. Gabrielle.

Okay. Now that you've yelled at yourself and stomped your feet, do you want to figure out *why* you're having this reaction? (The old me rolls my eyes in my head.) Yes, yes, I do. Obviously, you know he's in Rome. You know he is there without you. So it's really not the pictures that are plugging you in so badly.

Here is where I came up with what I like to call the Thought Onion. It's a tool that is used to dig deeper into whatever you're feeling, to get to the root of it all. The Thought Onion is layered, like an onion, with different thoughts covering up the core issue. The outer layer is the superficial thought, the thought we automatically have when we are reacting to something. The next layer is what I like to call the authentic thought, which is the emotion under the reaction. And finally, you have the subconscious thought, which is the meat and potatoes, what is really at the core of it all. So as I walked through the streets, I said to myself, *Okay, Gabrielle. Use the Thought Onion.* So... what is the superficial thought?

- WHAT THE EVER-LOVING *FUCK*, JAVIER?

No, no... that's a little excessive. Okay *really*, Gabrielle. What is the superficial thought?

- There is something around this situation that I am not dealing with.

Yes. Clearly, as Zen and woosah as I have been pretending to be the last seventy-two hours, there is definitely something around Javier that I am not dealing with. Okay, so then what is the authentic thought?

- A part of me deep down doesn't believe the change in his feelings for me is possible because of grief.

Hmm. Is that because when my friends experience the "it's not you, it's me" stuff with men, I'm always the first to say that it's a huge typical male cop-out? No, because I know this is different. But there is definitely some small part of me that just can't believe it all. Fine. So now what is that subconscious thought? What is at the core?

- I have to accept the fact that I am—and allow myself to be—angry at him.

Oh shit. It seems so simple, doesn't it? Still, over the last five days, I had been defending him, protecting him, making sure my people didn't judge him. Loving him, trying to take care of him, all the while not even realizing that I was just mad at him. This realization didn't make me go, "Aha! I'm healed!" It actually made me...*sad*. I didn't *want* to be mad at him. I didn't *want* to feel angry. I didn't blame him, I didn't think he had "done this to me." I didn't want to feel anything negative toward this person I loved.

When I finally arrived back at Emma's, I sat on my guest bed and wrote out what I had just pieced together on my way home. I had felt liberated, free, and empowered. I had explored, ventured, experienced, and wandered. And now, as I felt the tears coming and my chest tightening, I lay down, by myself, and cried. Holy shit. This was only day one.

Fuck
Emotions

(They can be such a bitch sometimes.)

DAY TWO

"If there's even a slight chance at getting something that will make you happy, risk it. Life's too short and happiness is too rare." - A.R. Lucas.

I sat in bed as I posted this quote to my Instagram story. It spoke to me in some way; I just couldn't put my finger on what exactly it was. I had slept a whole five hours but was still up before the sun. So I decided to Thought Onion why this quote had grabbed me. Superficial thought:

- Why am I not fighting for the love I was very clearly experiencing so strongly? Why am I not flying to Rome, smacking Javier in the face, and telling him to wake up and realize what we could be together?

Well, Gabrielle, because 1) you're not fucking crazy and 2) you're a woman and you already stood by his side when he decided he just had "friendship" feelings toward you. Yes, I call bullshit, but nevertheless, those were his words. Who am I to say that's not what he's feeling? Authentic thought?

- Why is *he* not fighting for what we were both so clearly experiencing? Why is he not fighting for...me?

That layer of it made me *angry*. And frustrated. I've experienced tremendous grief in my life, but it's never made me just completely flip a switch like he had. How had we gone from planning months and months down the road to just nothing? It made no sense to me, his family, our friends, no one. Well, what's the subconscious thought?

- Am I blind to the fact that maybe what everyone has been saying is true? Did he just flat out play me?

No. I refused to believe that. I had watched tears stream down his face when he said, "I don't understand why this is happening, everything has been so perfect with us." I saw his heart breaking when he told me he needed to go alone. There was just no way, even with how good of an actor he is, that all of that wasn't real. I'm not a stupid woman. In my logical mind, it felt like he was running from what was so clearly apparent. Love. So if it was all real, but he now suddenly didn't want me, what was left for me to do? Sit with that shitty realization, I guess.

There was a certain sense of freedom that came with knowing I didn't have to follow anyone else's agenda. The only plans I had for the day were to meet the twins, two London actors I had met and clicked with back in the US earlier that year. Other than that, it was another day of adventure.

I put on 90s Pandora and started to get ready. Seriously, that station can get me out of almost any funk. They just don't make music like that anymore. Missy Elliott's "Work It" came on, and I danced by myself while putting my makeup on. I was determined to make the most of this day.

I headed out and down to the train station. I grabbed a seat and opened up *The Alchemist* to continue where I had left off. As I looked up I noticed a sign on one of the train walls. It read:

Making Friends On The Train
1. Establish eye contact.
2. Oh no, you made eye contact.
3. What were you thinking?
4. So much sweat.
5. FOR THE LOVE OF GOD LOOK AT YOUR PHONE.

I couldn't help but laugh. It was so sadly true. Our world today is completely sucked into our phones and technology that we've forgotten what it's like to interact with people, to smile at a stranger for no reason or make small talk with the person next to you. It's truly sad when you stop to think about it.

My first stop of the day was to see the Tower of London. It was like walking into a page of a fairy tale. While taking in the giant castle, I couldn't help but notice I was feeling...off. The first day I had been so empowered and excited. Today, I just didn't feel the same rush. Maybe it was because I was tired. Or maybe it was because I couldn't stop thinking about the Rome photos Javier had sent me and how they were still making me feel.

Once I had seen everything I had come to see, I walked along the river to a coffee shop to warm up a bit. Thank God Emma and I are the same size in everything because I *so* did not pack for London weather. It also helped that I didn't have to dirty any of my limited clothing until my next destination.

As I stood in line looking at the menu, a very good-looking barista asked me if I had any questions.

"What's your favorite?" I asked.

"Ah, that's easy. I'll make it for you." He smiled at me.

He handed me whatever he had whipped up without telling me what it was. I grabbed it and reached for my wallet.

"Your eyes are beautiful. It's on me," he said with another charming grin.

"Thank you," I said, returning the smile. It was a very welcomed compliment during all of the shit I was feeling. I sat in the café and began to write. DAY ONE. From the moment I started writing, I could feel that this book was what I was supposed to be doing. I felt that it was one of the big reasons I was going through everything I was going through. Then I remembered the session with the psychic medium that I'd had before everything with Daniel fell apart.

"I need you writing. I really need you to be writing," she had said. Touché Madame Medium, you were correct yet again.

After about an hour in the café, and a good amount of writing, I headed out to meet the twins. Feeling funky, I was looking forward to having some company and familiar faces. With some serious luck and some help from strangers, I successfully took the tube to Russel Square Station. I hopped off to see the two smiling twins waiting to greet me.

We headed over to the restaurant where the three of us started to catch up on life. It was so nice to have some good conversations about our industry and the crazy ups and downs we had all been experiencing. Of course, I eventually had to tell them about Daniel, who they had both met before, and the Javier situation that had led me to be sitting at a restaurant in London with them.

"Wow, I had no idea," one of them said. "I mean I knew something was going on from your social media but I didn't realize it was... that," he continued.

We talked for a while about how much social media can paint a different picture than what is actually going on. We sat, ate, and talked for three hours. The time flew by and we touched on a million different topics, some of which were quite deep. I definitely got to know them much better during that one meal, and they are both really amazing humans.

Once we realized how late it was, they walked me back to the tube entrance. We snapped a picture before saying our goodbyes, then I headed back to Emma's. We opted to spend the night relaxing. Emma had gotten work off the next day (it pays to tell your boss your best friend just went through a heinous divorce and flew to London), so we were planning on spending the day and evening out.

"Have you heard from Javier?" she asked, obviously knowing what had taken place the day before.

"Nope," I said. It was 10 p.m. and it was the first day since Javier and I had gone dancing that first night that we hadn't spoken. Not a single word.

"Wow," she said.

Yeah. Wow. It was only the second day of this crazy journey, and he didn't feel the need to even check on me? I mean, sure, he had been watching every single one of my Instagram stories and knew that I was alive, but hello, you just broke my heart, put me on a plane, and are calling yourself my best friend. WHERE ARE YOU?

I decided I was going to take an Ambien and pray to anyone who was still listening up there to give me a break and let me sleep. I hopped in bed and finished up some writing and tried not to think about how weird it was that we hadn't spoken. And then, just in time, my prayers were answered and the magic little pill kicked in. Sorry brain, you'll have to overthink tomorrow because right now, I'm passing the fuck out.

Fuck
Appearances

**(Be transparent—that's the only
way you'll serve yourself and others.)**

DAY THREE

I slept. I finally fucking slept. Thank you, sweet baby Jesus. Yes, I woke up twice during the night and couldn't fall immediately back to sleep but regardless, I slept till 9:30 a.m. and that, my friends, is a win.

I snuggled in bed, allowing my body to revel in the fact that it wasn't some ungodly hour, and I began to think about the discussion the twins and I had had about social media. When I had left for this trip and posted the announcement about my divorce and the journey I was about to embark on, I had gotten so many messages. People told me they felt connected to what I was going through, that reading it had gotten them through their day, and how thankful they were to read something so open and honest. So I thought, although I had been sharing all the awesome things I was doing on my Instagram story, I should probably continue to be honest about where I was on this journey. So I did.

"Yesterday I was talking with two people about the façade on social media. In the hopes of continuing to be honest and transparent, I want to be clear: I am not 'okay.' There are days that will be amazing highs and days that will be awful lows. It is all part of the process and soon enough you'll be on the other side, seeing why it all needed to happen. Don't be afraid to meet yourself where you are, even if that is a dark place at the moment. There will eventually be light."

Posted. I started getting ready for my girls' day out with Emma when my phone went off. It was a picture. *From Javier.* There, on my WhatsApp screen, was the journal I had given him and his usual mate set-up, with a text that read:

Javier: Beautiful post, Gab. I was literally just writing about similar things. Have a great day today.

Ahh, hello surge, so *not* nice to see you again. To be honest, I didn't know how to respond. So I didn't right away. In fact, it took me four hours to figure out what the hell to write back.

"Why don't you just say 'Thanks, you too' with a smiley face?" Emma suggested.

"Because I'm not happy. I'm angry. And irritated," I said.

This was such uncharted emotional territory for me regarding Javier. Up until now, I had been so loving and compassionate and had just wanted him to be okay. Now I was realizing how not okay *I* was. The revelation I'd had the first day in London when he sent me all the photos of him in Rome really was...*real.* I was angry. And that anger had festered yesterday when I didn't hear from him. And now, for the life of me, I did not know how to answer. Finally, after putting it off for hours, I wrote back.

Me: You too. Keep writing.

Honestly, that was all I could muster up with the way I was feeling. Needless to say, there was no response. We headed off to our girls' day.

It was pouring. Like, really pouring. However, as you can read on my Twitter bio, life's too short not to dance in the rain. We ran around and took pictures in Trafalgar Square in front of the fountains and giant statues before purchasing some seriously necessary umbrellas. Again, thank God for Emma's clothes. We walked for a bit before ducking into an underground pub that was pretty empty, as expected at 1 p.m. We grabbed two cider beers (because, obviously, it's five o'clock somewhere) and sat and talked for an hour. I was so content. It felt so good being with my best friend whom I hadn't seen in so long and having no set schedule except to talk and explore at our leisure. I had made the decision that Amsterdam would be my next stop. A family friend had reached out to me on Facebook, letting me know his friend who lived there had offered to host me at her apartment. Emma helped me book my plane ticket and, boom, the next stop was chosen.

Once we finished our beers, we walked around the city. The rain had thankfully stopped by then. Walking down the street, we happened to turn to our left and see giant bedazzled Magnum ice cream bars in a window display. It was a Magnum pop-up shop and thank goodness we saw it because it was freaking amazing. Inside this little party of an ice cream store was a florescent sign that read: *A day without pleasure is a day lost*. Hell yes. We chose our flavors, and they had endless toppings you could choose from. It was literal sugar heaven—and worth every freaking calorie.

By this time we were stuffed. We walked around the city, through different squares and outdoor shops. I decided to buy a cheap selfie stick because Emma's had seriously come in handy that day when we wanted to snap some pictures. Emma had been raving about a spot called Dirty Martini (I mean...the name alone made me want to go) so we headed for some more liquid fun now that it actually *was* five o'clock.

Dirty Martini was so cool. It had a speakeasy vibe and an extensive menu with tons of amazing concoctions. Literally, you guys, best drink I have ever had. We each got three. Don't judge us, it was happy hour. We sat and talked about the never-ending saga of Javier and how pointless it was to try and analyze what was going on. During this conversation, a text from his mom came through.

Ana: Hi, Gabrielle! How are you doing? Loving London? Enjoy each and every second of this trip!

Yes, loving London under the circumstances, I suppose. I was slightly buzzed at this point, so I made sure I filtered what I was actually feeling. She had been so sweet and honest to me during all of this.

Me: Hi! It's been amazing, but lots of ups and downs emotionally. Really trying to navigate all the feelings I have around Javier. It's been tough. But having an amazing time. Adventuring around alone was liberating and wonderful. Saw two actor friends yesterday and the girlfriend I'm staying with and I are having a girls' day today.

I sent her a few photos I had taken in London so far.

Ana: Nice photos! Thank you for sharing! Have a wonderful day, sweetheart!

Emma and I finished our delicious third round and headed back toward home. The constant energy and conversation was a welcomed break from the never-ending thoughts by my overthinking brain. Once home, I said goodnight and got tucked into what was now my own little room. I started to write. It really was crazy. In the past two and a half months, I had found out my husband was having an affair, filed for divorce, fell madly in love, had my heart broken like my husband never could have done, and here I was sitting across the world as a result of it all. If you would have told me this back in the beginning of June, I would have laughed in your face. Crazy how the universe has a way of surprising you. Well, to be fair, this was not a surprise. This was like me standing on a basketball, being balanced on a chair, on top of a table, with a rug underneath—then having the rug vigorously pulled out and me falling flat on my fucking face. Still, I smiled because even after the tornados known as Daniel and Javier had swept through my world, leaving broken pieces and debris all around, I was still here. And that, was badass.

Fuck
Coincidence

(There ain't no such thing.)

DAY FOUR

I woke up that morning happy that my jet lag had started to level out. I wasn't sleeping nearly as much as I did back home, but at least it was more than a few hours every night. It was Saturday and the weather was thankfully much nicer for the day Emma and I had planned.

I sat in bed and read another chapter in *The Alchemist* before getting up for the day. One of the lines smacked me right in the face, so naturally, I posted it on my Instagram story.

"People need not fear the unknown if they are capable of achieving what they need and want."

Literally everything in my life felt unknown at this moment. I hadn't known I was going to be going on this trip alone. I didn't know what other cities I was going to end up in. I didn't know what the hell was going on with Javier and me. That is such an issue for my type of personality. I'm a planner. My friends make fun of me for how far ahead I plan our nights out. Hey, blame my mother, but regardless, being in the unknown is *really* fucking uncomfortable for me. I've always had struggles with authority and control. I don't like not having control over things in my life, especially important things. This trip was so clearly making me (at least attempt) to let that shit go.

Emma was still asleep, so I headed down the street to an ador-able little coffee shop and sat down for some writing and a delicious latté. Once I had finished the chapter I was working on, I headed back to get ready for the day. Our first stop? A proper afternoon tea.

We had found a great little spot that did a full tea spread. We spent two hours talking, laughing, and stuffing our faces with tiny sandwiches and delicious scones. There was probably enough for four people but we managed to clean the three tiers of food.

"So how are you feeling about everything with Javier? Do you think you're going to end up seeing him?" Emma asked.

"I don't know at this point. I mean, on the plane he was the one saying that was the plan but now after not hearing from him...I don't know," I said.

"Do you think there's a chance you guys will get back together? I mean, he clearly has feelings for you. That doesn't just disappear," she continued.

"I don't know. What I do know is that I have to not even let that be in my mind. I can't hope, plan, or think that anything is going to change or work out a certain way. I have to move forward," I said, trying to convince myself.

"Yeah, you can't wait around for him. It's all so messed up. You need to just enjoy your trip, have fun, and hook up with some hot men." She laughed.

"Literally, that is the last thing on my mind." I laughed with her. A handful of my friends had told me I needed to go find a hot Italian man and forget about all the bullshit that was going on. I have never been one for one-night stands. I had only had one in my twenty-eight years, and we kept in touch afterwards. Casual hookups, sure, but I most definitely was not feeling the urge to go "fuck my heartbreak away." Besides, this trip was about new beginnings and changing old patterns, not searching for a man to fix my feelings.

After tea, we seriously needed to walk off how uncomfortably full we were, so we took the long way to Camden.

Camden was like an entirely different world. Ever been to Venice Beach in Cali? Well, it's like that...on crack. It was a mile of street with endless shops on both sides, then a bunch of paths and walkways that branch off to even more incredible shops and food spots. It was never-ending and freaking awesome.

I had decided I needed some type of souvenir from each country I was going to visit. Since I was traveling with my one giant (but fully stuffed) backpack, I didn't have a ton of room for souvenirs, so I decided to get a meaningful bracelet from each place I traveled to. Since they would each go straight on my wrist when I bought them, they wouldn't take up any room, and it would be a cool representation of each place.

We walked through rows and rows of stands until one jewelry stand caught my eye. Each piece had a paper with a saying on it that explained what the jewelry meant. I zeroed in on one that was two little sterling silver hearts on two black bands. The piece of paper read "adventure awaits." Done. That would be my London bracelet. I also bought two little gold rings from a different stand. One was an infinity symbol that I unconsciously placed on my ring finger.

After shopping for a bit, we stumbled on a stand that had a bunch of different stones. I was immediately drawn to it and knew that I wanted to get a few to take on the rest of my trip with me.

"Pick which ones you're pulled to choose. They all have different meanings, but it's best if you choose without knowing them," the older lady said to me.

I stood there for a moment, looking at the different stones. My mother is a healer, and I'm very spiritual, so it didn't seem weird to me that stones will energetically "pick you." Once I had selected four of them, she began to tell me what they were and the meanings they held. Are you ready for this shit?

Orange Calcite – Balances Emotions. (HA. Shocker.)
Green Calcite – Opens and Clears Heart Chakra. (Which is so most definitely closed right now.)
Rose Quartz – The 'Heart Stone,' Love, Compassion, Trust. (Oh, the irony.)
Pyrite – Protection and Grounding. (Lord, do I need some of that shit right now.)

I mean...COME ON. How incredibly appropriate. Emma and I just looked at each other and laughed. I was so happy to have these stones in my possession, and they would prove to be very helpful in the coming weeks.

Emma and I went back home and relaxed a little before heading to dinner at a delicious Thai place right on the water. It was my last night in London. My last night with Emma. My last night in any type of comfort zone.

We talked about Amsterdam and what I had planned there so far. A girl I had worked with on a film had messaged to tell me her younger sister was traveling alone in Amsterdam and sent me her information. Her name was Cally, and we had chatted online and decided to do a pub crawl together on my second night in town, which would be her last. That was all I had planned, which of course, was super unlike my planning-ahead self. We talked about where I might go after Amsterdam. I knew I wanted to go to Barcelona. It felt like something was pulling me toward Barcelona, and I told Emma I felt like something important was going to happen there. Although I didn't know when I would go, it was definitely on my list.

"So you know you put that infinity ring on your ring finger," Emma pointed out.

"Shit. I did," I said, just realizing it. It hadn't been intentional but sure enough, I had put the little gold ring directly on *that* finger. "Well...," I said, "it will be a good reminder to never stop loving myself," I concluded. From then on, whenever I looked at it, I was reminded of that.

That night when I got in bed, my brain was flooded with thoughts. I hadn't spoken to Javier in almost three full days. I knew he was viewing all of my travels on my Instagram story, but the fact that I hadn't heard from him was crazy to me. Did he not want to hear my voice and ask me if I was okay? Did he just flat out not want to talk to me? Or did he just not care? Again, trying to analyze this human was literally impossible. Still, I knew a Thought Onion might give me some type of clarity on how *I* was feeling. What's the superficial thought here?

- Does he think this is normal? That everyone is like him and can just run off with a fucking backpack and be super strong and be fine? Because *this*? *This* is not fucking normal. Especially for me.

And it wasn't. Sure, I'm a strong freaking woman. My mother would say that, my friends would say that, hell, my ex-husband would say that. But my mom was right when she pulled Javier aside the day he brought me back from camping. I was fragile. I was really fucking fragile right now. And yes, I'm strong and have done some amazing things in my life. Pick up and leave the country to travel *by myself* for a month without any research or plans in place? No. That is not me. Nor is that normal. And it was fucking scary. Now, what's the authentic thought?

- Why doesn't he care about me? And if he does, why the hell isn't he doing anything to show it?

I mean, yeah...here I was thinking this man loved me. I mean *really* loved me, the way that I loved him. But there is no way you would just cast someone you love out into the ocean and hope they freaking float. Uh, hello, the least you could do is give me a fucking life jacket. Jeez. And, finally, what's the subconscious thought?

- Why do I need a man in my life? Why can't I just take care of my damn self?

DING DING DING. There it is. Welcome to having your father die at age six and your boyfriend die at eighteen. The second I lost my dad, I felt like I needed that male figure in my life. Once I got older, that male figure naturally became a boyfriend. When I lost Jake, it made it all the more real. I was not safe if I didn't have a man in my life. It was as if there was a hole in my heart that I kept trying to repeatedly patch with different men. I honestly can't remember the last time I was single for more than a month. Why can I not just be okay by *myself*? Why can *I* not be enough? That is where the real core issue of my genetic makeup is, and that is what I need to begin to adjust and heal. Ah, so much easier said than done.

I was more than a little freaked out. To be honest, I was slightly panicking. I took a Xanax, partly to not have a freak out and partly to make sure I slept. I mean, yes, I was taking this bold trip by myself but let's be honest—up until this point I'd had one of my best friends there for comfort and security. Tomorrow, that would all be gone and I would really be on my own. Without Emma, and without Javier.

All this thinking really brought my emotions out. I sat there in my guest bed on my last night with tears rolling down my cheeks. I just wanted to pick up the phone and call him. I just wanted to hear his voice and have him tell me everything was fine and that he was there. But I didn't. Instead I called my mom, the one constant in my life. Talking to her made me feel better, although I could hear in her voice that she was *hoping* I would be okay, and that was a new sound for her.

After we hung up, I took deep breaths, trying to calm myself down. *Amsterdam will be amazing*, I thought. *It's going to be an adventure.* I thought about what I might do in this next country. I needed some type of rebalancing. I wanted to find a meditation center, take a yoga class, reconnect with myself. Oh, silly Gabrielle, that is definitely *not* what Amsterdam would bring.

Fuck
The Safety Net

(You just have to jump.)

DAY FIVE

I hugged Emma and Mark, thanked them for everything, and slung my ridiculously heavy pack onto my back. I took a deep breath and walked away—away from the comfort of my friend, the comfort of familiarity, the comfort of London. I still hadn't spoken to Javier. It had been three full days now, and it was driving me crazy.

Once my bag was checked and I was through security, I had lunch while I killed some time writing. I finished a chapter just as it was time to board. Here I come, Amsterdam.

I was off to meet the woman who had graciously agreed to host me. She had even offered to pick me up from the airport that evening. When I arrived, I got my backpack and headed out of the gate. There was Ineke, a young sixty-year-old in a polka dot dress and leggings, hair in a high bun with thick bangs on her forehead, and glasses so thick they could have been shields.

She waved to me with a smile, and I headed toward her. She greeted me with a big hug, and I instantly felt safe and a little more relaxed. Ineke looked like an adorable real-life cartoon character, like she had just stepped off the pages of your favorite nursery rhyme.

We rode back to the apartment that would be my home for the next few days. It was unlike anything I had ever seen. Filled with color, the living room was clumped together in reds, oranges, and pinks. The kitchenware was colored plastics that felt like what you'd find in Minnie Mouse's house at Disneyland. There was a giant red vintage refrigerator, an actual diner booth as the kitchen table, and organized stacks of brightly colored chaos everywhere. It was borderline hoarder yet so fun and vibrant it just...worked. The living room had small chairs pushed together with red, orange, and pink pillows on top that made it into a makeshift couch. This couch looked out a big bay window onto the most perfect patio I had ever seen, with a quaint table and two chairs that had a view of the striking brick building surrounded by massive, gorgeous trees. It was beautiful. That window would become my spot for the next few days.

After I settled into my room, which oddly enough was all white and had strange little life-size mannequin dolls in the corner (still not sure what those were for), Ineke offered to take me to dinner.

We went to one of her favorite spots that was literally in the back courtyard of her apartment building. It was an old factory that had been converted into a restaurant.

She ordered us each a glass of wine and some strange sausage I agreed to try, all in Dutch. What an interesting language it is. She said something about the sausage being made with blood, so I tried not to think about what I was actually consuming. It was pretty delicious, honestly.

While we waited for our entrée, I asked her how she had come to know my friend in the States. What an incredible story she began to tell me. She and her friend had left home to travel the United States for a year. Along the way, a friend had put her in contact with my friend's mother in Los Angeles. She ended up becoming dear friends with the mother and father, often babysitting my friend (who was two at the time and is in his forties now) and staying much longer than she ever anticipated. She lived with them for some time, working and enjoying LA, and they've been close friends ever since. I was in awe listening to her story. What a brave adventure to have experienced so young. I mean, I was on a trip across the world but not really by my choice. It more or less had happened *to* me. I don't think I would have ever been as brave as Ineke and just decided to leave home without a plan for that long. Yet, here I was, on my own little version of self-discovery. Why did I admire her story and not recognize my own?

"And what about you, Gabrielle?"

Ah yes. My insane last three months. I told her the semi-long version, a few times actually getting choked up a bit. She didn't interrupt, she didn't ask questions, she just listened intently with sympathy and compassion in her eyes. I finished with the most recent events—the photos Javier had sent me in London and the fact that we hadn't spoken for three days. When I was done, she looked at me and after a long beat said, "You are so strong. You need to do what is best for you now." I kept hearing that from people, and I knew they were right. But knowing that wasn't the problem...figuring out how to *do* that is what is fucking hard.

She graciously insisted on paying for dinner. Back at the apartment, she gave me a set of keys and showed me what bus to take to get into the city. After we said goodnight, I went to my room to decompress before bed.

I couldn't stop thinking. Why had he not reached out to me? Why hadn't he checked on me? The countless options that came from attempting to analyze it and him were exhausting. Fuck this. I texted his mother.

Me: We haven't talked in 3 days. I've been struggling with so many emotions trying to deal with how I'm feeling about...everything. And now with the distance from not hearing from him, I don't know if I should be trying to love and support him still or just be giving both of us space to be by ourselves.

She responded right away.

Ana: Well, it is interesting how things can be interpreted differently. He told me that he sent you a text, and your short response made him think that you needed space, and it was not a good idea trying to ask how you were doing. I think that you need to do what is best for you, and if contacting him makes you sad, don't do it. But I cannot believe that the connection you two had just vanished. It is impossible to go from everything to nothing, but if a little something hurts you or keeps you from enjoying this trip, you know what to do.

Okay...so it *had* been because he knew I was affected by the pictures. But still, silence for three days? I explained to her what had hit me in London after seeing all his photos and how I came to realize that deep down I was angry with him.

Me: And when I asked myself, "Well, why am I angry?" it's because some small part of me, deep down, doesn't believe he can just fall out of love with me that quickly. No matter what the reasoning. But I'm aware that is not my judgment to make. Simply saying that's where it was all coming from. But I love him so much I pushed a lot of that down because I want him to be okay. Contacting him doesn't make me sad. I haven't stopped thinking about him for more than a minute. I just don't know how to try and begin to heal my heart, because he made me feel that what we will be is friends.

Ana: Dear Gabrielle, he is my son and I love him deeply, but I am also a woman, and I know exactly how you feel, and I believe every word you say. Javi had girlfriends that I didn't like for him. However, I opened my house and I did my best to embrace them. With you I felt exactly the opposite. I was happy for him. I felt relieved that someone will care for him. When Javier came to us crying, he told us that he needed to believe that he could be happy without feeling guilty. He said that he was empty, disconnected from life. His father and I felt so much pain that I cannot describe. I want him to be okay, and I feel that he will probably regret pushing you away in order to heal, and to be alone. I understand what you feel, more than you know, but if you were my daughter, I would tell you to love and take care of yourself first. I cannot ask you to be his friend, or wait for him. You are such a wonderful and kind person, you deserve to be loved without any conditions. What I'm trying to tell you is: do not let anyone, not even my son, treat you or care for you less than what you deserve.

God damn. She always hits me with all the feels when she texts me. I was so impressed with how unbiased she was toward her son.

Me: I know. I feel the same about you. I can't even begin to tell you. And believe me, a big part of my brain and a huge part of my heart wants to hold onto the thought that maybe he will heal, maybe he will come out of this on the other side and all those feelings I saw in his eyes will come back. But the way he explained everything to me…when I flat out asked him if he felt anything more than a friendship toward me and he answered "no"…I just can't comprehend how that is possible. It is one thing to need to love yourself and find your way back to peace. It's another to fall out of love and into a friendship. So when my heart wants to hold onto that what if, I know that I can't wait in limbo in hopes something may change. It is genuinely one of the hardest experiences I have ever dealt with in my life. And I've had many. Every fiber of my being wants to be back in whatever it was we were in three weeks ago. But my brain is telling me that I need to protect myself and try and move forward. I just literally don't know how to. The thought of meeting him at the end of the trip is so confusing to me. But I would be lying if I didn't say a part of me thinks I should fight him pushing me away because I know that's what he's always done when he hurts. I can't describe the conflict constantly going on in me the past week.

Ana: I'm so sorry that you are hurting. I know that I'm not helping you by saying all this, but I was also shocked when he told me. There are people who hurt other people on purpose, or that simply do not care. Javier is the exact opposite, and he thought, and thinks, that he has to be honest, and because he cares about you, he didn't want you to suffer with all the ups and downs of his grief. I know that his good intentions do not make things easier for you, not now. I honestly want him AND you to be fine. I do not want his well-being to be the price of your pain. I do not know how to help, and I wish he will soon find his way back to you, but you do not have to wait, you have to live to the fullest for you, and only for you.

Me: It's not making it easier but it is helping me. I will never not be his friend. I've told him that. I just don't know how to be right now. And I know there is nothing you can say or do. It's his life and no one really knows what he's feeling. But I can't thank you enough for your support and your words. It truly means the world to me. I've only spent two days with you, but you feel like a mother to me.

Ana: And you feel like a daughter to me too. Perhaps you have to be angry at him to be able to move on. I'm not saying anger is a good feeling but may be the necessary phase to be strong and to truly believe that someone will love you unconditionally. Do not ever, ever accept less.

Me: I won't. That is one thing I am certain of. Thank you for talking me through some of this. I appreciate it more than you know. It's 3 a.m. here, I'm going to try to sleep.

Ana: Please count on me always.

Me: I do.

And with that, I left another safety net. I texted Javier.

Me: Can we talk tomorrow?

Fuck
Limbo

(Peace begins when you make a decision.)

DAY SIX

I just hung up. I literally *just* hit end on the FaceTime call. So why have I already forgotten everything that was just said? Why is it all running together like one big blur? I can't say I got any clarity from that whatsoever. But I did feel a little...better. Okay. Let's try and recount the hour and forty-five-minute conversation.

The call came in. I answered. His face looked so different, yet exactly the same. His beard was much more filled in. He wore a dark blue baseball cap, and a heavy heart looked at me through sad eyes. I wanted to jump through the phone and throw my arms around him. He sat on a floor in a mall somewhere in a small mountain town in Italy. We were so far away yet I felt so incredibly close. After he told me about the Russian woman's home he was staying in and how shitty the Wi-Fi was, I gave him a quick peek at Ineke's eclectic apartment, which I already felt so at home in.

"Your mother is...absolutely incredible," I said. He nodded. But he had no concept of the conversations we'd had and how our connection had grown. He told me he knew I was upset when my answers became short, and I explained what I had just told his mother a few hours earlier. Only this time tears immediately escaped my eyes. I struggled to keep them in the best I could. I was so worried he would feel guilt or pain knowing what I was going through and hearing what I had realized that first day in London, and that was the last thing I wanted. I could barely look at the screen as I spoke. I knew that if I saw the pain on his face, I wouldn't be able to finish or say everything how it needed to be said. He said he knew. Right after he sent the first twenty-two photos he knew. And again, when he sent the photo of the journal and the mate.

"Why are you sending her that?" he told me he questioned himself. He knew I had been affected by it all. I told him that the last three days of not speaking had been awful. I explained that, after the initial twenty-two photos, the first day without speaking had made my emotions fester and grow, which prompted the short response. "Cold," as he described it. I told him I hadn't intended to be cold, I just didn't know how to navigate what I was feeling. And that during the following three days, I went back and forth between "I should just reach out and talk to him," and "This motherfucker hasn't even checked in on me."

"I have been!" he cut me off. "I've been watching your whole trip. You sent a postcard to your mom..." Of course, I knew this. I could see he had been watching every Instagram story I posted.

"It's not the same," I said. He nodded. He said I deserved to feel anger, and that he understood all that I was saying.

"I had to open the letter you gave me," he said. *Oh*, I thought. My heart hurt knowing that during those three days he had needed me. "Thank you *so* much for that." He told me that one night he had taken his hammock deep into the forest and had an intense meditation with the sunset. He had almost frozen, but it had pushed him through a lot of stuff.

We talked about our connection and how different it was. How *instant* it was. How powerful it was.

"I was seeing your posts and you seemed to be enjoying yourself and I thought, 'Yes. Good, she's happy. She's ok,'" he said. "And then when I saw other things it made me feel so bad. I wanted to put aside all I was dealing with to try and help you. I care about you so much."

"Stop," I said. "That is why it took me three days to decide if I should tell you all this. Because the *last* thing I want is for you to put everything on hold or feel more guilt. I do *not* want that. The best thing you could do for me is to go heal yourself and learn to love yourself. And not for me or what that could mean for 'us.' For you. Because I want that for *you*."

That was when I realized that this—what I was in, knee deep—was full and complete *selfless* love. This was new.

And that's when he said it for the first time.

"I love you, Gabs," he said. A pause.

"I know," I replied. And I did. I knew when we woke up camping on the beach. I knew when he texted me in Argentina saying, "I can't believe I get to be with you." I knew when he couldn't let me go when I left his mom's house for the first time, and every other time he hadn't wanted to let me go. I knew when he said, "This is my girlfriend, Gabrielle," to every friend I met at the wedding. I knew the first time we made love, and every time after that. I knew when we were in Vegas, lying in the bathtub. I knew when he sat on my bed in tears explaining how unfair it was that he was experiencing these feelings. And I even knew on the phone that Friday night when I asked, "Do you feel anything for me right now besides friendship?" I had known all along. I wish I could say that I felt nothing hearing him say it out loud for the first time. Oh, how I wish. But that would be too simple. Instead, I felt the surge. The same surge I'd felt when he'd responded "no." The same surge I'd felt when I saw the photos. I was so damn tired of this fucking surge.

We went on to talk about my book. About his journaling. About everything.

Finally, I said, "There's still that little piece inside me that feels like this is a cop-out." His face fell. Although he could see it from that perspective, I think it still hurt to hear it come from me.

"I'm not running," he responded.

"Okay," I said. We talked about plans (or lack thereof) for the rest of our trips. "When is it you're in San Vito with the boys?" I asked.

"The twentieth for ten days," he said. Ding. The surge. Why did I think he was going to be there much earlier, leaving a good week at the end of the trip? That left only two to three days before our flight home. Even with my conscious decision not to fantasize and play out scenarios, apparently a week together had still MacGyvered its way into my damn head. Well, time to actually live what I had been preaching to Emma the past week. I cannot plan, hope, wish, decide, or think about that possibility. Not a week, not three days, not a day. And with that, the last little bit of fairy-tale ending left. And it *hurt*.

I told him I didn't want him to be cautious with sending me things. If he wanted to talk to me, he should reach out. Because in my soul I knew that he needed me, even if he didn't know it...although I think he did. He agreed.

"My phone's at 8 percent," he said with a longing in his eyes that showed this talk had brought comfort to him.

"Okay," I replied. Our talks always seemed to last longer than necessary but felt unduly short.

"I'm glad we got to talk. I'm proud of you. I miss you. Please be safe," I said.

"You too, please." His voice cracked.

"I love you," I said.

"I love you," he said back. I hit the end call button. A few moments later I sent him a picture that read "Fear has two meanings. Forget Everything And Run or Face Everything And Rise."

Me: Don't run.

Javier: I won't.

I sat back on the couch and looked out at the green trees blowing in the wind. Jesus. Fucking. Christ.

Fuck
What Was His Name Again?

(Yeah...It was *that* type of night.)

DAY SEVEN

had spent the whole day writing after Javier and I had spoken on FaceTime. For six hours, I sat in Ineke's beautiful apartment looking out the big bay window at the vibrant greenery and the rain falling between rays of sunshine. At one point, I went out on the balcony and sat on the ledge with my four stones as I sipped on a cup of tea. When I got up to go back inside, I heard something fall. I had dropped one of my stones and it had fallen where I couldn't see it and had no hopes of retrieving it. It was the balancing of emotions stone. How incredibly ironic. I continued to write. Every time I finished a chapter, it gave me some type of...completion. I had needed this day. I had been up until 3 a.m. talking to Javier's mom and then up at 6 a.m. before talking to him. Between all the emotions and the lack of sleep, it was all starting to take a toll. But sitting in this little slice of heaven, reading and writing, felt really good.

Around 3 p.m., a FaceTime call came in from Javier's sister, Sophia. Seeing her face instantly made my heart smile. She had such an energy about her that radiated through her face. I updated her on what had happened in London that had led to Javier and I not speaking and on the conversation we had just had that morning.

"Javi is so fucking stubborn," she said. She always kept everything so real. I told her that the core of my anger stemmed from not believing that he could just go from being madly in love with me to feeling nothing.

"None of us do," she agreed. "It's not possible. You must not be able to trust anything he says right now. *I* don't even trust what he says right now. He's all over the place." Okay, good, it wasn't just me. I told her she *had* to visit Westminster Abbey when she got to London. She told me about a week-long love affair she'd had with a German girl in Spain, and we laughed like we had been best friends for years. What was it about this family that made me feel so instantly connected? It was the polar opposite of everything I had experienced with Daniel's family. I always used to tell myself, "You're marrying him, not his family." No. Fuck that shit. I have never been so thankful to disconnect from a family. That may sound harsh but every person reading this book that knew Daniel's parents is sitting there nodding their heads. I will never again venture deep into commitment with someone who doesn't have a family I want to be a part of.

During my hour conversation with Sophia, she said something that really resonated with me. After I explained to her that I couldn't wait in limbo for Javier to hopefully wake up and feel for me again, she asked, "Why?"

Why?! Because I'm fucking heartbroken. Because that's the smart thing to do. Because *fuck* that.

"You don't have to sit and wait around for him, Gabrielle, but you don't have to cut off all ties and possibilities for the future. Then you will always have a little piece of you that says, 'What if?'"

Well...yes, she was right. But I also knew I couldn't keep feeling like this. It just hurt too much. So how would I decide which to attempt?

"You have to grieve this relationship. What you two had the past month and a half was, and is, very real. But no matter what happens in the future...whether you two have a friendship or a relationship, it will never be what it was the past month," she said.

Wow. What an incredibly accurate fucking statement. I had to admit that, although it profoundly resonated with me, I wasn't sure what it meant I needed to do. But I knew it was an important piece of this unfathomably complicated puzzle.

"Are you and Javi going to see each other?" she asked. Good fucking question. As of that morning's conversation, I would say no, whereas on the plane ride to London, I had thought yes. I talked it through with her.

"It doesn't feel right that all this has happened and we're just going to...what? Fly home and say see you in four months after you go film in Mexico? Where is the closure in that? I'll need to do a lot of work to get a certain amount of it, yes, but I feel that after all this, all we have been through—and are still going through—it deserves *some* type of something," I explained.

"You're absolutely right. You 100 percent deserve that," she said.

"But why should I have to be the one who initiates seeing him? And what if it's not what he wants or needs?" I asked.

"Who cares?" she said directly. "You need to do what is best for you. If that is something you want and need, you need to say that and put it out there. Then at least you've done all you can do and it's out of your hands." Seriously. His sister was like fucking Yoda.

* * * * *

After hanging up with Sophia, I showered and got ready for my night out. Jeans, a one-piece bathing suit that was doubling as a bodysuit/top, flats I had bought with Emma in London, and a light jacket. Not bad for living out of a backpack. I locked up the apartment and hopped in an Uber to Dam Square.

I met Cally, who I had been Facebook chatting with the past few days, for dinner at a cute little restaurant, where we sat at a table with a big window looking out at the city streets. Cally was only twenty and talking with her made me realize how insanely long ago that seemed. I felt like I had lived ten lifetimes since I was twenty. We ate a delicious meal, and I told her my "story," which was now always being referenced as "the ridiculous Netflix show that has become my life."

After dinner we had about thirty minutes before we were supposed to meet for the pub crawl we had booked. We decided to find a coffee shop, grab a latté, and share a joint. I mean, when in Amsterdam... I don't smoke, although I have socially in the past, more so in my younger party years. But weed has always made me want to eat everything in sight and go to sleep, which is really not conducive to my lifestyle of not wanting to be fat.

Afterward, we went to the square where we were supposed to meet for the pub crawl we had signed up for. By this time, it was fucking pouring, and my light LA jacket could be rung out like a towel. It was a monsoon, and we both looked like drowned rats. There we met one of the two guides who worked for the pub crawl company. For purposes of this chapter, we will call the two guides by where they were from, which will also paint a picture of the accents they spoke in.

"Here for the pub crawl?" Australia said.

"Yep!" we said through uncontrollable shivering. We were the only two who had chosen to meet at the outdoor monument. All the smart people had apparently just headed to the first bar location.

"Great! Let's go!" he said. "It's about a fifteen-minute walk to the first spot." Um...you're fucking kidding, right? Wrong.

Halfway through it thankfully let up a little bit. By the time we finally arrived at the first bar, my feet felt like I would for sure be getting frostbite by the end of the night. We were greeted by the second guide, a tall, sandy-brown-haired guy with crystal blue eyes who asked for our tickets. This was Ireland. We handed him the tickets and walked inside.

"He's gorgeous," Cally said. And he was. But the last thing on my mind was anything to do with men. Ugh, men.

We headed to the bar. At each location, we were all given tokens to get either a beer or a glass of wine. We each got a Heineken (which was all they offered), and I was immediately taken back to beer pong in college. We met a group of people traveling together from Jersey. Not Jersey Shore, Jersey, but Jersey as in the coast of France by Normandy. The two girls were super sweet, and we all began chatting. The two guys they were traveling with talked and joked with us, as well. Then there were Josh and Yeung, who had met each other at their hostel. Josh was from San Fran and Yeung was from New York.

I chatted with Yeung for a while, as we were both traveling alone for the first time. He was super cool and down to earth. I asked him how old he was, and he told me he'd be twenty-five in a few days. *God I'm old*, I thought. And divorced. I laughed at myself.

Australia began walking around with a giant bottle of watered-down blueberry vodka. The pub crawl included unlimited vodka shots the first half hour. Now, although I used to drink and party with the best of them, that is *so* no longer the case. More than five drinks and I am for sure puking the next day. My hangovers are *no* joke. Like, it doesn't matter if I'm scheduled to go see the president, I'm not going. I knew I needed to try and watch how much I drank and how many types of alcohol I mixed. Cally and I had already had a gin drink at dinner. But Australia was fucking relentless, walking around pouring shots into everyone's mouths. We probably had at least...eight? Now, mind you, I'm 99 percent positive they had filled a third of that bottle with water, but nevertheless...

We were all given T-shirts that were kind of lame but super comfortable and, more important, dry. Almost all of our huge group put them on, including me. Then it was off to bar number two.

We got to the second bar and were given our tokens by Ireland. It was more like a small club than a bar. They had a fog machine going with loud (and great) music. We headed to the bar, and Yeung told us he had heard about these shots called Harry Potter shots that they light on fire.

"I love *Harry Potter*!" Cally squealed. Oy, here we go. We ordered three of them from the obnoxiously good-looking bartender. I still have no idea what was actually *in* the shots but what a fucking display! After they were poured, the bartender lit them (and a good portion of the bar) on fire. He then shook some type of spices or something onto them, which made the whole thing spark and fly around even more. It was pretty freaking cool. After that magical display, we headed over to where the Jersey group and Josh were dancing. "Despacito" came on. In case you were living under a rock during the summer of 2017, it's a famous Latin song that became even more famous when Justin Bieber jumped on the remix.

"I'm waiting for the day I don't want to burst into tears when I hear this song come on," I said to Cally, laughing, only kind of kidding. We danced for a bit and then saw an electronic menu of all the different kinds of shots they had at the bar. So, you remember back in chapter one when I told you my mom was an actress? Well, one of the roles she's widely known for is playing the mother in *E.T.*—and what do I see on the menu? An "E.T. shot." HA!

"We have to get an E.T. shot!" I said to my new group of random friends.

"Okay!" one of the girls said. "Why?"

"Have you seen the movie *E.T.,* with the alien?" I asked.

"Duh," someone answered.

"My mom is the mom in that." My buzzed self laughed. Everyone got super excited, either because we were slightly drunk or because they thought it made me slightly famous. Either way, we got the shots, which were a mint-chocolate-green liquid. I sent a video of it to my mom.

After that shot at the bar, a guy came over and introduced himself to me. He was very sweet and seemed like a cool, down to earth guy. Let me give you a mental picture:

-Brazilian

-Dark hair and features with a beard

-Spoke five languages

-Latin accent

Sound fucking familiar? He was literally a slightly less attractive version of Javier. Really, universe? Why? His name was Paulo.

Paulo and I spoke about many things that night—where we were from, why we were traveling alone, and where we were going next. He too had just broken up with someone a few months earlier. Paulo worked on a cruise line seven months out of the year. I told him about Daniel, about Javier, and the ridiculous events in the last three months that had led me here.

"How could anyone be so stupid to have someone like you and let you go?" he asked in his Brazilian accent. What a seemingly simple question, yet it made me feel so many different things. To Thought Onion that little statement was quite interesting. The superficial thought:

- He's an idiot and made the biggest mistake of his life.

Although that implies I think way more highly of myself than I actually do. The authentic thought:

- Clearly, he wasn't deserving of me and all I have to give.

Hmm...I felt that way about Daniel. Not about Javier. And the subconscious thought:

- Maybe I'm just not good enough.

Fuck.

As we walked to the next few bars, Paulo stayed close by, and I introduced him to the others in our little group.

"Find me on Instagram!" one of the Jersey girls yelled. Everyone began to connect on social media before we got any more intoxicated. She handed me her phone, and I typed in my name.

"Oh my God, you're verified!" she shrieked, and she and everyone suddenly became very excited again. As they all asked who I was and what I did, I laughed. This silly little blue checkmark had made them suddenly think I was important, when I knew that I wasn't. Not in that way, at least.

They all wanted to know where they could see my films and what I had been in. I've never been good at talking about my career because I don't feel that I'm anywhere near as well established as I'd like to be. Most of the time when people ask what I do, I won't even tell them. But on this journey, I wanted to meet people as my authentic self, with no reservations or cover-ups, and part of that is my acting.

We continued hopping from bar to bar, dancing at each. Paulo and I found ourselves in more than a few deep conversations, shouting over the music.

"If you ever want to come on a cruise, you tell me and I will take care of it all, and you can stay with me. A week, twelve days, whatever you want." What was it with these Latin men wanting to immediately whisk me off on some grand adventure? Knowing my recent track record, he would probably leave me on an island in the middle of the ocean two days in. Paulo was very sweet, and I really enjoyed talking to him. I felt a friendship with him similar to the first time I met Javier. But there was nothing beyond that.

"I have to tell you, Gabrielle. I know you've been through a lot, but I feel a connection with you. I feel like I have to say it or I may regret it. You are an incredible woman," he said over the music. *Incredible woman*. Something Javier says to me. Says *about* me. What the hell does that even mean?

"I'm so far from being able to be with anyone or even think about that," I said with a smile, because his honesty was genuine and commendable. "We can go to lunch tomorrow if you want?" I offered. He smiled and said okay.

By the time we all walked to the last bar, it had, thankfully, finally stopped raining. I went to the bar to get a much-needed water and found myself standing next to Ireland.

"Water, huh?" he teased. "Are you really that old?" He smiled.

"Yes. I'm really fucking old," I replied.

"Oh, please, you can't be older than me," he responded.

"I guarantee you I am," I said.

"Give me your ID," he said, putting his hand out.

I slapped it down and said, "Twenty-eight."

"Ah. I don't believe it." He looked at it. He was twenty-seven. He handed it back to me and stared at me, then smiled.

"What?" I asked.

"You ready for some wild sex?" he said. I literally laughed out loud. Good one, dude.

"Maybe tomorrow night," I joked.

"Why? Why not tonight?" I just laughed. He couldn't be serious. I could feel Paulo's eyes on me watching this exchange. Well, this was...*awkward*. I grabbed my water and headed over to Paulo. Josh and Cally had joined him. The night was ending and we were hungry.

"Crepes?" Cally suggested. Everyone's drunk munchies agreed. I walked back over to Ireland and asked where we could get crepes close by.

"Right there." He pointed across the street a few doors down. "Are you ready?" he asked. Forrrrr...? He couldn't be serious.

"You can take my number, if you want," I offered to dodge this incredibly weird exchange that was taking place.

"No, just come with me," he persisted.

"We're going to eat!" I said as I began to walk toward the others. He grabbed my arm.

"Fine," he said. He handed me his phone. I put my number in his WhatsApp and walked out with Paulo, Cally, and Josh to the café.

We ordered two "pancakes." First of all, these were not pancakes. They were fucking pizza-size dessert pies of heaven and diabetes waiting to happen. We all sat and laughed and talked about our night.

Everyone began to decide on their routes home. It was around 2:30 a.m. Paulo gave me a hug and asked about lunch tomorrow.

"2 p.m.?" I suggested.

"Perfect," he said as he put his number in my WhatsApp. We said goodbye and I stood with Cally and Josh. A text popped up on my phone.

Ireland: Ready for some fun?

Fuck. I had completely forgotten about Ireland.

Me: Yes, Sir.

Wait...Um, no? Why did I even just respond?

Ireland: Where are you now?

Me: At the café across the street you pointed at.

Ireland: Haha
Ireland: Wanna go do bad things?

That was so not sexy, bro.

Me: You're awful.

Me: What part of tomorrow did you not understand? Is it an Ireland thing?

Ireland: Pffff (accompanied by a snoring emoji)

Me: And how do you expect me to get home?
Me: I'm gonna grab an Uber unless you're still at the bar.

Ireland: I'm close. You want to meet me in front of Burger King?

No, Gabrielle, you want to go home.

Me: I'm right outside Burger King.
Me: To go where?

Ireland: My place.

Me: Ok.

Ireland: Gimme 5 min.

Me: Ya.

Fuck. What the fuck am I doing? I'm literally standing here, having an inner dialogue with myself. Gabrielle. Go home. No part of you wants to have sex right now. No part of you wants to do this. You are literally already regretting this decision. Go. Home.

He walked up and grabbed my hand, and we walked over to the taxi line. He asked the driver a few questions, and then he opened the door for me to get in.

Just say "I can't" and go home. It is seriously that simple.

I got in. The cab started to move, and Ireland immediately grabbed me and started making out with me. I felt like I was back in college. This poor cab driver—how incredibly awkward. After a minute of making out, I pulled away and let out something between a laugh and a sigh.

"So give me the two-minute version of your story, why you're here," he said. HA. Do you even know what you just asked, dude?

"It's uh...a lot," I said.

"Well, you have one hundred and twenty seconds. Go."

Pause.

"Three months ago, I found out my husband of two years had been having an affair with a nineteen-year-old for six months. I filed for divorce and left. Met a guy, fell madly in love with each other, and he convinced me to go on a month-long trip to Italy with him. He started experiencing a ton of grief over something that happened to him, and he decided two days before the trip he needed to go on his own. Broke my heart. So I decided I could either sit at home and be heartbroken or come travel for a month by myself, so here I am."

Another pause.

"Oh shit," he said.

"Yep," I agreed.

"So you're like...fucked up."

I laughed. "Yep. Okay, your turn."

He proceeded to tell me just as quickly how he'd left Ireland at seventeen to travel. He told me about all the different places he had been and lived, including how he'd fallen in love with a blonde from Chicago. He'd moved there for her, but she turned out to be bat-shit crazy. He'd torn his ACL, so he'd had to stop everything and rehab his body and mind. He ended up in Amsterdam a year ago and hadn't been home in years. It was actually quite deep for one hundred and twenty seconds in the back of a cab in what was such a ridiculous situation.

We hopped out of the cab and he paid.

"That cab driver just got *so* much more than he bargained for." I laughed. I followed Ireland inside and we took the elevator up and into the apartment.

"I have to pee," I said, clearly giving a shit about being *super* sexy. He opened the door to the bathroom, and I went in to pee while my inner dialogue continued.

Why are you doing this? No part of you wants to do this, Gabrielle. Besides the fact that you know this is the last thing you need, is it because everyone has been saying you should go be wild and have fun on this trip? What are you trying to prove?

I left the bathroom and walked up the steep winding stairs that were so typical in Amsterdam but *so* fucking impractical. He was lying on the queen-sized bed fully clothed. I sat my purse down and sighed.

"I'm trying to decide if I should ask you what your name is or just...not," I said.

"No," he responded.

"Yeah," I agreed.

I climbed onto the bed and we started to make out. I literally couldn't even try to convince myself to relax and get into it. I was already waiting for it to be over and wondering what I could snack on when I finally got home. He flipped me over and took off my clothes. Then he stood up and undressed. Don't get me wrong, Ireland was a pretty perfect specimen of a man. I mean, even as I yelled at myself inside my head, there was a definite moment when I just stopped and said to myself, *"Well, good for you, Gabrielle,"* just for the sheer fact that he was drop-dead gorgeous.

I watched him put a condom on as I rolled my eyes at the fact that I had let this night get to this moment. The worst part? All I could fucking think about was Javier.

I will spare you the fifty shades of details, but I will tell you it was oddly...rough. Like, if he wasn't so hot and if I had taken a moment to consider that I was in a foreign country with a random stranger, it might have been a little scary rough. I faked an orgasm because Lord knows there was a *zero* percent chance of that happening, and God forbid he actually cared enough to keep going until it did. He finished and fell back onto the bed. I instantly stood up and grabbed my jeans. As I put them on, I said, "Okay, I gotta go!" He slowly stood up and grabbed a pair of sweats. "Can you call an Uber from my phone? Here's the address," I said, handing him the phone. He smiled and did.

We walked down stairs and into the elevator.

"You gonna be all right?" he asked.

No. Probably not.

"Yes," I said with a forced chuckle. We waited in the lobby for the Uber to arrive. "Okay, tell me your name," I finally said.

"Really?"

"Yeah, it'll make me feel like less of a terrible person." I laughed.

"Chase," he said. "You?"

"Gabrielle."

"When was the last time you slept with someone besides your husband and the other guy?" What an interesting question.

"Six years ago," I said.

"Damn," he responded. And then we high-fived. And *laughed*. The Uber arrived and he gave me a quick awkward side hug.

"It's been real," I said, letting out a laugh. I walked out the door—never to speak to Ireland again.

I FINALLY opened the door at Ineke's after fucking with the weird locks on her door for five minutes and literally *crawled* up the two flights of the death-defying Dutch stairs. I plopped down on the bed in my room and allowed myself to check in with all the feelings that were flying around inside me. First up? Guilt. A lot of freaking guilt. Disgust. Disappointment. More disgust. Okay, more-than-slightly-drunk-Gabrielle, what is the Thought Onion? Yum, onion rings. Okay seriously, focus. Superficial thought?

• You're a fucking whore.

Ok, that may be *slightly* harsh. Valid, but harsh. Authentic thought?

• Why did you knowingly go through with that when you knew it would lead to you feeling like this?

Good freaking question, Gabrielle. Finally, the subconscious thought?

• Were you hurting *that* badly that old habits were too scary to let go of?

Okay...that actually made sense, even in my drunken state. I would always run to a guy when I was hurting or in fear of something, as if that would somehow make it better. Did this make *anything* better? No, it made it ten times worse. What a prime example of my old habits coming back to bite me in the fucking ass. Doesn't help the feelings. Doesn't change the fact that I thought of Javier every second it was happening. God, I am still so fucked up.

I started aimlessly scrolling around on social media. I saw Javier had *just* viewed my story. It was 4:31 a.m. Naturally, my drunk brain thought it would be best to text him.

Me: Veto.
Me: Why are you awake?

Javier: Hey.
Javier: I don't know.

Me: Are you okay?

Javier: Yesterday was an intense day so I went to bed at 10 p.m. and woke up at 4 a.m.
Javier: Yeah I'm okay.
Javier: I feel rested but it's too early.

Me: Yeah, I'm jealous.

Javier: I'm gonna go for an early hike.

Me: I slept two hours last night.
Me: And I haven't gone to sleep yet.

Javier: Looks like you had a blast.

Me: It was fun. Lots of cool people.
Me: I FaceTimed with Sophia for an hour.

Javier: Nice. I did as well yesterday.

Me: Why was yesterday intense?
Me: Actually. Tell me to go to sleep.

Javier: Haha you should.

Me: Before I ask you and tell you a million things that don't need to be discussed right now.

Javier: Get some rest, Plum. I'm going on a hike.

Me: If you keep calling me that it will help me dislike you. A little.
Me: Have a good hike.

Shut up, Gabrielle, you're drunk.

Me: Lastly, I wrote an entire chapter in my book today. I didn't leave the house until 5:30. And I feel like I got at least a small amount of clarity today after making some decisions.
Me: OK, I'm slightly drunk, have a good hike, I love you, blah blah. Goodnight.

Javier: Love you too, Plum.
Javier: Goodnight.

What, so it's just a thing that you say I love you now? Ugh. It should have ended there. Of course, it didn't.

Me: Okay last thing.
Me: And I'm only saying this after talking to Sophia. And because if I don't say it now, I feel like I won't say it at all and wait for you to say it, which you probably won't because you're you.

How eloquent of you, Gabrielle. Eye roll.

Me: I think I want. Or need. Or want. To see you before we go home. The last few days. If only for some type of discernment or closure or whatever the hell it will be because I know when we get home you leave. And I'm done trying to do what's right for everyone and trying to figure out what's best. I just want to be. And where I want to be at the end of the RIDICULOUS journey that I never thought in a million years I would be on, is with you, as whatever the fuck we are, together.
Me: Okay, now I'm really going to bed. Have a good hike. Literally eating, praying, fucking my life right now. Stop laughing at me.

Maybe it had taken this poor decision to make me realize that Sophia was right. All I wanted to do right now was tell him everything that had just happened that night...but why would I need to? He left *me*. He broke *my* heart. Intentional or not. He sent *me* off into the unknown on this trip. I knew very well that if I had learned of him doing something—anything—on his trip, it would have absolutely shattered me. But he'd told me he only had friendship feelings toward me. So why did I feel so goddamned guilty, like I had done something wrong? Maybe the ever confusing *I love you*? Regardless, I had said my piece, and it had felt good to say. Now, I just had to wait for his response.

Don't be expecting an answer quickly. It didn't come.

I took my makeup off, crawled into bed, and attempted to shut my mind off from all the bullshit I had allowed that night that I knew I wasn't capable of handling. I rolled over and felt an earring poke me. I went to take them off and realized there was only one. Where the hell was my other earring? Oh. Ireland's bed. Icing on the fucking cake. Goodnight.

Fuck The Morning After

(The quicker you face the music...the better.)

DAY EIGHT

I opened one eye slowly and *waited*—waited to see how vastly hungover I was and if I still felt as awful as I had when I'd finally gone to sleep. After a few moments, I opened the other eye. Slight headache...I could live with that. I popped two Excedrin and glanced at my phone. It was 9 a.m. Why was I incapable of sleeping on this damn trip? How was I even still alive? And what the *fuck* was I thinking last night?

A call came in on my WhatsApp. It was Jess. I clicked *accept* and her smiling face popped up on the screen. She, however, was met with my disheveled lion's mane hair, a look she'd come to know all too well over the years.

"Good morning, sunshine!" she teased.

"Fuck my life," I responded. We chatted for about two hours while I told her about my ridiculous night and the pool of regret I was now drowning in.

"I don't understand why you feel bad. He broke up with you and sent you on a trip by yourself." Jess was one of the friends who was actually somewhat understanding of Javier's situation, but by this time she was really over the roller-coaster ride he had been taking me on.

"So then why do I feel like I have to tell him?" I asked.

"You don't," she said. Of course I didn't. I knew I didn't *have* to, but the thought of keeping something from him felt so foreign and wrong. Still, she and Emma convinced me there was no reason I should. This trip and this journey were about finding myself and making mistakes. And who knows? Maybe he wouldn't even be bothered by it. Maybe he really did only have friendship feelings for me. And they were right, I was single. No. All of that was me trying to make myself feel better. It was more than guilt about Javier, it was sheer disappointment in myself. I had just been starting to feel like I was changing old patterns and handling things so differently. I felt like a piece of shit.

"So has he read the last message you sent yet?" she asked.

"No," I told her. That was the double-edged sword when it came to WhatsApp. You could see when a message had been delivered, when it had been read, and when the last time that person was on the app—all things that make already crazy women even more crazy.

"Where are you going to next?" she asked excitedly.

"I'm thinking Paris. I'm gonna buy my train ticket tonight."

"And then where?! I've always wanted to go to Paris. I'm so jealous," she responded.

"I'm not sure...I know I want to do Barcelona. So probably there. I need some sun after London and Amsterdam." I laughed. "I'm gonna get ready for the day, I'll call you later." We said our goodbyes.

I got dressed, grabbed one of Ineke's two hundred coats, and headed out. It took me about an hour to walk through the park and streets to get to town. I turned on random streets and walked up and down the canals. Amsterdam was a breathtaking city. The buildings were like nothing I had ever seen, and the canals were stunning. It was quite beautiful. I stopped in a random shop and bought three postcards, one for myself and two to send.

I finally found myself in Dam Square, the main center of town. I sat at a café and hopped on Wi-Fi. He had read the messages. I told myself I had to let it go and not obsess over it. Sophia was right—all that mattered was that I had said what I felt and needed. That's all I could do.

It was about 3 p.m. I hadn't heard anything from Paulo, and I decided not to message him. It was probably for the best. I didn't ever want someone wanting anything more from me than I was capable of giving—and right now, that was nothing more than a friendship. I sat at the café and finished the first book on my list. Well...what to do? I put my headphones in, picked a direction, and began to just walk. It's funny how music speaks differently to you depending on where you are in life. Songs that I'd heard a million times suddenly had completely different meanings to me. Songs that had never affected me now made me want to cry. And that day, I didn't want happy music or songs that were surface level. I wanted emotional music that felt how I was feeling. So I walked for hours, listening to "Stars" by Grace Potter and "Over the Love" by Florence and the Machine.

I began to think about the night before. *Why was I unable to just say no?* Having sex with Ireland was clearly something I hadn't wanted to do. Yet I'd gone right ahead and done it anyway. I started to look back at my history with men. Was there something related to my abandonment issues that had to do with intimacy? Hmm. Part of me didn't even want to Thought Onion that. Especially while I was still mentally drowning in this shitty regret.

Once I had finally grown tired, I stopped at another café for a late lunch. After ordering, I pulled out my two postcards. I wrote one to my mom and one to Javier's mom. She had been so instrumental in helping me through my emotions the past week. For whatever reason, I truly felt like she was a second mom, and that type of feeling was rare for me.

When I finished my meal, my headache had still not subsided, so I decided to head back to the apartment. I somehow magically hopped on the correct bus and made it home. As I patted myself on the back and headed upstairs, I looked at my Facebook page on my phone and *froze*. The first post was from one of my cousins. My uncle had passed away.

I stood in the kitchen and my hand involuntarily smacked my chest, as if to stop the pain my heart was feeling. There I was, all alone, across the entire world. I sat down and sobbed. Not the kind of cry where heavy tears are merely pouring down your face, but the kind where you have to remind yourself to *breathe*, where you feel the pain in your tears, and you wonder if it will ever stop. This cry had needed to escape for a week and a half, so I finally let it.

I didn't hear back from Javier that day, or that night. I wanted to call him, to have him tell me I was okay, to feel comfort. But in that moment, I realized that the only comfort I needed was from myself. I took a Xanax, got into bed at 10 p.m., and cried myself to sleep.

Fuck The Roller Coaster

(You have to choose to step off.)

DAY NINE

I finally slept *nine* full hours. Thank God, it was about damn time. My body needed it. My soul needed it. I poured myself a bowl of cereal and sat in the living room watching the rain in my new favorite spot. I felt...*anxious* isn't the right word...*uneasy*. My gut is usually pretty accurate. This time was no different. I FaceTimed Jess.

We caught up on things and talked about the previous day. I told her about my uncle. I was still pretty emotional.

"Has he answered yet?" she asked.

"Nope. But if the whole thing with Ireland taught me anything, it was that I do want to see him...for a reason that isn't clear to me yet. So at least I stepped up and put my feelings out there," I reasoned.

"Yeah, absolutely. You have to do you and focus on yourself," she said.

"I know. But in my heart I feel like he's going to say he doesn't want to meet." And just then, like the fucking movie that is my life, a message from Javier came through. I told Jess to hold on.

> Javier: Hey, Gab, I know you want and need closure of some kind, but I don't feel like that plan would be the healthiest thing for me to do right now. I would much rather fly to LA one week-

end from Mexico to sit down with you and talk for hours once this trip is over. Emotions are all over the place right now so I don't want to make a mistake. We can talk tomorrow night when I arrive in Napoli if you want.

Damn, did I literally call that one or what? Still, the surge. I read the message to Jess. She was over the roller coaster. And you know what? So was I. After all, *he* was the one who had made a point on the plane to say we were going to meet. Talk about flip-flopping. Although, considering his feelings had flipped so suddenly, why was I even surprised? I told Jess I would call her back. I texted Sophia.

Me: So after you and I spoke about everything, I told Javier that I wanted to see him at the end of the trip. He finally wrote me back and said this: (I sent her a screen shot of the message).
Me: You're right. He's all over the place. One second he says I love you, then he doesn't want to see me. So I just have to somehow move forward.

After about ten minutes she responded.

Sophia: Okay love, I am so sorry. He is processing a lot and that's not your place to figure him out. That's his. You decided you wanted to see him and put it out there, now it's on him. He decided one thing but I know he is thinking about it. It's important for you to just state your needs and then let go. I love you and I am going now, but I'll be thinking of you. I have lots to say but don't have the time…I want, if you want it, to give you advice on how I would proceed…but Javi is an amazing man who is figuring out that there is more to self-destruction right now…if you can, be patient and loving with yourself and know that this will pass.

Fucking Yoda. Oy. So I gave myself permission to let my emotions and thoughts word-vomit freely into my journal. Are you fucking kidding me? Weren't you the one on the plane and at the airport that said, "We'll meet at the end of our trip in Amalfi and spend some time together"? Let me answer that for you...YES. You're scared of making a mistake? Like the giant fucking one you already made? Like what? Sleeping with me? Kissing me? Making me hate you? What the hell does that even mean? If you really loved me, you would want to be with me. Isn't it really as simple as that?

And then, no more than twenty minutes after his message had come through, my FaceTime rang. It was him.

What now? I thought. Well, he probably saw my Instagram story post about my uncle and feels like an ass for sending me that before checking on me. Wrong.

"Yeah," I said as I answered.

"Hey...I uh...can you talk?" he stuttered.

"Yeah...What's up?" My voice cracked.

"What's wrong?" he immediately asked, concerned. Well, besides the message you just sent me?

"My uncle passed yesterday." I failed to keep the tears in.

"Oh fuck." I could see all the different meanings behind that response. He didn't know. And he knew he had just sent that message at the worst possible time. "I'm so sorry."

"Yeah..." I said searching for words. Instead I found more tears. "My heart just needs a fucking break, you know?" He looked at me the way I look at him when I just want to wrap my arms around him and make everything better.

"What can I do?" he asked.

"Nothing." I tried to pull myself together. "What's up?" I asked, in regard to the reason for the phone call.

"So...I'm sorry. I know I'm all over the place but can you please disregard everything in that message?" he asked. *All over the place?* Understatement of the fucking year.

"What does that even mean?" I asked. Javier wasn't the best at clearly communicating what was happening inside his head, and he knew that.

"Right," he began to explain. "I talked to Sophia and was telling her why I'm worried and unsure of meeting you and she asked me why I was only looking at the worst-case scenarios. She said, 'Well, can you imagine a scenario where it's positive and you guys have a good time and a lot of positive things come from it?'"

"Okay..." I continued to listen.

"And I said yeah...and I think when you sent me that message, I got so in my head about it all instead of just talking it through with you. Which is why it took me so long to respond. So, I think it's better if we can check in and talk on FaceTime so I can see you and see how you're doing and not get so in my head. I do want to spend some time together. I know we'll have a good time regardless of anything. So, I'm sorry. I feel like I just need to apologize before I even say or do anything." We laughed. Somehow, we always ended up laughing in all of our heavy conversations.

"Okay," I said. "But you really have to like...stop." For lack of better words. "I get it and I know you're working through a lot right now but I am so done. I am so done with this roller coaster. I can't do it anymore," I said firmly.

"I know," he said nodding. We continued to talk for a while. I was firmer with him than I had ever been before. When he would say something vague I would say, "Stop. What does that mean?" And he would go on to explain it more clearly. I must say, when we communicated, we did it very well. It was when we didn't that so much got lost in over-analyzation.

We briefly talked about where we would meet, but to be honest, I didn't feel like anything was decided. At that point, I felt like he was capable of changing his mind five more times over the next three weeks. I would believe we were seeing each other when I was standing next to him in Italy. *If* I was standing next to him in Italy.

We agreed we would talk the next night once I arrived in Paris and he in Napoli. As I sat in my new spot on my last full day in Amsterdam, I decided it was time. It was time for me to get off the roller coaster. Time for me to focus solely on myself and not allow what Javier was dealing with to affect me so vastly. Oh, darling Gabrielle... that is so much easier said than done.

Fuck
Narrow-Mindedness

(Red light, marijuana, prostitutes, and peep shows.)

DAY TEN

A fter the emotional whirlwind with Javier, it was time to do some writing. I wrote for three hours, drinking lots of tea while listening to the wind and rain outside. Every time I finished writing about an experience, I felt a certain amount of peace around it.

I had made plans with Yeung, from the pub crawl, to do some of the tourist stuff Amsterdam had to offer that night. I got ready and headed into town on the bus. The weather had thankfully cleared and the city was bustling with people. I found Yeung at our agreed-upon meeting spot and we were off. First stop? The sex museum of course!

It only took about twenty-five minutes to walk through the whole place. I must say, staring at so many explicit things with a seemingly reserved Asian I had just met was an experience. We stopped by two giant penis statues, and he insisted I get a picture with them. I mean, who am I to turn down a photo-op with dual dicks? There were just *so many* vaginas and penises in this place. They had animatronics like you see on Pirates of the Caribbean at Disneyland. Some would pop out and flash you, others were in mid-sex positions, and there were even ones that were spanking each other. There was a little of everything—paintings, porn, body part statues—all with lots of pubic hair on them. Apparently, waxing wasn't a thing back then. Lucky bitches. We walked through laughing at how outrageous it all was.

Afterward, we stopped to grab a snack to share—Amsterdam's famous fries. It was just a paper cone filled with fries and your choice of sauce. We got the garlic mayo. Holy, fucking shit. I could literally feel my ass growing with every bite, but they were *so* delicious it didn't matter. We shared the fries and walked along one of Amsterdam's many unique and beautiful streets. Stumbling into a shop, Yeung pointed out some bracelets. I zeroed in on a red one made of yarn with a dream catcher on the front. It was perfect. I paid the three euros for it and asked the Rasta man who sold it to me to tie it on.

At dinner, I said to Yeung, "So, tell me your story," since I had given him the highlights of mine at the pub crawl. I sat and waited as he searched for what to say.

"My story?" he asked. "Umm..." He stuttered around for a few minutes until he gave up. "I'm blanking right now." He laughed.

Blanking? I thought, *On your life?* On what has happened to you in your first quarter century? Part of me felt sad that he had no stories that he felt defined him. Like he had just gone through the motions of life the way you're "supposed" to. The other part of me felt sort of jealous that his story was so simple. No death, ugly divorce, or love being ripped away from him. Or maybe he just didn't want to open up about it all.

Next it was off to the canal tour, which was a great way to see the city. It took us up and down numerous waterways and allowed us to admire all the incredible architecture. It was truly beautiful. I could see why people loved this city. The sun set as we floated along the water and the city's lights came alive.

Last on the list, but certainly not least, was the famous Red Light District. It was a famous section in town (mostly one huge street) where women stand in windows illuminated with red lights, waiting for men who wanted to...well...pay for their services. They rented the windows out like you would a booth at a farmers market. It sounds completely crazy. Seeing it in real life? Fucking mind-boggling. Even more insane? Watching men *actually go in*. Yes, this was an actual thing. Some of the women stood seductively in their windows and some tapped on the glass to get the attention of men as they walked by. But the majority sat there using their phones, looking bored out of their minds, which I found incredibly amusing. One was even eating a bag of Cheetos. It was a sight to see and didn't even feel real.

We walked around, taking in all the craziness. We passed dozens of live sex shows, in which I'd heard bananas were a popular prop. It was like walking through another world.

After grabbing a drink, we headed out to walk "the alleys." Yeung knew *all* about the alleys and was strangely excited to go see them. They were specific sections of the Red Light District set aside for certain categories of women. There was "fatty alley" (which I found rather mean), "tranny alley" (self-explanatory), and—wait for it— "granny alley." Yes, ladies and gentlemen, for the right price, you can have a wild time with women seventy-five years old or older. They'll even take their teeth out for you. No joke.

We found fatty alley first. Let me tell you, *this* is what is wrong with our world. Curvy? Yes. Voluptuous? Definitely. Fat? No fucking way. It made the name even worse. Tranny alley was next. You could definitely tell that there was something...different. But by no means were you like, "Oh, shit, that's a fucking dude." It was actually impressive, and I thought they all looked beautiful. Kudos ladies. We never found granny alley, and quite frankly, I was just fine with that.

"Have you heard of a peep show?" Yeung asked as we continued to walk the crazy streets.

"Uhh...No?" I was hesitant to even ask at this point.

"So, you go into a booth and pay two euros and then a window opens, and you watch whatever is happening inside," he explained.

"That sounds fucking terrifying," I responded deadpan.

"Let's go," he said.

"Oh God," I agreed.

Standing in the incredibly long line for what apparently was a super popular thing in Red Light, I made a comment about how insane this all was.

"Where are you from?" a guy standing in the line next to us asked.

"California," I responded.

"Where?"

"LA," I said.

"Where?" he asked again.

"Woodland Hills," I answered.

"Shut up. I'm from Fullerton." He laughed. I'm telling you, the number of American people I had already met on this journey was hysterical. His name was Jason and he was with a Canadian named Travis. They had met the night before at their hostel and had done the same pub crawl we had done on a different night. The four of us talked for about fifteen minutes as we waited in line.

Jason and Travis went in right before us. When they came out after the two minutes they'd paid for, they were both hysterically laughing.

"I'm going to stand outside the door so I can hear your reaction," Jason said. He laughed at how clearly dumbfounded I was by this and the rest of the Red Light District.

Yeung and I stepped into a space the size of a phone booth. He dropped two euros in the slot, and the window opened.

"OH MY GOD," I said involuntarily and rather loudly. You could hear Jason and Travis laughing at my reaction outside. There, separated from us by only a window, was a man and a woman full-on having sex on a circular rotating bed. Legitimately real-life porn. I stood there flabbergasted with my new friend watching this...show? It was one of the most bizarre things I had ever witnessed. To top it off, the man and woman would make eye contact with the people watching. So. Fucking. Weird. It was the longest two minutes of my life.

We left the booth and walked to the street where Jason and Travis were standing. We spent five minutes discussing what the fuck we had just witnessed.

"I just can't believe this is like...their *job*. Like 'Hey, I'm heading to work to go have sex while people watch,'" I said.

"Do you think they know each other?" Yeung asked.

"Well, he wasn't wearing a condom," Travis pointed out in his Canadian accent. No, he definitely wasn't. His very large, very uncircumcised penis was out for all to see. Jesus.

"You guys wanna grab a drink with us?" Jason asked.

"Sure," Yeung and I agreed. The four of us walked to a bar where we grabbed a spot on the lower level that was tucked away from the busy crowd.

Jason was twenty-two and traveling alone as well. Travis was twenty-one and traveling with another Canadian friend who was back at the hostel, sick.

"So, are you traveling alone, Gabrielle? What's your story?" Travis asked. Sigh. The ever-loaded question.

"Well...It's kind of a long story." I chuckled as I looked at Yeung.

"Let's hear it," Jason said.

I gave them the short version that I had perfected by that time. When I finished, everyone's mouths were hanging open. That seemed to be the typical reaction.

"What a story," Jason added.

They asked me some questions and we discussed where I'd been so far. The guys and I seemed to have quite a lot in common, even with our age gap, and we had a really good time talking. We all swapped Instagrams.

"I don't know what your trips look like after this, but I have a big hotel room in Mykonos if you wanna come meet up," Jason said to Travis and me while Yeung was in the restroom. I had heard about this happening with travelers. You meet cool people and they're like, 'Hey! Come here next!' and you say why not? I definitely didn't say no. Greece had always been on my wish list.

The four of us left the bar and went to a lounge. We all shared two joints and continued to talk. Travis insisted I pull up one of my movie trailers online. At that point, I was high enough to laugh and say okay. They were insistent they would all be watching it when they got home.

After a while, we were all hungry and went to grab some more of Amsterdam's delicious fries. Once we finished, we headed back toward the beginning of Red Light.

"We have to take a picture," I said. Everyone agreed. After they made fun of my selfie stick (and then admitted what a badass picture it took), we said our goodbyes.

"Maybe I'll see you guys in Mykonos," I said as I hugged Jason and Travis goodbye.

"Seriously, let me know," Jason said.

Yeung and I walked back to the main central station where I called an Uber. It was too late, and I'd smoked one too many joints to try and figure out which bus would eventually get me home.

As my Uber arrived, I hugged Yeung goodbye.

"Have a blast in Munich, keep in touch, dude! Great meeting you," I said.

"You too, Gabrielle. Maybe I'll see your book on the shelves one day," he said with a smile.

"Yeah. You will."

Fuck First Impressions

(Always be open and decide for yourself.)

DAY ELEVEN

After a whopping two hours of sleep, I got up to say goodbye to Ineke before she went to work. She insisted I take the coat she had let me borrow during my time there (which had saved my life, since I only packed for warm romantic Italy...HA) and it would most definitely come in handy in Paris. We took a picture together—looking like absolute hell, I might add—and she asked me to sign the guestbook before I left. I forced myself to go back to sleep for another two hours before getting up to shower, pack, and say goodbye to Amsterdam. I signed the guestbook and left a postcard I had written for Ineke next to it. I was just the slightest bit sad leaving this eclectic little apartment I had felt so at home in.

I took the bus to the central train station and found the first train I would be taking in Europe. Off to Paris I went. I really enjoyed taking the train. It was comfortable, peaceful, and way less stressful than flying. I wrote, read, and gazed at the countryside out the window. A short three and a half hours later, bonjour Paris. I had arrived.

Walking into my first hostel, I wasn't sure what to expect. A lot of my friends had suggested I stay in hostels for a better travel experience. They're known for being the best way to meet new people and it's a hell of a lot cheaper than a hotel. I checked in and headed up to the top floor. There were *so* many rooms. St Christopher's was a chain and known (unbeknownst to me) to be a party hostel. I walked into my room and it was quite cute. There were six beds—three bunks—all with little curtains to shut you off from the room. We had two of our own private bathrooms (thank God), and we even had a little window with a view of the Eiffel Tower.

I went down to the bar/restaurant and ordered some food while I dug into book number two: *The Four Agreements,* by Don Miguel Ruiz. *The Four Agreements* was the prequel to the book *The Fifth Agreement,* which Javier *insisted* I had to read. I was only thirty-five pages in and already had mixed feelings about it. Some of the notions being proposed seemed to suggest you didn't have to take responsibility for your actions, that if someone else is having a reaction to you or something you did, it is *their* choice. While I saw many good points and truths in some parts of the book, I couldn't help but think that the way Javier dealt with things was influenced by these "agreements" that he swore by...and not necessarily in a positive way. For example, agreement number two: "*Don't take anything personally – Nothing others do is because of you. What others say and do is a projection of their own reality, their own dream. When you are immune to the opinions and actions of others, you won't be the victim of needless suffering.*" Okay...really? Correct me if I'm wrong, but doesn't this sound like they're saying, "Don't worry if you hurt someone or cause them discomfort or pain because it has nothing to with you or what you may have done to them. They are choosing to feel that." Can't say I'm in total agreement with that in every situation, and certainly not the one I was currently in. I'm not having this reaction because I *feel* like it, Javier, I'm having it because you decided to put my heart in a blender and drink it like a smoothie. I would hope he would take that personally. It was really eye opening and explained some of the way Javier was—or wasn't—handling all of this.

After eating, I headed up to my bed for a nap. I was exhausted. When I got to the room, a baby-faced blond-haired New Zealander popped his head out of his top bunk.

"Hi, I'm Gabrielle," I said.

"Greg," he replied with a smile and an accent.

People from New Zealand, or 'Kiwis' as they're sometimes called, are known for being such lovely people. I had spent time in New Zealand when I was young and my mom had been filming there. I had such fond memories of the people I had met. Greg was only eighteen and had been traveling for nearly three months. We chatted for a bit before I climbed into my cocoon and dozed off.

A FaceTime call from Javier woke me up. Groggy, I put my headphones in and stepped outside to answer. He was in Napoli, planning to take a day trip to an island the next day before heading to San Vito Lo Capo, where his friends lived. Part of me was hopeful that he would find some healing with his friends. The other part of me wondered if they would all go out and party and pick up girls. And *all* of me knew I had to not allow myself to think about it.

Javier told me about an amazing experience he'd had with a young boy playing soccer. He had gone up to this little kid kicking a ball around on a dirt road and began playing with him as his mother watched and smiled. After they had played for a bit, Javier gave him a hug and asked him what his name was. His name was Chris, the same as Javier's brother.

"That's amazing," I said.

"Yeah. There was also a girl at a restaurant that I had a conversation with. When I asked why she was on her trip, she told me her father had just passed. I was getting up to leave and asked her what her father's name was and she said Chris," he told me.

"You're kidding." I chuckled.

"Crazy, right? It's like there are signs from him all over the place," he said.

"Good. I'm glad you're choosing to see it that way." I've always been a huge believer in signs from loved ones who are no longer with us. I could hear in his voice that it had all had a positive effect on him. I was happy to hear that he was finding the lighter side in all the grief.

After we hung up, I felt like I had to do something my first night in Paris, so I decided to head down to the hostel's bar.

It was *not* a bar. It was a club, complete with a DJ, a ridiculous number of people, and tables lined up for beer pong tournaments. I walked around once and was like...nope. Way too much for tonight. I decided to go find a nice Paris café, get a good meal, and write. That is *not* what happened.

I only got about two blocks (in the rather sketchy neighborhood my hostel was in) when a short younger guy who looked to be of middle-eastern descent accidentally bumped into me.

"So sorry!" he said in a familiar London accent.

"No worries," I replied with a smile.

"Holy shit, are you American?" he asked.

"Yes."

"From where?" he continued.

"Los Angeles," I answered.

"You're kidding! Where are you off to?"

"Dinner somewhere," I responded.

"Walk with me. I'll take you around," he said as he offered me his arm.

Now, I know this sounds super shady on all fronts, but he was a small guy and seemed harmless. In hindsight, it was probably *not* the smartest decision but at that moment...I don't know...it felt fine. We began to walk, and we talked about where we were from and all that basic stuff. He was from London originally, and I told him that I had started my trip there and let him know what I had done during my stay.

"You are so beautiful," he kept saying every few minutes. I would laugh and continue talking about whatever we were discussing at that moment. He was also excessively fond of the phrase "I swear on my mum's life" and used it as often as a Valley girl uses the word *like*. For the first ten minutes, everything seemed fine. He said he would take me for food and show me around a bit. Then it all started to get... *strange.*

"Let me tell you what I want, Gabrielle. I swear on my mum's life, I want to get married and have children. I could take care of you," he said.

Okay. First of all dude, just...no. Still, I would laugh and brush it off, saying, "I'm not looking to be with anyone right now." And I wasn't.

He bought me a slice of less-than-stellar pizza, and we sat on a corner as I ate. He asked me what my story was and what had brought me here. Sigh. Okay, super vague bullet-point version for you, buddy. I didn't even get past the cheating husband when he jumped up and exclaimed (as if you couldn't guess the typical answer that was about to come out), "You're kidding me! If I had you, I would…"

Really? You're going to go down *that* road? Oy vey. I finished my story, leaving out most of the important details. He then randomly asked me how much a bed cost at my hostel.

"Uh, I don't know…" I said, confused.

"I'll come back with you."

"HA! No, I will go by myself," I responded, mildly shocked.

"There's another cheap hostel we can go to for the night," he said. I literally could not believe this dude actually thought he could buy me a shitty slice of pizza and then take me to a hostel to sleep with me, even though I had blatantly told him I did not want anything more than a friend. It was comical.

"Again, I'm not looking for anything more than a friend," I said firmly.

"Okay, okay, let's grab a drink," he said.

By this time, I was fully regretting committing to this little adventure in the first place and was wishing I was by myself at a nice café eating calories that were actually worth it. He grabbed my hand and started walking and before I knew it, we had stumbled into the legit drug-dealing part of Paris. Awesome. And that's how I died.

Just kidding. He spoke in French to a few different people, grabbed a cigarette from someone, and then we continued (thank God) to walk.

"They all know me," he said. Great, I feel even better knowing that you're on a first-name basis with all the drug dealers, bro. I'm walking around the shadiest part of Paris with someone who knows all the shady characters. Fantastic.

"Can you walk me back now?" I asked as we were leaving the store.

"Let's have a drink, Gabrielle, come on!" he whined.

"I'm really tired, I'm ready to go back," I said firmly. Thankfully, we started to head back. All of this had gone from normal to incredibly uneasy and creepy so fast. He eventually agreed to take me back but was hell-bent on getting my info so he could "take me out" in Paris. Yeah, right.

"I'll take yours," I insisted. I added him on WhatsApp without putting the proper country code in. His name was Sid. Yep, like the evil human kid in *Toy Story*. Do I even need to crack a joke at this point?

"Please, Gabrielle, call me, please," he said.

"Yeah, okay, thanks for the pizza!" I replied, so ready to get the hell out of there. He gave me an awkward hug and squeezed me like he was saying goodbye to a puppy he had just gotten. I turned around and walked straight back to my hostel without stopping.

When I arrived, there were a good fifty people outside trying to get into the hostel's club. While assessing how to get in, I felt a hand touch my hand, which was holding onto my phone inside my coat pocket. Holy shit. Someone just attempted to pickpocket me. Thank God I'd had my hand on my phone. I would have lost my fucking marbles.

I finally made it upstairs, feeling so gross and uneasy. This was the first time on this journey that I had felt unsafe. I picked up my phone and FaceTimed Javier.

I told him about my night and that I just needed to have someone familiar and safe tell me I was okay, and he understood. I can't say he helped very much that night. Yes, he was there to answer the call and talk but something was just...different. It felt like there was a little less love and not a ton of compassion, and this was the first time I had felt that from him.

I got ready for bed while meeting another roommate in the hostel, a thirty-two-year-old from San Francisco named Brad, who was in the tech business and was very nice.

I climbed into my bunk, shut my curtain, and put my headphones in. I looked down at my phone screen that read, "You Can." Come on, Gabrielle...*you can*. Oh fuck, Paris, please be better than this.

Fuck Karma

(It's a fucking bitch...act accordingly.)

DAY TWELVE

I awoke to a plethora of messages on my phone. I groggily rolled over in my bunk to see what was happening, then sat straight up, eyes wide. It was a mutual friend of mine and Daniel's back home. Daniel had been fired. Whoa. This was the job he had worked so hard for and was meant to be his career for the rest of his life. How is it possible he let that fail? I texted Emma and Jess. They quickly responded.

Emma / Jess: Karma's a bitch.

Yeah. It really is. Still, even after all that Daniel had done, how violated he had made me feel, how incredibly disrespectful he had deliberately chosen to be for so long, and how truly thankful I was to be out of such a toxic union, I found myself feeling bad for him. I never went into the divorce saying, "I'm going to ruin you and take away everything you've worked for." If I had wanted to do that, I would have walked into where he worked and slapped down the giant packet of proof I had. I never wanted to take him down or ruin his career. I just wanted to be divorced and to get what I was entitled to. I called the friend who had given me the news.

"They had to have security escort him off the property. He was throwing things and yelling. It was like someone had taken over him," he said.

"I don't understand. What was the reason they gave him?" I asked.

"Gabrielle, he had been showing up late all the time because he was with Laurel. They had told him to not post stupid stuff on social media and he continued to. They even told him he wasn't allowed to be with Laurel at the facility and then caught him making out with her on the security cameras right off the property. There were a million reasons. He was being a terrible employee," he shared with me.

"I just don't get it. That was everything he had worked for," I said as I listened, stunned. Of course, Daniel and his lawyer would claim that he was fired because of an email I had sent to the fifteen sports people I was friends with, the ones who had come to my wedding. A quite mild, adult, and restrained email, I might add. That email had been sent two and a half months earlier, and he had kept his job just fine since then. But I get it—when you're incapable of taking responsibility for anything in your life, you have to find someone to blame. Daniel may have been able to convince his own brain that it was my fault and that's fine, but good luck ever convincing a judge or anyone who actually matters. Still, I felt bad for him. I guess that means I'm human and not a terrible person. Still, Emma and Jess were right. Karma's a fucking bitch.

Enough of the drama happening back home. I was in freaking Paris, the glamorous city that was in all the best films, where people dined on coffee and crepes and strolled through parks looking up at the Eiffel Tower. As I was getting ready for the day, Greg, the young Kiwi, popped his head out from his bunk.

"Morning!" he said, still half-asleep.

"Good morning!" I replied.

"I'm thinking of doing Versailles tomorrow. There's a shuttle that takes you right from the hostel lobby."

"Nice! I was going to try and hit Versailles tomorrow too. I'm up for going together if you want," I offered.

"Yeah, that sounds great."

"Cool." I smiled. He was such a young spirit. I instantly felt like an older sister. I finished getting ready with our plans now in place.

That night I was meeting a friend for dinner. When Daniel and I were on our incredible honeymoon at the St. Regis Bora Bora, we had become friends with the sommelier (wine expert) at the top restaurant. His name was Timothée and he was originally from Paris. When he finished working in Bora Bora, he and his wife, Alice (who he had adorably met while working there), moved back to Paris. They had even stopped through LA, and Daniel and I had met them for dinner. He was so sweet and I was looking forward to seeing a familiar face later that day.

I grabbed Ineke's coat and headed out to explore Paris for the day. First up was taking a bus toward the Eiffel Tower. I hopped off at a random stop and walked through the streets of the city. I was searching for a café where I could grab some breakfast and read for a bit. While walking, I ran smack into the Eiffel Tower. I looked up at the massive structure and yet again found myself feeling felt so incredibly small. This feeling seemed to be a recurring theme on my trip. It made me feel helpless, to be honest. I'm just this one human in a sea of billions. Where do I really fit in to all that? Still, it was pretty amazing to look up at. I walked through the park situated right in front of it and snapped a photo (again, the selfie stick comes in clutch). I posted it with the caption: "In French, you don't say 'I miss you.' You say, 'tu me manques,' which means, 'You are missing from me.'" It felt so appropriate to how I had been feeling from all this love and heartbreak mess I was in the middle of. I didn't miss Javier. It literally felt like someone was missing from me, as if a little piece of my heart had been taken.

I found a café close to the Eiffel Tower and sat at a little table right outside on the street. It was beautiful. I ordered a café latté and a crepe with strawberry jam. It was freaking delicious and reminded me of my childhood. My mom would sometimes make crepes on the weekends when I was younger and taking my first bite was like experiencing a sense memory from when things were so much simpler. I took out *The Four Agreements* and continued where I had left off.

I finished my delicious crepe and headed back toward the Eiffel Tower. There are two ways you can get to the top of the tower: walking up the hundreds of steps or taking the elevator. I figured with the amount I had been eating, my body (and ass) could use a natural stair stepper. I started the long hike up. On the first level, there was a restaurant, an ice cream and coffee stand, and a bunch of places to sit and enjoy the views. And let me tell you, those views were absolutely incredible. You could see the entire city in every direction. It was so beautiful. I spent fifteen minutes walking around, enjoying the city from this vantage point, and then I started up the next batch of stairs. The next level up was even more beautiful, which I hadn't thought was possible. Luckily, I don't have an issue with heights because it was *high*. There was a macaron shop on that level, so I grabbed a few and walked around the railing, snacking on the incredible little desserts. Once on that level, the only way to get to the very top is to take an elevator. I stood in line and hopped on to head even higher. Being at the very top was a pretty epic feeling. You felt so small looking down on everything. It was like being a bird perched on a mountain. I turned on my data quickly and tried to FaceTime my mom. No answer, so I called my stepdad and showed him the view. Again, technology is so crazy to me. The fact that I could stand at the top of the Eiffel Tower and see my stepdad's face in Taos, New Mexico, is mind-blowing. I think we take for granted how incredibly connected we can be even though we're across the world. I spent some time looking out at the view below before I started the long descent to the bottom. I took the stairs down from the second level until my feet were back on the ground.

I headed to Palais de Chaillot, where I was supposed to meet Timothée. I took pictures of the grand statues and of different perspectives of the Eiffel Tower. It was all really beautiful. I was so nervous I wasn't going to be able to find Timothée on this random street corner at the specific time we had decided on. There were so many people out and about. Then, out of the crowd, I heard in a thick French accent:

"Gabrielle!"

"Hi!" I shrieked as I ran over to hug him. Timothée had a small build, dark features with light eyes, and a sweet smile. He looked very French. His English was good with only the occasional wrong word, but I did sometimes need him to repeat something three times before I could decipher it through his accent. He was a manager of Aquarium de Paris Cinéaqua and offered to take me on a private tour.

We walked through the empty aquarium, which had just closed for the day, and looked at a variety of fish, sharks, and other sea creatures. The coolest part of this aquarium? It was also one of the most popular nightclubs in the city. Timothée walked me into the giant room where the main dance floor was. Behind the bottle service tables there was a giant glass wall with fish swimming around behind it. It was *so* freaking cool. It shit on any Vegas nightclub I had been to.

"We usually have a mermaid that swims in here when the night-club is open," he said.

"I'm sorry, what?" I asked.

"A mermaid," he repeated.

"Like an actual fucking mermaid?!"

"Well, like a human but dressed as a mermaid." He laughed.

"Obviously, but that's so freaking cool!"

What a cool place to have a nightclub, and how great that a friend I had met in Bora Bora on my honeymoon was the manager. So funny how life works.

"We can come to the club tomorrow if you want," he offered.

"Um, YES," I said.

"Good, I'll get us a table," he said casually. Great.

We left and walked around the city for a bit, down the famous shopping street Champs-Élysées as he pointed out all the notable spots. Then it was time to go pick up Timothée's wife, Alice, from the gorgeous hotel she worked at. We grabbed her and headed to dinner at a little place called Shirvan Café Métisse. The food and drinks were absolutely delicious. We spent hours talking, eating, and drinking. I loved how nothing was rushed in Europe. It was totally normal to enjoy a meal for hours on end. I told them the details about Daniel, which I'm sure they were dying to hear all about but were too polite to ask. I told them about Javier and how I'd ended up on this big European adventure all by myself. Alice was quick to say how insane it all was but how incredible that I had chosen to still come.

"It really shows your strength. It's amazing," she said. I had heard that a lot on this trip. And I mean, yeah, I can recognize that it is a fact. I just wish I felt it more. Part of me definitely felt like a badass for deciding to go on this trip and the other part of me felt so broken and so defeated. Hmm...I feel like there's a Thought Onion there. The superficial thought?

- People must think my life is a joke.

To be fair, everyone had seen me be lied to, cheated on, divorced, back in love, and broken up with, all in the span of three months. Authentic thought?

- I feel like a failure.

Yeah. I definitely felt that, big time. Failed marriage. Failed relationship. Failing at not resorting back to old habits. Just failing. Now, what's the subconscious thought?

- But you're still here.

And there it was. The subconscious golden nugget. Who cared if I had been lied to, cheated on, broken up with? None of that was in my control. What was in my control? Having the freaking courage to *keep going*. To go on this trip. To not let myself crumble into a million little pieces. So no matter how beaten and broken I felt, I knew what a strong woman I was.

After a long and wonderful dinner, and being so stuffed we couldn't breathe, they offered to take me back to my hostel. I was so relieved that I didn't have to figure out the trains and buses in the not-so-safe-feeling city this late at night. Alice had offered to take a bag of my laundry and do it at their house for me, which was so beyond sweet and needed at that point. I ran upstairs and grabbed the bag to give to her, said goodbye to them both, and planned to meet Timothée at the club the following evening.

I walked into my hostel and chatted with Greg and Brad for a bit before turning into my bunk. I welcomed an early night that ended before 1 a.m. I checked my email and saw that there was one from my lawyer. The surge. It happened every time I saw an email from him. Not because I had any feelings left toward Daniel because, believe me, I didn't. But because it reminded me of what I was eventually going to have to go home to. Reluctantly, I opened the email to see what was happening in the circus of the divorce.

Daniel's lawyer (who was a criminal defense attorney, not a family law attorney) had emailed my lawyer (who was, as he should be, a family law attorney) in a manner which I can only describe as that of a five-year-old who had watched too many *Law and Order* episodes. Sounding like a complete moron, his lawyer ranted and complained that *I* was the reason for Daniel losing his job (did I not call that?) and said they would be coming after me for slander. Quick educational moment: the definition of slander is "the action or crime of making a false *spoken* statement damaging to a person's reputation." See the problem here? I didn't run around telling the sports community that Daniel had been sleeping with a child. I had simply written an email to a small group of people whom I had come to know personally in the past five years, stating only that we were separating because of a six-month affair. It never ceases to amaze me how full-grown adults can act like such temperamental children. After reading that long, threatening, and rude email from Daniel's lawyer, I suddenly didn't feel quite as bad anymore. I got under my covers, popped in my headphones, and turned on my white noise app (which had literally saved me on this trip). I took a deep, cleansing breath, smiled, and thought: Yeah. Karma *is* a fucking bitch.

Fuck
Bucket Lists

(Do as much as you can...even if you're by your damn self.)

DAY THIRTEEN

I awoke rested, rejuvenated, and ready for the epic day I had planned. Greg and I were planning on adventuring through Versailles during the day, and for the evening I had booked myself a ticket to go see Moulin Rouge. Those who know me know what an insanely amazing thing this was. *Moulin Rouge* is one of my all-time favorite films, and I was beyond excited that I was *in* Paris and able to go see the *actual* show. Big-time bucket list. After the show, I would head to the aquarium to meet Timothée for a night at the club. Pretty epic schedule for the day, if I do say so myself.

Greg and I headed downstairs to catch the shuttle that took us from our hostel to the Palace of Versailles. In the van, we met a really cool guy from Uruguay who happened to be staying in the room right next to ours. We all chatted during the thirty-minute drive over to Versailles. When we got out of the van, everyone's jaws dropped. The palace was really indescribable. The massive structure was so impressive to look at, and it was *covered* in gold. I don't think I've ever seen more gold than during that day.

Once we were inside, we ventured through the huge palace. In every room we walked into, Greg and I would stand wide-eyed, with one of us saying, "Oh shit." After a while, we had seen more gold and rooms than we would have thought possible and decided to go see the famous gardens. I had been wanting to walk through the gardens and find a perfect spot to write. Let me tell you, they didn't disappoint.

The gardens went for miles and were filled with fountains, trees, statues, flowers, and beautiful landscapes. You could get lost there for hours, and we did, chatting about our travels as we walked. Then, out of nowhere, it started to absolutely pour. People pulled out umbrellas and took cover, and I handed Greg my phone.

"Snap a photo for me!" I said as I ran over to the fountain and began to dance around in the rain. Soaking wet, we took cover under a row of huge trees that were close by.

Once the rain had cleared and we had walked around for about an hour, we found our way back to the entrance of the gardens. We decided we would go our separate ways and meet up at the shuttle pick-up a few hours later. I found a ledge that looked over the maze-like landscaping, which reminded me of a labyrinth. I was feeling optimistic and inspired. Sitting on the ledge, I took a photo to post. With it, I added the quote: "Today I choose life. Every morning when I wake up I can choose joy, happiness, negativity, pain...To feel the freedom that comes from being able to continue to make mistakes and choices—today I choose to feel life, not to deny my humanity, but embrace it." This was something I needed to continually practice. *Choosing* what I wanted to feel, not simply letting outside forces dictate what that would be. Not letting news about Daniel, the saga of Javier, or any other variables I couldn't control affect me. Easier said than done. I sat on my little ledge and wrote a chapter in my book. It was a creative, magical place.

Two hours flew by and I headed back to meet Greg at the shuttle. When we got home, it was time for me to get ready for the long night out I had planned. Before getting ready, I booked my hostel for my next destination. I had decided I would go where my heart had been pulling me this whole time. *Barcelona*. I was still deciding whether I was going to take a short one-hour flight or a longer six-and-a-half-hour train ride. Since I wasn't leaving Paris until Monday and it was only Saturday, I still had tomorrow to decide and book my travel route. That's what's so great about Europe—you can book things last minute on a whim. I had packed two dresses and decided that this was the night to wear one of them. It was freezing out, so I again thanked the Lord I had Ineke's coat to throw on. Once I was ready, Greg, Brad, the Uruguay guy from next door, and I headed downstairs to grab a drink before I headed to Moulin Rouge. We all chatted about our travel plans, where we had been, and where we were headed next.

"Where next for you, Gabrielle?" Uruguay asked.

"Barcelona."

"Ah, you'll love it. It's beautiful there," he said. He had come from Spain and had stopped in a few different cities, including Barcelona. We were all traveling on our own, which was cool. We went around the table explaining why we had decided on solo trips. Then it was my turn. Cue the extra-short story. Cue everyone's mouth hanging open.

"Wow," Brad said.

"Seriously, wow," Greg agreed. "Is that what the book is about?"

"Yep," I replied.

"Shit," Brad responded. "Cheers to that." We all toasted. I snapped a photo of the four of us for my Instagram story and hashtagged where everyone was from: LA, Uruguay, San Francisco, and New Zealand.

It was time to call my Uber to head to the show. I stepped outside the hostel and hopped into the car. The driver dropped me off right across from the lit-up windmill with the giant sign that said Moulin Rouge. I stopped by a little crepe stand and asked the guy to make me whatever his favorite crepe was to go. He handed me an insanely delicious crepe with Nutella, banana, and some type of cinnamon sugar powder. I could feel my ass growing in my mini dress, and it was so good I didn't care.

I asked a girl on the street to take a photo of me in front of the show's entrance. I stood smiling on the corner with my gigantic crepe and the beautiful background of this iconic location. Then I realized—I'd had absolutely no reservations about asking her to take my photo like I had back in London. I was no longer embarrassed that I was by myself. In fact, I was proud.

After finishing what was technically my dinner, I hopped in line and posted the photo with the simple caption: "Fucking. Bucket.

List." I was so freaking excited—even by my damn self. I walked into the beautiful theatre, which was filled with dimly lit tables, sparkling curtains, and purple and red mood lighting. I handed my ticket to one of the French men who was seating people.

"Just one?" he asked.

"Just one," I said with a smile. He looked surprised that I wasn't with anyone, but this time, I didn't feel weird or awkward. I felt *empowered*. He walked me over to one of the front tables and winked. The waiters proceeded to bring me free champagne the rest of the night. I guess it pays to be alone. In fact, I was slowly but surely learning that it paid to be alone in a variety of ways. Especially in the case of a significant other.

The show was wild. If I'm being completely honest, the dancing was subpar, especially the male dancing. However, the unbelievable costumes made up for it. I hadn't been aware that the show was true cabaret style. Most of the women were topless the entire time. I looked at their flawless bodies and thought about how awful it was going to be heading back to the gym once I got home from a month of eating like an asshole. Oh well. The circus acts were amazing. I had seen tons of Cirque shows, but this had acts I had never seen before. At one point, a huge glass pool rose up from out of the stage with giant ten-foot snakes swimming around in it. A woman dove into the tank and swam around with them. It was absolutely insane. There was even an act set to the movie version of *Roxanne*, which I had choreographed and danced to in high school. It was such an amazing thing to do in Paris. I finished my free champagne as the show was ending and the adorable waiter who had been bringing it came up to me as I headed toward the exit.

"Where are you heading to for the night?" he said in his French accent.

"Out with some friends," I replied with a smile.

"Lucky friends," he said. It was sweet, but I was not looking for another Ireland situation.

I hopped in my second Uber of the night and headed to meet Timothée at the club. It was almost 1 a.m. by the time I arrived, and the club was just starting to get full. The aquarium had been fully transformed into a top-of-the-line night club. We headed downstairs to the bottle service section, where the fish swam behind the humungous glass as everyone danced and partied. Timothée and I talked and drank...and drank. The one downside of being at a club in Paris (and most places in Europe, for that matter) is that literally *everyone* smokes. It looked like there was a smog machine inside the aquarium from all the cigarette smoke. I danced at our table and talked to all the people who came over to say hi to Timothée. Before I knew it, it was 6 a.m. We had one last drink and headed out.

"I'm going to swing by my office really quick," a just-as-drunk Timothée said to me. We headed to the back entrance of the aquarium to where all the offices were.

"I kind of want to go to Barcelona today. Like not wait until tomorrow," my drunk self said.

"Do you want to look at train times?" Timothée offered as he opened up his computer. We looked and saw that there was a train leaving at 10 a.m.—just a few hours from then. We were both so drunk that we decided it was totally doable to run by his house to pick up my bag of clean clothes, go back to my hostel so I could pack and change, and get to the station for a 10 a.m. train to Barcelona. We tried to buy the ticket on the computer but it wouldn't work, so we decided I would just buy it there.

At 6:45 a.m., we hopped in an Uber to head to his place to get my clothes. Halfway there my drunk spirit animal left the fucking building and I hit a wall. *Hard.*

"I need to sleep," I said to him.

"Probably a better idea," he agreed. Thank God we hadn't been able to purchase the ticket. When we got to his apartment, I waited in the Uber and he grabbed my bag of clean clothes. The Uber brought me back to my hostel where I stumbled in (full-on ratchet style) in my mini dress and coat at 7:30 a.m., smelling like a giant cigarette. I didn't even wash my face guys, I was *that* tired. I threw on my sweatpants, glanced at the two bunkmates who were already waking up for the day, and fell into my bed. No, I would not be in any shape to be getting on a train in two hours. In fact, I would be pretty out of commission for the next twelve hours. Paris 1, Gabrielle 0.

Fuck Alcohol

(I'm too old for the hangover life.)

DAY FOURTEEN

Remember in the Amsterdam chapter where I told you I don't do hangovers? How it doesn't matter if I'm scheduled to see the president, if I'm hungover, I'm not going? Well, *this* is why. I awoke still semi-drunk in my bunk not knowing what time it was. What I did know was that I needed to puke. Thank God I had been smart enough to choose a hostel with en suite bathrooms in it because my day would consist of traveling from my bottom bunk to the bathroom and back to my bunk. I was miserable. The fact that a mere few hours earlier I had thought I would be in any condition to be getting on a train for six and a half hours was absolutely comical. My hangovers are the freaking *worst*.

After a long day of puking, sleeping, and more puking, I finally woke up from a mini nap feeling like I was on the other side of the death hangover. It was 5:30 p.m. I mean, did you expect me to go on a month-long trip to Europe and not have *one* hangover day? Come on.

I finally took my makeup off and washed my face. I felt like a new person. I hardly ever sleep with my makeup on. I came out of the bathroom, and Greg popped his head out from his top bunk.

"Alive yet?" he laughed.

"Ughhhh," I groaned in response.

"What time did you get in?"

"7:30...ish," I answered.

"Damn!"

"Yeah," I agreed.

I lay in my bunk going through my phone, which I hadn't checked all day. There was a direct message on my Instagram from Javier's friend Manny.

Manny: Hope you're having an amazing time, Gabrielle! Looks like it!

Manny was getting ready to fly to San Vito Lo Capo to meet Javier and the rest of the guys. It was crazy to think I was supposed to be there right now instead of Paris.

Me: It's been a lot of ups and downs, but amazing nonetheless. I hope you have an amazing time in San Vito! Take care of him.

Take care of him. God, Gabrielle, even after all this, you're still worried about him? Who the fuck is worrying about me? I guess it just showed how much I really cared about him. I was still worried that he wasn't okay.

Manny: I will. He will be okay. He's needed this for a long time.

Me: I know. It's just been really difficult. I don't understand it.

Manny: Trust me, I saw how he was with you. He's never been like that to anyone before. That doesn't just go away.

Yeah. Says you, his mother, Sophia, all my friends. Unfortunately, according to him, it can.

Manny: I'm here if you need to talk ever.

Me: Thank you. I appreciate that more than you know. Fly safe.

Manny: Besos.

It was crazy to me. Every single person in his life was telling me the same thing. "We saw how he was with you," "He's never been like that with anyone," "We knew this was it for him." And I had felt all of that too. How do you just wake up and have all that be gone? Isn't that the million-dollar fucking question?

That night was the earliest I'd been in bed the entire trip. I spent time writing and then finished reading *The Fourth Agreement.* I came across a line that jumped out at me. It read: "The first step toward personal freedom is awareness." Hmm. How interesting. *What am I not fully aware of right now?* I thought. Well...I'd just recently become aware of the fact that I wasn't fully in love with my husband and that I'd married him because he was "safe." I was aware of the fact that I was terrified to truly be by myself, which this trip was forcing me to get over rather quickly. I was aware that I had learned more about myself in the previous three months than I had in twenty-eight years. So, what was I *not* aware of? I Thought Onioned the big issue here to see if I could find out. The superficial thought:

- I always need/want to have a man in my life.

Again, this sounds ridiculous but when a little girl loses her father and a young woman loses her boyfriend, you get textbook serial monogamist with a dash of abandonment issues. My mom is the same way. We're just relationship people. Healthy or not. Now the authentic thought:

- I don't know who I am when I'm not in a relationship.

This made sense to me. I had always been known to pick guys that I had to "fix." Obviously, I wasn't doing this on a conscious level, but I was doing it, nonetheless. I generally felt more confident, empowered, and motivated when I was in a relationship. But why? What was the subconscious thought in all this?

- I don't really know how to love myself.

Yep. There it was. I really did not know how to love myself. Everyone is always saying, "You have to love yourself before you can love another," or "Loving yourself is the most important thing you can do." But what the hell does that even mean? And how does one go about learning how to love themselves? I mean, I was sitting there thinking, *Okay, I'm ready to now, but how the hell do I do it?* This wasn't a question I could answer at this point because I genuinely had no fucking idea. I just knew that I had to figure it out.

It had been two days since I had heard from Javier. The last time we'd spoken was the day I had arrived in Paris. I booked my train ticket to Barcelona for the following morning. After packing up my stuff, I snuggled into my first hostel bunk for the last time. Okay, universe. Show me the reason I'm supposed to go to Barcelona.

Fuck
Expectations

(When you have none, they can only be exceeded.)

DAY FIFTEEN

Ever since London, I had told Emma I felt like something important or amazing was going to happen in Barcelona. These next few chapters will prove my intuition is like a fucking ninja on steroids. I had run out of time in Paris and settled on a gold bracelet from a shop at the train station to add to my collection. The six-and-a-half-hour train ride from Paris to Barcelona gave me time to write and reflect on the city I was leaving.

When I arrived in Barcelona, I was greeted with warm weather, which was *so* welcome after the sporadic rain and lower temperatures in the first three cities I had been in. This was the first city with no Uber, so I hopped in a cab and headed to my hostel.

I had read a bunch of amazing reviews on this hostel, about how it was unique and friendly with family-style dinners and group nights out. It's kind of incredible how much information you can get on apps these days. Hostelworld is like a full-on Airbnb where you can see reviews, ratings, pictures, the whole deal.

When I checked in, I signed up for the family dinner that night, as well as the night out, which consisted of going to a bar and then a club called City Hall. After checking into my room, which was co-ed with eight other people, I decided to text Javier. I hadn't heard from him in over three days. I was so over the waiting game.

Me: What's going on with you, Veto?

Javier: Hey, Plum. I'm here in San Vito.
Javier: You seem to be having a blast in Paris! New friend! Good food.
Javier: Makes me happy.

Me: I'm in Barcelona now.

Like you cared to even ask...or know...because we haven't talked in three days and you didn't feel the need to check on me at all...Sorry, let's continue.

Javier: Oh nice.
Javier: When did you arrive?

Me: A few hours ago, took the train.

Javier: Hostel?

Me: Yeah.
Me: I haven't heard from you in three days...Just wanted to make sure you were okay.

As if *I'm* the one who needs to be initiating this.

Javier: Oh yeah, all is well. Took me a day to get here from Napoli. It's so hard to get here. Limited buses.

Totally missed that insinuation.

Javier: But now with the boys and I really needed it.

Me: Good.
Me: My lawyer emailed me yesterday.

Javier: About?

Me: Daniel got fired.

Javier: Not surprised.

Yeah, I'm fine, thanks for asking.

Me: Half of me feels like karma's a bitch and the other half of me just feels…sad, I guess.
Me: But I guess that means I'm human.
Me: Anyway, have fun with the boys.

Javier: Of course, you're not evil.
Javier: Ok, let's talk one of these days. The Wi-Fi here is the worst of all. I can write but video sucks.
Javier: Be careful and have fun.

Me: Sure, whenever.
Me: Have a great time.

He always ended up saying, "Let's talk soon," and then just wouldn't initiate it. Such a guy thing. Not even. Such a *him* thing, which of course drove me crazy. *Whatever*, I thought, I'm finally in the place I've been so excited to go, and I'm going to be in the moment.

After settling into my room, I went outside to a beautiful terrace. Now, because there will be so many people in this chapter, I'm going to call our supporting characters by their state/country and our main characters by name. I immediately met Arizona, who was in the same room as me. I found it so funny that you could be on the complete opposite end of the world and meet someone who lived a six-hour drive from you. I sat and had a long conversation with Quincy, a petite bleached blonde from Australia with a bull ring nose piercing and long acrylic nails. She was very sweet and had a wonderful energy about her. We also chatted with Denmark, a girl with dark features who had been traveling alone as well.

After freshening up, we all headed down for the family dinner. There were two guys from the hostel who had been mentioned in all the hostel reviews: Damian and Alejandro. They were both Latin, Damian from Argentina, and Alejandro from Mexico. They were cooking up a storm in the kitchen where about twenty of us had gathered, taking advantage of the unlimited sangria and dinner for only five euros.

I plopped down at a table next to Denmark, where six guys were also seated. After shaking hands and getting everyone's name, my eyes went to the guy sitting directly across from me. He was well dressed and had light eyes and an overly cool haircut. He had a definite *style* to him. I immediately realized my brain going, "Well, if anyone, it'll be him." Whoa, Gabrielle...where had that thought just come from? Another old habit creeping back in. I didn't need a guy to have fun in this city nor did I need to jump back into the pool of regret I had cannonballed into in Amsterdam.

"I'm Chris," he said. "This is Jacob." He introduced his friend. Jacob had tan skin and a fun and outgoing vibe mixed with a quirky personality. They were traveling together from—take a guess—California. Chris grew up in Orange County (pause for eye roll) but they had attended college together and were now living in San Francisco. They were both twenty-three (again, why am I so old?).

After talking for a while and eating a delicious meal cooked by Damian and Alejandro, it was time to head out. Our group of fifteen or so headed to the metro station. On the walk over, a spunky reddish-brown-haired girl from New York introduced herself.

"Hi! I'm Mallory." She smiled.

I introduced myself and some others that were around. Mallory was my age (finally) and traveling alone as well. She was well into her third month and had been to Israel, Greece, Italy, Croatia, Slovenia, Hungary, Czechia, Germany, Netherlands, Belgium, and Spain. To top it off, after her crazy adventure, she was heading straight to Australia, where she was moving to work and live for a year. I was immediately impressed with her fearlessness. Being away from home and family for that long is a lot. We talked a little as we walked through the warm streets until we bumped into another girl who looked about our age as well. She seemed a little less open, so Mallory and I introduced ourselves. Her name was Rhonda, and she gave off a serious Eva Mendez/Rosario Dawson vibe.

"Where are you from?" I asked.

"California," she replied. Seriously, why does it even surprise me anymore?

"Where?"

"LA." She smiled.

"Where?"

"Reseda." She laughed.

"Shut up. I'm in Woodland Hills." We were literally fifteen minutes away from each other. Again, the smallest freaking world.

We all piled onto the metro and headed to the first bar. Similar to Amsterdam, I wouldn't really call it a bar. It was definitely a small club. We ordered drinks that were literally the size of the giant ones you get at a day club in Vegas. Our core group (me, Chris, Jacob, Mallory, Rhonda, and Quincy) stood around dancing, drinking, and laughing. We were joined by two French Canadians, both with heavy accents, one of them with crystal blue eyes, brown hair, and a sweet smile.

I found myself standing next to Chris.

"So, what brought you on this trip?" he shouted over the loud music.

"It's such a long fucking story," I said as he looked at me and smiled, waiting for me to elaborate. "Okay, I'll give you the Cliff Notes version." I proceeded to fill him in while standing in the middle of the very loud bar.

"Damn, what a story," he said. "Well, for what it's worth, you seem like you're doing great." That was actually really nice to hear. A few people had said that to me along the way but for some reason this was the first time I didn't roll my eyes. He told me about his trip to Southeast Asia and how it had really changed him as a person.

"After a while back at home, I reverted back to the typical Orange County douche bag." We laughed. You could tell that he was definitely a different person when he was traveling, as opposed to when he was home. And although you could see the flickers of "bro" and "frat guy," there was definitely a way deeper side to him that I could already sense. I told him about the book I was writing and that the title was *Eat, Pray, Fuck My Life*. He laughed and told me how awesome it was that I was taking all of the nonsense going on in my life and making it into something. Even in the craziness of the bar, we found ourselves in a rather intimate conversation.

After some more dancing, we went on to the second spot of the night, which was a much bigger two-story club called City Hall. Apparently, City Hall was the place to be on a Monday night and it was so appropriately titled *"Fuck Mondays."*

While in line, we all swapped Instagrams so we could coordinate the rest of the time we were all there. As had happened before, everyone freaked out about my stupid little blue check mark, but with this group it would become a frequent running joke. Jacob and I chatted as we waited.

"We're going to the Barcelona soccer game tomorrow. You should totally come with us."

"Hell yes," I said without a second thought. Javier and I had talked about going to a game in Italy. It would be such a memorable experience, especially in Barcelona.

Everything here started *much* later (like most places in Europe do) so we didn't even arrive at City Hall until about 1:45 a.m. After grabbing drinks, we all headed to the dance floor.

I must admit, growing up as a dancer, I'm immediately judgmental about people's dancing. While I always appreciate and applaud effort and fun, it takes quite a bit to actually impress me. Let me tell you, for a white boy, Chris could fucking get down. We all danced and freaked out when amazing songs came on, and we all rapped Eminem's "The Real Slim Shady" together. Suddenly, the French Canadian grabbed me to dance. After about a minute he grabbed my arm and yelled, "Gabrielle! Don't worry! I'm gay!" We laughed. I absolutely *love* my gays, and they love me. I have many gay friends and they are some of the most amazing people in my life. I swear I could live in a house of gay men and be the happiest person on the planet. Our new little group was quite content in the middle of the crowded dance floor. Five minutes later, I turned around to see the very drunk, and apparently very gay, French Canadian making out with an equally as drunk *Mallory*. Oh, Barcelona.

Around 4:30 a.m. I saw Chris drunkenly look at Jacob with a look that said, "I'm done," and they quickly disappeared without a word. Mallory was nowhere to be found, nor were the French Canadians or our guides, Damian and Alejandro.

After another thirty minutes of dancing, Rhonda, Quincy, a few others, and I walked back to our hostel around 6 a.m. What a fun first night with such a great group of people. I felt like it was going to be an eventful four days. Oh, Gabrielle, you have *no* idea.

Fuck
Connection

(When it's there, it's undeniably strong.)

DAY SIXTEEN

The day before, I had booked a ticket to go to the famous Park Güell so I could get my tourist stuff checked off early in the trip. After falling asleep at 7 a.m., getting up at 10 a.m. wasn't the most ideal thing. I threw on shorts (finally) and the shirt Javier had bought me in Argentina. It felt like it fit the feel of this city. I headed off to make my way to the park.

It was just as beautiful and breathtaking as everyone who had recommended it had said, with views of the entire city. You could feel the culture in the streets. People sat playing live music, and the sounds of Spanish guitars filled the air. It was truly magical. There were vendors with blankets laid out selling a variety of trinkets. One with a bunch of bracelets caught my eye, perfect to add to my growing collection. They were six bracelets for five euros, so I picked out one for each of my girlfriends back home and one for my mom. For myself, I settled on a black and turquoise one with an owl charm and a blue one with a heart charm that read "Be true to your heart." Owls had been my favorite animal since I was a little girl. After my dad passed, we planted a tree in our backyard on Father's Day in memory of him. That night an owl came, perched in the tree, and made it it's home for months. Ever since then, I have had so many random occurrences with owls, which my mom and I always take as a sign from my dad.

I walked around by myself, taking in the beauty of my surroundings. At the top, I looked out over the epic view. A couple asked me to take a photo for them. After I did, they took one for me. In the photo, I turned around and looked out over the city. The shirt Javier had bought me read my last name on the back. It made for quite a powerful picture. I posted it with the caption, "Barcelona, you have my heart." And it already did.

I made my way down to the more decorated part of the park. Beautiful ceramic tiles lined giant archways, and grand architecture decorated the beautiful grounds. I stopped and sat on a bench to write a page in my journal.

> Walking through the breathtaking Park Güell my heart feels...full. Something about the architecture, the sweeping views of Barcelona, the lush greenery surrounding the strong stonework—something about this place made me feel at home, like I did that day on the beach with Javier. Walking along the dirt road through the park, I heard his language everywhere. I had been immersed in his culture for a month and a half, and I wasn't ready to let that go. Something about it made me feel awakened and alive, as did Barcelona. Clearly it was for the same reason that my heart was hurting, because everything here made me think of him. I'm ready for this to lessen. To go away. To move on. But a part of me just doesn't want to believe I have to.

Now, you KNOW there is a juicy ass Thought Onion in there. Superficial thought?

- I have some type of pull to this culture.

It was true. I looked back to before I apparently fell into a white boy coma, better known as my boring white boy phase (sorry to my exes who *weren't* boring...you know who you are). Looking back, I have always had a pull toward Latin men. My first serious boyfriend was Mexican. The guy I lost my virginity to was Salvadoran. Another one of my exes was Peruvian. There was a definite pattern here that I had somehow forgotten about. What's the authentic thought?

• Javier really fucked me up.

Now, that may sound superficial but it's really not. This man really did a number on me. I had never felt so many relationship scars from someone before. That's saying a lot after my fair share of long relationships, a marriage, and a divorce. And at this moment in Barcelona, only a few scars had formed, and there were more to come. So, what's the subconscious thought?

• My heart isn't safe with a Latin man.

Okay...let me remind you it's called a *SUB*conscious thought for a reason. It's not like I'm walking around saying, "I can never date a Latin man again," because I guarantee you that is *not* the case and it will most likely occur in the future. Let's think of it as...oranges. What I am saying is that these three thought patterns make up something that looks like this: I love oranges. I have always loved oranges. I got a really bad orange. Now oranges are ruined for me.

I mean, it kind of makes sense, right? How frustrating to have this feeling toward something and have it feel ruined for you. Not that it was necessarily Javier's fault. It was me who was subconsciously feeling this way. But it was real, nonetheless. I didn't want to take this into any future relationships. I mean, how awful to try and date someone and not trust them because of one bad orange? Maybe I need Latin Lovers Anonymous.

After my journey through the park, I walked twenty minutes to La Sagrada Família. It's a famous church that is still under construction and probably always will be. It was designed by Antoni Gaudí, who also was responsible for the beautiful park I had just come from. I'd never seen something so dauntingly magnificent. It didn't even look real. It looked like something out of an imagination, like one of those sandcastles you create by dripping wet sand out of a bottle. It was breathtaking. I didn't go in, I just stood on the street taking in the grandness of this vision. A text from Javier came in.

Javier: Any picture is better with the Argentina shirt.

Sigh. He never failed to pop back in the second I finally get my mind on something else. However, it was slowly beginning to affect me a little less every time. I headed home to shower and get ready for the soccer game.

I was thinking about where I would go after Barcelona. I had kept in touch with Jason from Amsterdam and had really been considering going to meet him in Mykonos. Getting there was definitely expensive, but I had always wanted to visit Greece, and he had a free place for us to stay. I decided why not? I messaged him and told him I was booking my ticket. The Canadian Trevor was going to be meeting us for a night too. How cool that I met two people by chance in Amsterdam one night and now we would all be reuniting in Mykonos. This was one of the awesome things that came from traveling by yourself. *See Gabrielle? You would never be able to just go meet new friends if you had a man around to worry about.* Solo travel for the win. So there, on the streets in Barcelona, I booked my ticket to Mykonos.

* * * * *

Later that day I met Mallory on the terrace and helped her buy a ticket to join us at the game. She was planning on doing the park at sunset but wanted to meet us after. I met Chris and Jacob downstairs where Arizona and a newbie from Culver City asked to join us for dinner, since they were heading to the game later as well. In the lobby stood a tall dark-haired Australian girl.

"Karly!" Jacob and Chris exclaimed as they all excitedly said hello. They introduced me and she smiled warmly. The boys had met Karly in Granada, where they all spent time together before they had come to Barcelona.

"Come to dinner with us," Jacob said. "We're going to the game after if you want to join us."

"How much is the game?" she asked in her Aussie accent.

"Like seventy euros," he replied.

"Ha! Fuck that." She laughed. Karly had been traveling for over a month already, so she had to pick and choose where her money went. She agreed to join us for dinner.

Chris quickly gained the nickname "TripAdvisor" because he knew all the amazing places to go, which was nice since I had obviously done zero research in regard to this trip. Let me tell you, this restaurant was *amazing*. Unreal blackberry mojitos, delicious appetizers, including ceviche, octopus, artichoke, and breads. Then two different paellas for the main course, one seafood and one duck. The duck paella was what the restaurant was famous for, and it was *incredible*. Even the ambiance was perfection.

After an insanely delicious meal, Karly and I headed to the bathroom. We chatted about being solo female travelers, and she asked if I had found it easier to connect with guys as opposed to girls. I had. Was it because society expects women to compete against each other and automatically compare ourselves to other women? That's such bullshit. We decided we needed to break whatever "thing" that was and start being more open with other women.

We said goodbye to Karly, Arizona, and Culver City, and the boys and I made our way to the bus, where we met Mallory. Walking up to this huge stadium was amazing. You could feel the energy and the excitement. We walked up to security, and they checked our bags. My Moroccan hairspray was still in my bag from the night before. The security guard told me I couldn't bring it in and casually tossed it in the trash. My soul died a little. It was literally the *only* hair product of any kind I had brought on this trip. Mallory sympathized with me while the boys laughed.

We headed to our seats, and the view was unreal. The vibrant colors, the thousands and thousands of people, the lights...it was amazing. We watched the game with one of the most passionate crowds I have ever been a part of. Messi, one of the most famous players in the world, scored four goals that night, making it 6-1 Barcelona. The boys, Mallory, and I took a picture overlooking the epic stadium. I posted it with the caption, "Bucket List in Barcelona." What a freaking moment. Just then, my phone went off.

Javier: You made it to a game.
Javier: Amazing. Have a blast.

It's stuff like this that felt so strangely...*friendly,* and I was never sure what to make of it.

Me: I did.

Javier: Great.
Javier: I'm talking to my friends in Mexico City right now. I'm anxious and scared.

Me: Wait what?
Me: What do you mean?

Javier: Huge earthquake in the city.
Javier: 22 buildings collapsed already.

Me: Are all your friends okay?

Javier: As of now, yes. Haven't heard from my best friend yet.

Me: I don't want you to go.

To Mexico City...and I didn't want him to go for a million reasons.

Javier: How was the game? Did they win?
Javier: Who did they play?

Me: We're still here.

Javier: Amazing. Watching the best player in the world. Messi. Numero 10.

Me: Yeeep. He's been killing it. Playing Eibar.

Javier: Enjoy Plum! Really fucking happy for you.

Again, really happy...that I'm not crying over you? Happy that I'm okay? That I've made friends? Happy about what, exactly?

Javier: Look at you learning the team names.

Me: Hope you're having a good time with your friends.
Me: Let me know when you hear from your friend in Mexico.

Javier: Yeah I will. Thanks.

Sigh. Just when I start to feel some distance from him, he pops back in. It's not intentional and I know that. He's damned if he does and damned if he doesn't.

We watched the rest of the epic game, listening to the chants, songs, and energy of the crowd. On our way out I joked with Mallory, "I'm gonna look for my hairspray." I kid you not, walking out the same gate we entered, I glanced into the trash can. There, in a perfect corner away from the trash, right on top, sat my bottle of hair gold. And yes, you're damn right I fucking grabbed that shit.

The four of us decided to take our time getting back and we walked home. Chris and I found ourselves in a few deep conversations yet again about our traveling experiences. We all grabbed food and decided to call it an early night. And by early, I mean 2:30 a.m. And let me tell you, thank God we did. Because the next two nights wouldn't be *anything* of the sort...

Fuck How You "Should" Be

(Just let yourself be in the moment.)

DAY SEVENTEEN

Today was different. On this seventeenth day abroad, in Barcelona, on Wednesday September 20th, I woke up...*happy*. I felt excited for the day, my new friends, this city. I just felt *good*.

Mallory and I had made plans to get brunch at a spot Chris (aka TripAdvisor) had highly recommended. We met in the common room of the hostel and headed to Brunch and Cake. Walking through the streets made me feel energized and alive. There was just something about this city. We arrived and each ordered a coffee, some delicious sounding pancakes, avocado toast, and the cheesecake pot Chris and Jacob had raved about. Don't judge. I'd been eating my way through this trip, and I didn't want to fully think about it until I was home and living at the gym for two months. Every dish that came was like art on a plate. It put fancy LA restaurants to shame. The chef was a young Spanish guy in an open kitchen right next to us, rocking out to Drake on the radio. It was insanely delicious. Solid recommendation, TripAdvisor. Mallory told me about her journey and the job situation that had made her decide to move. She was so sweet, and for once, my age at twenty-seven.

After brunch, Mallory headed back to the hostel, and I ventured out to find two really important things: a nail salon and somewhere to get waxed. Hey, it had been two and a half weeks, and I'm a woman. I found a nail place and made an appointment for the following day at 11:15 a.m. I figured that wouldn't be too terribly early...Ha. I had gotten a recommendation on a spa for the wax. Slight TMI but, at home, I've only ever been to a wax lady who works with honey instead of actual wax. I've never had *actual* wax before, and I was in a random country, so I was slightly nervous. Luckily, the lady from the Philippines was incredibly sweet and we talked the whole thirty-five minutes. Also, it was somehow *less* painful. Win.

After my imperative spa trip, I walked back to the hostel where I was meeting Karly to head to the beach to join Chris and Jacob. I changed into my bathing suit, which by this point I was entirely too fat for, and headed downstairs. When we were about to leave, I noticed a guy checking in at the hostel. The one thing about traveling solo that is always nerve-wracking is getting to a new place and not knowing anyone. I decided to make his experience a little easier.

"Hey! I'm Gabrielle. We're heading to the beach to meet some people from the hostel if you wanna come meet us," I said.

"Hi! I'm John, that sounds awesome," he said with an English accent.

"Where are you from?" I asked.

"England."

"Oh, nice! I started my trip in London. Anyway, add me on Instagram and message me if you wanna come," I offered.

"Totally, thank you." He smiled and did so.

"And we're all going to dinner and then out tonight. You should come!"

"I'm in!" he said. It felt so damn good to be able to walk up to someone, have an open conversation, and make them feel welcomed. And at this point, in Barcelona with this group of people, I wanted everyone to feel as welcomed as I had felt.

Karly and I headed to the metro.

"So, what's your story?" she said in her adorable Aussie accent.

"It's such a long one." This had become my standard response so people could mentally prepare.

"I have time! If you don't mind talking about it," she said with a smile. I gave her the slightly more detailed version. When I finished, her mouth hung open, which had also become the standard response.

"Wow. You're so strong," she said. "I identify with so much of that. Well, not the divorce relationship stuff..."

"Tell me, girl!" I said as we changed stops at the metro. Karly proceeded to tell me that she had attended a music festival in Australia the year before and had nearly died when she was trampled in a huge crowd rush. She had suffered internal bleeding, damaged bones, and popped blood vessels in both eyes. She'd been in recovery in the hospital for two months. Originally, she'd had this trip booked for April, but she'd had to postpone it. She was still struggling with PTSD in crowds. It was a truly incredible thing that she had even come on this trip.

"*You* are so strong," I said back to her. We talked the whole way to the beach. We understood each other perfectly, and we instantly bonded. "My mom kept telling me, 'It's okay if you don't want to go. If you want to stay here, it's okay.'"

"Me too," she said. We had both taken a leap into the unknown and trusted it would be okay. And it *was*. So why was I still so afraid of other unknowns? Potentially seeing Javier and not knowing what emotions it would bring...going home to the unknown drama of my pending divorce. Why did I not trust that the universe was going to take care of those unknowns as well?

When we arrived at the beach, we met Chris and Jacob on the sand. What a perfect freaking day it was. We soaked up the sun, took pictures, and enjoyed discussing anything that came up.

An hour later I got an Instagram message from John, whom we had just met at the hostel. He was at the beach looking for us. *How cool*, I thought. I had been open and inviting to someone who had just walked into a hostel and he'd come to join our group. From that day on the beach until we left two days later, he was with us.

We were also joined on the beach by Chris and Jacob's new roommates, three guys from Toronto, Canada. One was of Indian heritage, one Italian, and the other Pakistani, and they were all traveling together. We instantly clicked. They were super friendly, cool, really open, and fun to be around.

We all sat for about an hour getting to know each other. The Toronto boys were heading to Ibiza next. After a good amount of sun, the eight of us decided to walk the whole way home. We were a little over an hour away, but we were having such a great time together, we figured we might as well see the city while we ventured back to the hostel. We walked along the boardwalk, past the harbor, and through what is called the Gothic Quarter. The Gothic Quarter was filled with incredible buildings that looked like they'd been pulled out of Harry Potter world. There were musicians playing Spanish guitars and you could feel culture pouring out of the fairy-tale buildings. We took group pictures at different spots along the way, pictures that all of us would hold pretty dear forever.

Back at the hostel, we got ready for our night out. Still getting by on a mere three hours of sleep, I had a cup of coffee and a much-needed shower. It's amazing how little sleep you need to actually function. After a few drinks in the hostel common area, Alejandro rounded up the massive twenty-five-person group that would be heading out for the night, eighteen of which were our newly dubbed "family." First, we were heading to a bar called L'Ovella Negra, which translated to The Black Sheep.

After about two blocks, we turned on a street where there was a huge protest happening. The street was packed with people marching and chanting, and the police were standing around, as well. We began to make our way into the crowd, which I must admit was slightly intimidating. Just weeks before, an awful terrorist attack had taken place in Barcelona, so everyone definitely felt a little...uneasy.

"Can I hold your hand?" I turned to see a nervous looking Karly. At first I was confused by the question. Then I realized, *Duh, Gabrielle—crowds*.

"Of course," I said and grabbed her hand. She squeezed my hand tight, like a kid holding her mom's hand at Disneyland. We made it about fifty feet before Alejandro decided this was not smart nor safe. Thank God because by this point poor Karly was in tears.

We got to the bar on a different route, and it was like what I imagine walking into a beer festival would be like. There were long wooden tables with chairs, and people slamming mugs in unison while chanting randomly together. The bar was known for its five-liter pitchers of beer and sangria. Naturally, our family got three. Once seated, Chris pulled out a pair of dice and explained the drinking game called *7-11 Doubles*. I'm still shocked that we managed to play any form of organized game with the noise level and amount of people in that place, but sure enough, we did.

After a good hour of this mayhem, we switched over to *Never Have I Ever*, which immediately brought me back to my college days. Everyone held up five fingers and, one at a time, people would say something they *hadn't* done. If you *had* done whatever was said you then had to put a finger down and drink. When all your fingers were down, you were out. Luckily, the Toronto guys were all twenty-eight and twenty-nine, so I wasn't the only older person playing with Chris and Jacob. John, Rhonda, and Mallory were all playing as well. I can't remember all the ridiculous sexual and drug-related statements that followed, but I do remember Chris and I smirking at each other every time we both had to put a finger down, which happened frequently. For twenty-three, this guy had done his fair share of...life, not only in the things we learned about in this game (which is always quite telling about people) but in his travels and experiences as well.

"Never have I ever been skydiving," I said and stared at him. He gave me a look, put his finger down, and finished his sangria. We had just talked about his skydiving experience the night before. I mean, that was the only way to assure he would be out before I was. No one said I always play fair. I was still out the next round.

After two hours at the bar and way too much sangria, it was time to head to the club. Everyone took a bathroom stop before hitting the road. Mallory, Rhonda, and I reconvened while washing our hands.

"You guys," I said. "Shit."

"What?" Mallory asked.

"Chris," I said.

"I KNEW IT!" she squealed. "Why shit?"

"He's twenty-three." I laughed, mostly at myself. "And like...my life."

"No, I totally get it. But it's so obvious," she said.

"Wait, what do you mean *your life*?" Rhonda asked.

"Oh! I haven't told you about the ridiculous last three months of my life," I realized.

"Tell me!" she shrieked.

"On the walk over," I agreed.

And I did. As Mallory, Rhonda, and I walked arm and arm, I told the Cliff Notes version I had come to know so well.

"Girl, you are a fucking inspiration," Rhonda said. "You're like Beyoncé. I want to be you." Oh girl, trust me, you so do not. However, it was insanely cool to hear that. Mallory nodded in agreement. I felt so supported and so empowered. For the first time, I wasn't sad when I spoke about Javier. I was...*irritated*. Huh. This was new. Shall we Thought Onion this bitch real quick? What is the superficial thought?

• What a dick.

I mean...yeah, let's not try and justify that one. It's called the superficial thought for a reason, after all. Now, more importantly, what is the authentic thought?

• This whole situation really isn't...okay.

Yep. It had taken two weeks for me to finally start to feel that the way he had handled all of this, and the way he was continuing to handle things on this trip, really *wasn't* okay. At all. In fact, it was very *not* okay, especially when you claim to love and care about someone. Finally, what is the subconscious thought in all this?

• Why am I allowing someone to continually let me down?

Because that is what I'd been doing this whole time. Every time Javier didn't reach out, every time he told me he didn't want to see me and then changed his mind, and every time he confused me by telling me he loved me—all of it would let me down. Why was I allowing this to happen? Another way I wasn't really loving myself. Damn that self-love concept I couldn't seem to grasp. Alas, as we arrived at Razzmatazz, I knew I would have to check back in with this new revelation at a different time.

You guys...this club was absolutely *insane*. Mallory, the three Torontos, Rhonda, Chris, Jacob, and I made our way to the main floor. Taylor Swift's "Look What You Made Me Do" blared and the DJ was dancing so fabulously with himself. It was literally the best thing I had ever seen.

"Let's go to the front!" Rhonda yelled over the music. She grabbed my hand and somehow our entire group made it right to the damn front. It was such good music, like every epic song from my life set to incredible dance beats. They played Avril Lavigne's "Sk8ter Boi" and Aqua's "Barbie Girl" (which is one of my personal all-time favorites. They even had dancers dressed as Barbie and Ken dolls that came out of life-sized toy boxes), all with this fierce DJ dancing, which was seriously a show in itself.

"Let's get shots!" Jacob yelled. We all headed to the bar except for Chris, who was dancing up a storm.

While Mallory, Rhonda, and the Torontos ordered tequila, Jacob and I stepped to the side and got two vodka shots each. After one, the alcohol was just enough for me to blurt out, "So. Uh...No, never mind," I said.

"No, tell me," he insisted.

"I feel, uh...I dunno, like a weird thing with Chris?" I said. His eyes widened a bit. I'm not sure what he was expecting me to say, but it definitely wasn't that. "I just don't want to ever mess up a friendship because I genuinely like you both, and I want to be friends with you guys," I continued. I truly meant that. In the short time we had all spent together, I knew I wanted to have friendships with all of the people I had met there.

"Chris isn't like that," he said. Such a typical wingman answer. "But how do you feel about the whole Javier situation?" he asked. That was interesting to me. Here was this twenty-three-year-old who had only known me for three days, but he knew enough about what I was going through to ask a really thoughtful question about my well-being, instead of just immediately trying to get his friend laid. Kudos to you, Jacob.

"It's kind of irrelevant at this point. He sent me on this journey. I'm just trying to navigate it, honestly," I responded as we downed our second vodka shots. "And ugh...he's twenty-three," I added.

"Age is just a number," he replied, the typical response of anyone who is trying to convince someone who is way older or way younger. Yes. It's a number that meant my ex-husband was too damn young. A number that made Javier look ideal. A number that made Chris look like a baby. All this was coming from me, someone who preaches that age is just a state of mind. And then I thought...*why*? Because he's young and it's not something I "should" do because it doesn't make any sense for future things? And that means I should not say yes to this experience or whatever it may bring? No. Fuck how you "should" be, Gabrielle. Just let yourself, for once, be in the moment. So I did.

With shots in our systems, all of us headed back to the front of the dance floor, where we found Alejandro and Chris. Rhonda, Mallory, and I started dancing while Jacob beelined it straight to Chris in the most obvious way possible. They stood on the dance floor for a solid three minutes discussing the information Jacob had just learned. Once they had finished the incredibly apparent exchange, Chris made his way over to me and we started dancing. I was trying to decide if it was lame or adorable that he had needed someone to tell him I was interested before he would do anything. I'll let you know when I decide.

After we danced for a little bit, he spun me around and said, "I have a question for you..." and kissed me. As typical Orange County and lame as it sounded, something about it was stupidly charming. And just like that, the twenty-three-year-old from San Francisco and I were coupled up for the night. We checked out all the different floors and danced our asses off on each. My personal favorite was the Latin floor. I have *always* loved Latin music, way before Javier ever entered the picture.

Around 4:30 a.m., Mallory and Rhonda decided to head home. Chris and I stayed with some of the others for another hour or so. It was a pretty perfect night of fun, amazing dancing, and great kissing. Once the remainder of our group had left, Chris and I grabbed a cab back to the hostel. I don't remember how, but we got to talking about my situation and the ins and outs of the whole Javier saga.

"Gabrielle, I want to say this, but know it's not meant to be mean. That's a fucking cop-out." Sigh. If he only knew how many times I'd heard that from people. And trust me, I am always the first person to tell my girlfriends, "That's bullshit. He just doesn't want to be with you." And I know that's exactly what this situation looked like to *everyone* on the outside. I'd been defending it for three weeks now. But something about the way Chris said it, or maybe the way Barcelona had made me feel, or maybe just the time that had passed, made me kind of agree. That car ride was our first of many deep conversations that night. Even through the alcohol and the partying, I could sense that he cared about me in some way.

Once we were back at the hostel, we were hell-bent on making quesadillas. Jacob had promised to make them but was entirely too drunk to do so. We found him sitting on the stairs, drunkenly spilling his heart out to his recent ex-girlfriend, who he was so clearly still in love with. Jacob was in all ways a very genuinely good guy.

Chris and I ventured off to the grocery store at what was now around 6 a.m. We continued to talk about whatever came up. He would randomly tell me I was cute, and we laughed and joked about the ridiculous night we'd had. On the way back from the store, I randomly stopped and said, "So can we just decide how this is gonna be so it's not awkward?" He started laughing.

"You're so cute," he said. I guess it was pretty funny. Here I was, the twenty-eight-year-old, telling the twenty-three-year-old, "Let's make a plan about what this is for the next forty-eight hours." Oh, alcohol.

We got back to the hostel around 6:30 a.m., and Chris made us quesadillas, which I can't confidently say were as amazing as they tasted at that moment in time. We kept talking as we ate. Everything seemed to flow really naturally with us. After we cleaned up, we decided to change and go hang on the terrace courtyard. Unfortunately, they locked it at 11 p.m. every night, so we ended up in the hallway between our rooms.

"Well...it is 7:30 a.m., we should probably get some sleep," I said as I stood there in my sweatpants. He smiled, and we made out in the hallway like teenagers for five minutes. I finally pulled away and casually said, "We're in a hostel, it's 7:30, and we can't do anything about this." Again, we laughed. "Goodnight," I said as I turned toward my room.

"Goodnight," he said back.

I walked into my hostel room, where everyone was already asleep. Of course, *I'm that girl*, I thought as I crawled into my bunk and set my alarm for 10:30 a.m. Yes, three hours from now for my nail appointment at 11:15am. And I had thought that wouldn't be too early. Ha. I closed my eyes and, for the first time that trip, fell asleep not thinking of Javier but of the twenty-three-year-old two doors down. Win for the night.

Fuck Your Plans

(Because someone will cross your path and change them.)

DAY EIGHTEEN

My alarm went off at 10:30 a.m. Holy. Hell. I closed my eyes for five minutes, contemplating whether or not I would actually get up. Yes, Gabrielle, your nails are fucking dreadful, and you have another two and a half weeks on this trip. You must get up. You must go.

I sat up and looked over off my top bunk. John sat up like a groggy Frankenstein with all of his clothes on and looked at me. We laughed. Then Rhonda popped out from under the covers on one of the other top bunks.

"When did you move into this room?!" I laughed.

"They moved me last night." She laughed back.

"Good morning!" Quincy popped her blonde hair out from the bunk under Rhonda.

"You too?!" We continued laughing. I had gone to sleep with one group of random roommates and had woken up with all my new-found friends in the room.

"What time did you get in?" Rhonda asked.

"7:30...ish." I groaned. This was serious dedication. Off I went to get my nails done, and honestly, *so* freaking worth it.

Right as I was finishing up with my much-needed manicure, I got a message from Chris. They were all awake and heading to get empanadas. I headed back to the hostel (looking like death, I might add) and met Chris, Jacob, Mallory, Culver City, and another Aussie in the common room. The empanada place was right around the corner and, oh my God, they were unbelievable. Everyone ordered and we all feasted on the best empanadas I have ever tasted. I had one with goat cheese and leek (which was unreal) and one with chicken and plum (which was somehow even better). We all talked and laughed about the night before—all the sangria and ridiculous games at L'Ovella Negra, how epic the DJ at Razzmatazz was, and Jacob pouring his heart out on the phone at 6 a.m.

"Gabs, how's the book coming?" Chris asked. I gave them some details about what I was writing and told them they would all be in it. They all made me promise to send them signed copies.

"Where are you going after Mykonos, Gabrielle?" Jacob asked.

"Well," I said, then hesitated. "It's really up in the air right now." Since I had only given Jacob the short version of my story, I had to fill him in on the fact that Javier and I were deciding if we were going to meet or not at the end of the trip.

"Oh fuck," he said. "That's intense."

"Yeah," I agreed. Especially since he had gone back and forth about three times now. It was exhausting. Chris sat listening to this, as did Mallory. In any normal situation, it would have been very weird to discuss a man I was in love with in front of a guy I had just spent the whole night kissing. But it wasn't. It was almost like he and everyone I was with understood that I was on this journey, and they were now a part of it.

"So, are you gonna go meet him?" Jacob asked.

"Honestly, I don't know right now." It was true. This was the first time the answer hadn't been a big yes. After all that had happened, I really didn't know if I wanted to. "I don't know if it would be good for my heart," I said honestly. "And although there has to be some type of closure, I just don't know anymore." This was a big step. Progress.

We finished our delicious lunch with an espresso and walked back to the hostel. I decided to head back toward the harbor and get two things on my last day in the city that had captured my heart. First, I wanted a large thin tapestry. They were sold everywhere, and I picked out a black and tan one with an elephant design on it. The bracelets from each country were great, but I felt I needed something more from this place. Although it would definitely take up space in my pack, it was the perfect thing to take home from Barcelona. Then I wanted to get some braids in my hair. I found one of the many ladies doing hair braiding and sat down to get four small braids on the left side of my head. Yes, the whole time I was secretly praying I wouldn't get lice from this decision. Luckily, my prayers worked.

I headed back to the hostel to do a load of laundry and pack, and I planned to take a seriously needed nap. I accomplished the first two. I've never been the greatest napper but I really did commit. I got in my bunk, put in my headphones to listen to my white noise app, and made myself lie there for two hours. Guess what? I DIDN'T FUCKING SLEEP. *What is wrong with you, body? You've literally slept six hours in the past two days.* Oy. Nevertheless, it was our last night out, so I showered and rallied. I felt like I had been rallying since I'd landed in Barcelona, quite honestly. To make the lack of sleep even more daunting, Chris, Jacob, and I were all flying the next morning around the same time, and we had decided to head straight to the airport after the night out without sleeping. I would be heading to Mykonos, and they would be on the long journey home.

Off to our last family dinner we went. It really was just that...a little family. Everyone felt it—Chris and Jacob, the Torontos, all the girls. It was just...*special.* We ate, laughed, and took a "last dinner" photo of the group. We all knew it was going to be a wild last night out.

We made our way to Opium, a club that was right on the beach boardwalk. It was literally like a Vegas club. We all grabbed a drink and headed to the dance floor where Rhonda quickly bulldozed a path to the front by the DJ. Chris grabbed me to dance almost immediately, which I found hilarious, since we hadn't flirted or anything the whole day. We danced, got more drinks, and danced some more. Soon our entire hostel was on the dance floor together—Alejandro, Damian, the whole group. At one point, Chris and I kissed and everyone started cheering. Apparently, they were unaware this had happened the entire night before but, regardless, it was hilarious.

Just then, in the moment of all this perfectness, my freaking wedding song came on. It didn't affect me at all, to be honest. By this time, I was beyond disconnected from that entire relationship, and it felt like a lifetime ago. I still, to this day, think it's a great fucking song. Nevertheless, I laughed.

"This is my fucking wedding song," I shouted over the music.

"Fuck him! We love you!" Rhonda screamed. And standing there with a group of strangers that had become family, I felt so incredibly supported I could've cried. But this time it would be tears of fullness and happiness. We headed back to the bar for another drink.

"I have to get a picture with you before I never see you again," Chris said.

"Why would you say that?" I asked very seriously. He kind of nervously chuckled. This was the moment I realized he actually cared for me, in whatever type of way it was, because it was apparent that he didn't want to never see me again.

"Let's go down to the beach, just us, and talk," he said.

"Okay," I agreed. The Torontos were leaving the club at the same time to go to the airport and catch their flight to Ibiza, so we walked out with them to say our farewells. We all hugged and promised to keep in touch, then took a group photo with the five of us.

After we said goodbye, Chris and I headed down to the beach and sat in the sand. This is one part of my trip I contemplated not fully writing about. The hour we spent on the beach that night felt really personal. But alas, it was a pivotal moment on this insane journey. Maybe even the *most* pivotal moment.

I asked him why he didn't have a girlfriend. To my surprise, he began to tell me about his ex, whom he'd gotten somewhat close to heading down the proposal road with. For the record, I'm really glad he didn't. Daniel was twenty-three when he proposed to me...and we all know how that turned out. Of course, there are many couples that get married young and are super successful. I had just learned how very true it is that your twenties are a huge growing period, and I could tell Chris still had some of that to do. When I asked him why it hadn't worked out, he simply said their love wasn't at the level it should be to last forever.

"You know what? Regardless of whether everything with Javier was a cop-out or not, it doesn't really matter. You're incredible and deserve to be treated so much better than that," he said. Hearing those words made a light bulb go off inside me. *You deserve to be treated so much better than that.* No matter how strong my feelings were about Javier or the situation, Chris was right. I deserved more than that. I deserved better than that. I deserved as much as I had been giving, and it was about time I start demanding that for myself. We talked about my past, his past, and would randomly stop and kiss in between it all. Out of the blue, he laughed.

"What?" I smiled, expecting to hear something humorous.

"I, uhh..." He suddenly got shy and seemed like he didn't know if he should continue.

"What?" I pressed.

"I want to come to LA and take you to dinner," he said. *Oh.* Well then.

"Oh, really," I replied.

"Yeah. I mean I'll be out there soon for work but I'd like to take you to dinner...if you want," he said. The ridiculousness of this entire situation was not lost on me, although neither was the overwhelming cuteness. Hmm, how to respond?

"Why do you want to take me to dinner?" I asked. He looked down and chuckled nervously again.

"I don't know how to explain it. I just feel like you challenge me. I feel connected to you, like, it's not just random that I met you," he said, fully vulnerable. What was happening? How was this fresh-out-of-college twenty-three-year-old and I connecting on such a deep level?

"Well..." I said. "If you really want to take me to dinner, you can kiss me goodbye at the airport and tell me then. When we're sober." I smiled. The past two nights, we had flirted, kissed, and stayed together the whole time. But during the day, he had been much more reserved, and we hadn't been anything more than friends in the group. Not that it mattered either way, but this would ensure he actually meant what he was saying. Although to be honest, I didn't feel like either of us were really *that* drunk at all.

"Okay," he said simply. Now it was my turn to chuckle, because I was having a realization.

"What?" he asked smiling.

"This place...and our group...and being here...I really feel like I healed a little bit for the first time from all of this. And I don't know what this is...and I can't say whether I'm going to want something with you or will just want to have a friendship with you...because I have no idea. But for what it's worth, you were a really big part of it. So thank you," I said. He genuinely understood, and he smiled.

"That's amazing," he said. And it was. "So when you write all this in the book, do me a favor."

"What's that?" I asked.

"Don't change my name," he said. I smiled.

"Okay," I agreed.

I wish I could end on that sweet romantic note, but then this book would just be called *Eat Pray* and not be nearly as entertaining. Around 5:30 a.m. we left the beach and headed back to the hostel. To both of our surprise, Chris's room was empty. We knew that the Torontos had left for the airport, but where the hell was Jacob?

I had decided ahead of time that I was *not* going to have sex with Chris. Best-laid plans, Gabrielle. We were both caught up in the moment...the night...the last four days. But it didn't happen like it happened with Ireland. It was strangely...intimate for being in a small rickety hostel bed. And ya'll thought I was crazy for getting waxed. HA! There was passion and kissing and a connection. But most important? Not a single thought about Javier. Then...the door opened.

I sat up on top of Chris to see Jacob and...RHONDA?! Wait... what in the hell? How? When? WHAT? The following ridiculous exchange then took place, all while I was topless holding a sheet up to me while still...ya know.

Me: "I'm definitely naked right now."

Jacob: "You definitely are."

We all laughed.

Me: "Who are you...Rhonda?!"

Rhonda: "Hey, girl!"

Me: "You guys can come in but I'm not going to be any quieter."

Got to love my drunken alter ego. Who the hell am I, a porn star? And hello, Gabrielle, of course they can come in, it's Jacob's fucking room. Oy vey.

Rhonda: "Girl, you're good!"

Everyone continued laughing.

Jacob and Rhonda made their way to one of the top bunk beds at the other end of the room. Oh, the awkwardness. I still did not understand how that had even come to be a thing, but I had the urge to air-five Jacob. Good for him. When all was...done, it was 7 a.m., and Rhonda had a flight to catch. She hugged me goodbye. Yes, I know, ridiculous.

"You better fucking call me when you get back so we can get dinner," she said.

"100 percent yes," I answered. She didn't say bye to the guys, which I found strange, she just kind of...left. I soon understood why.

"Dude. What the FUCK," Jacob said.

"What?" I asked.

"You have no idea how fucking ridiculous that was," he continued.

"Good!" I said, happy for him.

"No, no...not in a good way." His face said it all. He proceeded to tell Chris and me about their extremely awkward night, which consisted of her trying numerous times to have sex and him turning her down, and her almost biting off his finger. Yes, I said biting off his finger. Chris and I were dying, we were crying from laughing so hard.

We decided we might as well head to the airport a bit early. Quincy had set an alarm to come say goodbye to me, so when she texted me, I told her the room we were in. She hadn't joined us for most of the partying, but I was very fond of her. We had talked about my story in depth, as well as hers. She felt like a little sister. We all said goodbye and took one final Instagram Boomerang, which is still my favorite from the entire trip.

The boys and I headed downstairs, where I made sure to sign the hostel wall on behalf of our little family. Then it was off to the airport.

The bus ride to the airport was like a scene from *The Hangover*. Let me paint you a picture: 7:30 a.m. All three of us look like we just got run over by a car. I had no voice and sounded like a man from lack of sleep and yelling over club music night after night. Chris had scratches on his neck from my perfectly manicured (but still deadly sharp) nails. Jacob's eyes were bloodshot red. We literally looked like we hadn't slept in a week.

Jacob started to tell us the insanely ridiculous story of his night, in full detail, at normal conversation volume. Chris and I were dying of laughter. I laughed even harder watching the reactions of the people who were sitting behind us on the bus, clearly hearing the entire story. However, let me clarify that the whole story, although hilarious, was ridiculously endearing and sweet. I asked him why he hadn't just had sex with Rhonda.

"Because that's something I've only shared with her," he said, referring to the ex-girlfriend he had been pouring his heart out to the night before on the stairwell. Let's pause while all the female readers say "awww" out loud.

Once we got to the airport, the boys waited for me to check my bag. We took a pretty epic "Fuck, we haven't slept, just kill me" picture and headed to security. They were heading home and I was off to meet Jason in Mykonos. Of course, that night was the one night that the two Canadians from Amsterdam were going to be there as well, so that meant we had to make the most out of our one reunion night. All on six hours of sleep in the last three days. Pray for me.

We went to grab food and continued to talk and laugh about how dead we all were and the insanity of the night before.

"All right, dude, let's head to the gate," Jacob said. We stood up and grabbed our stuff, and they both put their numbers in my phone. Jacob and I said goodbye and hugged, and then he stepped to the side. Oh, here we go.

Chris and I hugged. We stood there looking at each other. Then he kissed me.

"I'll see you in LA," he said with a smile. Well played, TripAdvisor. Well played.

I walked away without looking back because I could already feel it. I, this twenty-eight-year-old, not even legally divorced, brokenhearted, full-on mess of a woman was going to miss this twenty-three-year-old.

Once I boarded my plane, it was time for some attempted processing. I say attempted because I was literally delirious from sleep deprivation. Now, let me be clear: I was fully aware I was an emotional basket case at the moment. I was also fully aware that there was a probable chance that Chris just wanted to bang a hot older chick. I was also fully aware that all of this could have been the romance of travel and a foreign country. Yes, he was twenty-three and probably the *opposite* of what I should have been looking for right then—and all of it was absolutely crazy. All that being said, whatever happened between us in Barcelona was real.

I thought about how the people I met in Barcelona would never fully realize what a profound impact they had on my life during this journey. I had been searching for something, some way to heal, and was chasing the idea of fixing my life. Then, unexpectedly, without any monumental "Aha" moment...I woke up happy. I can't say what piece of me healed or how it happened, but I know that I will forever be thankful to these people I now call friends and this city that now has my heart. I posted a picture from our night out that had the whole group together. I wrote: "To all of you, thank you for rooting for me, for seeing me for who I am, and for making the past five days absolutely fucking unforgettable. Until the book..."

As I sat on the plane ready to take off (or pass out) to Mykonos, I heard Chris's voice in my head.

"Don't change my name." And then it hit me. Just like Javier's brother, his fucking name was Chris.

Fuck
Sleep

(Is it really *that* important?)

DAY NINETEEN

I was now running on a mere six hours of sleep in the last seventy-two hours. Part of me was incredibly impressed that my twenty-eight-year-old self was capable of partying even better than my twenty-one-year-old self had. The other part of me was genuinely scared that at any given moment I was just going to fall over and die. You would think my body would say, "THANK GOD," and go right to sleep on the plane, but instead, I had a few random nod-offs but was then woken up by my head immediately falling. I maybe got a collective fifteen minutes. *Maybe.* Although I knew when I arrived in Mykonos I would have to rally, I once again had no idea of the crazy night that was about to take place.

While I was going to be staying with Jason for the three nights I was there, Travis and his Canadian friend were only going to be in Mykonos that one night. So, it was the only night we could take advantage of the Amsterdam crew being back together. Guys, I literally sounded like a man who had smoked his entire life at this point. Between the lack of sleep and partying every night, my vocal chords were like...Uh, bye, Gabrielle.

After a quick flight from Athens to Mykonos I landed in the very small airport and grabbed my bag. Waiting for the luggage to come out, I checked my phone and had a voice message from Javier. He talked about how happy he was to see my post about Barcelona and the people I had met there, and that he was so glad to see that I was having the type of experience that I was. He also said he wanted to try and talk sometime while I was in Mykonos. I responded with my nonexistent voice telling him I was heading to the hotel to meet the guys I had met in Amsterdam, and to tell everyone he was with in San Vito hello. I had to admit, this was the first location where I hadn't felt the surge when I heard Javier's voice come through my phone. In fact, I was almost irritated. I had found a new type of confidence in Barcelona, and my lightbulb moment on the beach with Chris had really stuck with me. I was so over receiving what I didn't deserve.

The hotel shuttle picked me up to head to meet the guys. Jason and Travis were only twenty-two and twenty-one. The other Canadian was twenty. I instantly felt like the mom in the group. We all caught up on our travels while I changed and attempted to fix my face, which looked like I hadn't slept in three days...oh, wait.

First, we headed down to the hotel beach, which had a club and a few restaurants. It was 10 p.m., which was ridiculously early for European nightlife, especially in Mykonos. They went hard in Paris, decent in Amsterdam, and raged properly in Barcelona. *None* of them had *anything* on Mykonos. Good. Freaking. God. The four of us grabbed some awesomely decorated fruity drinks from the bar and started dancing to what I would soon realize was a collection of songs that every Mykonos DJ would play during every set.

Dancing on one of the huge platforms, the energetic MC who had been hyping people up the whole time came over and asked where we were from. He was on the short side, suave, and had more energy than an Energizer Bunny on cocaine. It was literally his job to hang out, drink, and shout "LA in the house," and "Mykonos, put your fucking hands up!"

We danced for two hours while people watching all the characters on this crazy party island. I must say, I was glad to have people I knew in this particular place because it was definitely *not* like the other countries I had been to. It didn't seem like there were many solo travelers, and I couldn't imagine walking around the party scene by myself, trying to meet people. During our dance session, we turned around to find Travis making out with some overly drunk Indian chick and then, ten minutes later, another woman who was definitely old enough to be his mom.

Jason had heard of another famous club that was having its summer season closing night. It happened to be right up the street from where we were, so we decided to head over. Walking into Cavo Paradiso at 12:30 a.m. was like walking into a Hollywood hot spot at like 7 p.m. They *really* start late in Mykonos, and I was *so, damn, tired.* The guys grabbed drinks and we sat by the beautifully lit outdoor pool with incredible views of the ocean behind us. The club was like a Vegas club situated right on the most epic cliff on the island.

Finally, around 1:30 a.m., there was enough of a crowd there to dance. I was already thinking about what time I could leave, get food (priorities, people), and head back to the room for some much-desired sleep. I have to admit, I was impressed that three young guys were dancing hard, on their own, and not giving a shit about what they looked like. I had seen a lot of this on my trip. Maybe it was because everyone was traveling, but you would *never* see this in LA. I loved it.

At about 2:30 a.m., I said to myself, *Okay, after this song I'm going to tell them I'm leaving.* Then I happened to look up toward the balcony level where the tables with bottle service were situated. I locked eyes with a good-looking guy who was dancing up a storm at the table he was at. We stared at each other for more than a few seconds, then I continued dancing in our little group we had on the dance floor. Five minutes later we locked eyes again. He smiled at me while singing some lame lyrics of whatever song was playing and I laughed. This charade proceeded to go on for the next twenty minutes, until one time he looked at me and motioned for me to come up to his table. I smiled, but continued dancing.

Okay, Gabrielle, you are literally going to fall over. Go home and go to sleep. I turned around to tell Jason I was going to head out and came face-to-face with none other than—Javier. JUST KIDDING, but you know all your mouths just dropped open and you let out a gasp. No, but I did come face-to-face with the guy from the balcony. Shit. I guess I'm not going home.

I smiled and he pulled me in to dance. After a few minutes, I leaned into his ear (with my still barely there man voice).

"What's your name?" I asked.

"Marcus," he said. "You?"

"Gabrielle," I answered. "Where are you from?"

"New York." I laughed. Of course, out of the whole club, I would pick the hot white dude from New York, who oddly resembled Chris in some ways. "What about you?" he asked.

"LA," I said. "How old are you?"

"Twenty-four," he said. I rolled my eyes and laughed under the loud music.

"What?" He laughed. "Is that in your age bracket?" he asked while we were still dancing. Like I even had a fucking age bracket anymore. Let's be real.

"Yeah," I said with a laugh and another eye roll. We kept dancing for a bit. Then, for the first time on this trip, I had the urge to make out with a random guy that I had just met in a club. So I fucking did.

"Let's get a drink," he said, grabbing my hand and leading me up to where his table was. "We have a yacht on Sunday. You have to come with us." *Of course you do*, I thought. He introduced me to his friends at the table and then made me the worst tasting vodka soda (which was mostly vodka) that I had ever had. So much for leaving and heading to bed.

There was one definite negative about Marcus right off the bat. He smoked like a chimney. Although, I have to be honest and admit, while I don't like cigarettes or feeling like I'm licking an ash tray, kissing Marcus was oddly reminiscent of kissing Jake back in high school. Jake smoking had been part of the bad boy draw, and Marcus definitely had a little bit of that too. Honestly, he was just so fucking hot that it didn't bother me. The fact that he was a great kisser didn't hurt either.

"How am I gonna contact you?" he asked. He handed me his phone, and I added him on my WhatsApp, then I added myself to his Instagram.

After some hours of dancing, making out, talking, and more making out, we ended up at the table that was situated directly next to the DJ booth. Earlier in the night, Marcus had met (and had a hard-core bromance with) a forty-year-old billionaire whose family was apparently one of the most powerful families in Italy. Totally normal. At the billionaire's table, there were giant bottles of Dom Pérignon and vodka, and more than a few women who were clearly hookers. While the billionaire didn't speak great English, he and Marcus had no problem communicating through shots, high fives, and random screams. I sat down on the couch next to the DJ booth and a now-slightly-drunker Marcus leaned over to me.

"We're all staying in a big villa. You should come stay with me tonight." I smiled, although I knew I would not be staying at the villa that night. Somewhere deep down I heard a little voice say, *You don't need another placeholder, Gabrielle, you need to be with yourself.* But while I recognized this pattern returning, I wasn't quite ready to fully embrace that...yet.

FINALLY, at 6 a.m., people were ready to leave. I literally was so tired I couldn't think straight. I hadn't even had more than two drinks over the course of the night. Jason had texted me around 5:30 a.m. saying he was back at the room and would leave the door unlocked for me. Figures, after I'd attempted to leave early, all the boys had ended up back home before me. Standing outside the club it had gotten pretty chilly, so Marcus gave me his sweatshirt (which I have to admit was pretty stylish).

"Do not lose this sweatshirt!" he said very seriously. "I've lost it like ten times, and it's always come back to me."

The billionaire yelled something between English and Italian, and everyone hopped into a few taxis to head to his hotel. We drove right by the hotel I was staying at, and I looked out the window longingly as the hope of sleep became distant in the rearview mirror. Again, this inability to just say no. I was exhausted beyond belief, why on earth did I not just go home? It's like I subconsciously need to please people before taking care of myself.

When the billionaire, Marcus, a few of his New York friends, two random girls who were also staying at the hotel, and I arrived, it was 6:30 a.m. and still dark out. Even though the pool and everything was closed, the staff immediately suggested we sit in one of the cabana daybeds, and they brought out wine and beer.

"We need some uh...food too," the billionaire said in his broken English with a thick Italian accent.

"The kitchen is closed, sir, but I can try and prepare some sandwiches for you," the waiter offered.

As we sat eating and drinking at this insanely beautiful hotel next to a turquoise infinity pool that looked out to the ocean, the sun started to come up. How on earth did I go from needing to sleep hours earlier to watching the sun come up for the second straight morning?

Marcus offered to call me a cab and when it finally arrived, it was 7:15 a.m. People had begun to come out to the pool for breakfast already and the sun was now shining beautifully over Mykonos. He walked me out to the front of the hotel, gave me a hug and a kiss, and handed me twenty euros for the taxi.

"I want to see you tomorrow," he said, "and then boat on Sunday." Being it was Saturday morning by this time, I knew that "tomorrow" meant later today. I laughed.

"Okay," I said.

"And take care of my sweatshirt!" he said as I hopped into the cab. As I headed back to my hotel twenty minutes away, I caught myself nodding off more than once. Finally, I arrived back at the hotel room at 7:45 a.m. I opened the door to see Jason cocooned under the blankets in the freezing cold room. I shut the blinds, fell into bed, Marcus's sweatshirt and all, and finally passed, the fuck, out.

Fuck
Judging Yourself

(Everyone else does that enough for you.)

DAY TWENTY

I opened my eyes in a single bed that was a foot away from the one Jason was in. Ugh. Should I pick up my phone or attempt to go back to sleep? After a moment of contemplation, I picked up my phone. 12:53 p.m. Oh, thank God, I had actually gotten about five hours. I *so* needed that.

Jason groaned awake as I sat up. There was already music blaring at the hotel club down the way. It wasn't even the high season on the island but, goddamn, this town just *didn't stop.* I got up to look at the view that I had yet to see in the daylight and laughed as I realized I had slept in Marcus's sweatshirt. Jason joined me on the balcony as we caught up on each other's wild nights and admired the breathtaking view.

We decided to head down to the beach club...bar...whatever it was, to get some breakfast (or lunch by this time) and soak up some sun on the beach. Jason and I sat at a table eating and people watching. What a group of freaking characters, young people from all over the globe, already drinking and dancing. There were go-go dancers in bathing suits and an older, very tan dude walking around in a legit penis sock thong. And all at two in the afternoon. This was definitely a party town.

Before heading to the beach, Jason and I stopped in a store selling particularly trashy items to get obnoxious neon shirts that read "Mykonos Fucks Ibiza." It was so perfectly Eurotrash and especially fitting because the three Toronto boys from my Barcelona family were currently in Ibiza and had been sending me pictures of their adventures. I posted a picture of Jason and I in our new shirts with the caption, "To my Toronto boys who are in Ibiza right now." The whole Barcelona crew had kept in touch since we left. I had spoken to Mallory, all the Torontos, Jacob, and yes, even Chris.

The beach was amazing and, since I had only laid out one day in Barcelona, I really needed some color. The water was absolutely gorgeous. Jason and I were both still getting used to seeing random boobs on the beach. I know it's a cultural thing, and call me sheltered, but it never gets normal to see a pair of random tits sitting casually on the lounge chair next to you. A message from Marcus came in saying how dead he and all the New Yorkers were. After telling me to not lose his sweatshirt (again), he invited us to the villa. Every time he said villa, it sounded so...bougie. I explained that I was hanging with Jason, who I was staying with, and Marcus was quick to assure me he was welcome to join. *This* is what I loved about travel life. Back in LA, or in most of the US for that matter, most groups of dudes would only be interested in having females join them. I had noticed, in every place I had been so far, that most of these well-known stereotypes were not supported while traveling. I loved it.

After chatting with Marcus for a bit while Jason and I enjoyed doing nothing on the beach, we decided we would meet up with Marcus and his friends in town later for a night out.

After some good hours on the beach, Jason and I headed to a nearby restaurant for a low-key dinner. We were greeted by a stern Greek man and five stray cats that had made the restaurant their nightly dinner spot, and we sat and ordered.

He asked me more details about the never-ending Javier saga. I explained what the current status was and how, after Barcelona, my feelings had started to shift, and I was unsure about the meet-up.

"Damn, what a story," he said. He went on to tell me about his ex-girlfriend and the complications of that situation. Up until this conversation, Jason and I had only really spoken on a surface level about the prior party or future travel destinations. He came off as a young frat boy, but some of that started to peel away during this dinner. He was a good kid.

After dinner, we headed to the room to get ready. Since I didn't have pre-bought data (my one major fuck up on this travel journey) I could only talk with people when I was connected to Wi-Fi. When we were ready to leave, I had Marcus connect with Jason on Instagram so we could find them when we got to town. And, of course, I brought his damn sweatshirt.

It was our first time in town and it was everything you would picture in your head when you think of a Greek island town. There were uneven cobblestone streets, white adobe structures with rich blue accents, trees popping out of random places, and gorgeous bougainvillea plants hanging off branches. It was beautiful. Jason and I walked around the town, and it was bustling with energy. There were shops, restaurants, and tons of people. I noticed Jason staring down at his phone.

"What are you doing?" I asked.

"Finding them...they sent me their location on Find My Friends," he answered.

"On what?" I had never heard of this before. He laughed.

"You, like, send your location and then your phone maps you to wherever your friends are," he explained.

"There is no way that's gonna work here...right?" I mean, there weren't even proper streets here, much less names of the streets. There were just random turn-offs and little pathways. What could it possibly be saying? "Turn left down this random narrow alleyway, past the stray cat, and hang a right at the big white rock"?

"We'll see!" he said. Well, fucking technology, you guys. I kid you not, we walked for fifteen minutes, taking random side roads and pathways through the little town and all of a sudden:

"Yo!" Marcus yelled, while waving at us.

"No fucking way," I said as Jason and I laughed.

We headed into one of many ridiculously cute restaurants to meet them. There were three other New York guys with Marcus, and one from Germany, whom I had met the night before. After Jason had met everyone, and they bonded over their recent Oktoberfest adventures, one of the guys asked the ever-famous question.

"So, Gabrielle, why are you solo on this trip?" Everyone turned to me to hear my answer.

"It's such a long story, dude." I sighed with a small chuckle.

"And a fucking crazy one," Jason added.

I proceeded to give them the bullet-point version, which I was now a complete expert at. Everyone had the typical reaction—mouth hung open, eyes wide. Marcus was clearly taken aback by it but tried not to let it show in his reaction.

We all talked, laughed, and recounted the ridiculous night before. Then came the Instagram swap and the "what do you do?" with a much more "we're cool and from New York, so we won't act too excited" vibe. Then one of the guys pulled up an Instagram account called *Vodka Soda Boys*. They had made it one night as a joke but it had become a bunch of photos of different vodka soda drinks in different places. It was pretty freaking funny, to be honest, and it quickly became one of the jokes of the night.

After paying the bill, we headed out to walk around the town and decide where we wanted to go. We popped in and out of a few places before settling on a little outdoor bar/club right on the water. The boys all ordered vodka sodas. Something about the vodka sodas in Europe were fucking disgusting. I donated mine to the group and ordered a very fruity, very delicious blended mai tai that came with a small fruit salad on it.

The New York guys and Jason were all bonding over vodka sodas and smoking cigarettes. I swear, the number of people who smoke in Europe is unreal. Marcus would randomly come over to me and smile.

"Can I have a kiss?" he'd say. The whole charade of it was quite cute. There was definitely something about him that was undoubtedly adorable and intriguing.

"Wanna go see the water?" Marcus asked.

"Sure," I replied. We walked down the steps to a little sitting area right on the water. It was a lot quieter away from the music, and the apartments and shops lining the water were beautiful. We didn't talk about anything too deep. Mostly the basics. He was in commercial real-estate finance, originally from Boston, and had graduated from Northeastern University.

"I don't smoke back home," he said somewhere in the middle of our conversation.

"Right," I said, not convinced at all after seeing him chain-smoking the past twenty-four hours.

"Seriously." He laughed. "I do not smoke when I'm at home."

There was something that was just flirty and easy about it. After about thirty minutes, we headed back up to where the group was.

"So, tomorrow we have to take the ATVs back around 2 p.m., and then we can all grab lunch somewhere or something," Marcus said.

"We should try that famous brunch place where they get you wasted while you wait!" one of the New Yorkers chimed in. Somehow, everyone's drunk minds decided on a plan that went something like this: wake up at 10 a.m., take the ATVs back, head to the boozy brunch, then go out from there.

"I'll just have to figure out how we'll get back and forth," I said.

"Just stay at the villa. There's plenty of room," Marcus said.

"Jason too?" I asked.

"Yeah, of course," he answered. They had all made Jason part of their group, which made me like them even more.

"Okay," I agreed.

With a plan in place, we left the bar to satisfy our drunk cravings.

"Let's go to Jimmy's," the guys suggested. They all had been in Mykonos six days already, and it was literally like they knew the entire island.

Jimmy's was nothing short of life changing for my taste buds. It was a small shop and the walls were covered with photos of people who had stopped in. They were known for their gyros, and it was one of the best meals I had on my entire trip. And trust me, I had NOT been holding back on the food consumption. I felt like I had a fat suit on over my normal figure. But I mean...when in Europe going through heartbreak...right? Luckily, I had left with my very fit "fuck you" divorce body so I was still semi-okay, at least to the outside world.

We chowed down on these delicious creations. At 4:30 a.m., it was time to head home.

The villa was even impressive at night. Three floors, a huge pool, tons of rooms, all in white. We again went over the plan for the next day, and I was given the responsibility of setting an alarm and getting everyone up at 10 a.m. Welcome to being the one female in the group. By the end of this discussion, Jason was already snoring on the couch. Marcus and I said goodnight and headed down to his room, where he gave me a pair of sweatpants and the infamous sweatshirt yet again. I went to pee and while washing my hands, I looked at myself in the mirror.

Shit, I thought. I had no intention of having sex tonight, but the thought "Maybe he'll just want to cuddle and pass out" made me chuckle out loud in the bathroom. *Still, it's not happening*, I told myself. By now, you all know that last sentence is bullshit but, hey, at least my intentions were right.

I came back into his room and hopped into the very Greek and very uncomfortable yet aesthetically pleasing bed. I laid my head on his chest, and he put his arm around me. Cue the awkward "how is this about to start" moment.

Well, it did start, heated up very quickly, and clothes came off. Fuck. I guess this *is* happening. He tried to...well, you know, and I put my hand on his chest and laughed.

"Ha. You swear..." I said, insinuating the lack-of-a-condom situation he had going on. He smiled at me.

"Sorry, yeah, I have something," he said genuinely as he got up to head to his bag.

As I lay there in this gorgeous villa in Mykonos, butt-ass naked, all I could think about was how gross I felt naked. Remember the actual movie *Eat Pray Love,* where Julia Roberts says some epic bullshit about how it's okay to eat and gain weight on vacation because "Has a man ever looked at you naked and told you to put your clothes back on?" Well, no Julia, but she failed to mention how unsexy it makes *you* feel which, as far as I'm concerned, is way more important than what the dude is thinking. Ugh. Fuck you, Julia Roberts. Fuck you.

Marcus returned with proper...attire, and I yet again found myself staring up at a very sexy, well-built specimen of a man. This seemed to be a recurring theme on this trip. And again, good for you, Gabrielle. Three out of three. Jesus Christ, I'm a whore. Pat on the back, nonetheless.

No complaints. When we finished, he looked at me and said, "God, you're so sexy," which was beyond adorable. Okay, fine, touché Julia Roberts.

I threw his sweatshirt and my underwear on and we went outside to cool off on the ridiculous patio. We lay down on one of the lounge chairs, my head on his chest and his arm around me. It was actually really...*nice*. It was comfortable. We talked about his job and if it was what he wanted to do for the rest of his life. He asked about my work and had questions that showed he was genuinely interested. He told me about his brother and sister and his relationship with his parents. He asked me about my parents, and I told him about my dad and how close I was with my mom, which led to how much she'd helped me through the divorce.

"Yeah, I was blown away when you told us that story earlier," he said honestly.

I have to admit, although it wasn't the deepest of deep conversations, I felt like I saw a side of him that he didn't always let people see. Lying there listening to his voice, I saw a glimpse underneath the typical white frat guy who uses slang like "lit" and "legend," drinks beer, and gets really riled up over the Patriots game while high-fiving his bros. Don't get me wrong, at first glance he most definitely came off as a cocky douche bag. But, from what I was seeing, it was just a thick layer of protection that had been built up because of his environment back home. Underneath it, he was sweet and caring. I don't know if he had intended on me realizing that or not, but I did.

After about an hour of talking, we were both freezing and headed to bed. He put his arm around me and was fast asleep in five minutes flat. I fucking hate people with that talent. What I wouldn't give. I lay there for a good hour, not sleeping, as I tend to do, and felt a sense of relief. Because, like with Chris, I didn't feel any guilt. I didn't feel any negative emotions about what had taken place. And most important,

I wasn't missing Javier. Not at that moment, at least. I realized then that there was no point in judging myself on any of my actions. Don't outside forces already do enough of that? Judging myself only made me take steps backward from learning whatever lessons were being presented to me. Ultimately, if all of my actions were making me think and feel and grow and begin to heal, who the fuck am I to judge that? You all will do that enough for me.

It was 7 a.m. by the time I finally dozed off. It literally felt like I had just shut my eyes when my alarm went off at 10 a.m. I turned it off, rolled over, and looked at Marcus, who was sleepily staring back at me.

"Absolutely not," I said.

"Yeah, fuck that," he replied, and we went back to sleep for another two hours.

Fuck
Patterns And Types

(You have to learn why they exist before you can change them.)

DAY TWENTY-ONE

The island light poured into the room. I got up to see the day-light version of where Marcus and I had lay talking earlier that morning. I stepped outside and was hit with sweeping views of the crystal blue ocean. Past the pool was a cliff, and then the Mediterranean Sea as far as the eye could see. It was quite the location to wake up in.

Obviously, our original game plan for the day had been ruined, which I thought was a good thing. My body needed a damn break. We all hung out on the insanely awesome outdoor space the villa had to offer then hiked up to the third floor of the villa and squished together for a picture. The selfie stick I bought in London had seriously come in handy, as ridiculous as it looked.

After returning the ATVs that afternoon, we all headed into town, where the cruise ships had arrived with loads of people. Everyone was out and about, and it was a seriously beautiful day. We found some awesome spots to take some photos, and I uploaded some videos of our group and beautiful surroundings to my Instagram story. I immediately got texts from Emma and Jess.

Emma: Uhhh, who the hell is that?!

The question referred to Marcus.

Jess: He's fucking hot.

And he was. He was so typical LA frat-boy hot—the complete opposite of Javier. The notion was not lost on me. I had fallen head over heels with Javier to the point I had wondered why my mandatory checklist didn't include Latin, amazing dancer, speaks multiple languages, and at least thirty-five years old. I mean in all physical and sexual areas, Javier was a fucking *man*. He was sexy, gritty, and manly, and it just...*did* something to me. So, now here I was, comparing the two people I had attracted on this journey, who were freakishly similar to one another and the complete opposite of Javier. Let's compare, shall we?

Chris
- Twenty-three (Jesus Christ, Gabrielle)
- Lives in San Francisco (city boy)
- Jokes that he comes off as a douche bag
- Ridiculously good guy underneath
- Tall, white, great body, sandy brown hair
- Great job right out of school
- Looks great naked

Marcus
- Twenty-four (not any better, Gabrielle)
- Lives in New York City (again...city boy)
- Definitely can come off as a douche bag
- Has a sweeter, caring side underneath
- Tall, white, great body, sandy brown hair (uh...sound familiar?)
- Great job right out of school (ok...really?)
- Looks great naked (yes, it's ridiculous that I can say that about both. I'm aware.)

Okay. What the fuck, Gabrielle? I definitely didn't want to continue dating the profile that matched my ex-husband...although he lacked the good guy underneath the douche bag. So, why, after knowing how I felt about Javier, was I back to this...type? Oh, let's Thought Onion this one, shall we? Okay, what's the superficial thought?

- Why the fuck is Javier so damn sexy to me? How is the next guy going to compare to that?

Hey, it's called the superficial thought for a reason. Give me a break. Still, pretty freaking accurate. Now, what are the authentic versions of that thought?

- These qualities ignite a passion in me. How did I not realize how many things were clearly missing in my marriage?
- What is it about him and these qualities that woke something up inside of me?
- I don't ever want to settle for anything fucking less than those feelings.

I mean, it all makes sense. This is not to say I will never date a white guy again or would walk away from a potential soul mate because he can't dance or only speaks one language. It's simply about trying to figure out why I went from being adamant about wanting one thing (or type) and attracting two freakishly similar opposites. Okay...most importantly, what are the subconscious layers of those thoughts?

- Was I scared of having exactly what I wanted? Did I ever even really know what I wanted?
- What parts of myself was I guarding? Was my type before just *safe*?
- What if I'm alone for a long time because no one measures up?

Ah. There it is. The good old "Gabrielle doesn't want to be alone" theme. Hello abandonment issue, so *not* nice to see you again. Once this realization came, I felt a layer of emotions. Obviously, I had recognized that I don't like to be alone. But seeing how I had fallen back into old patterns with Chris and Marcus, I had a huge realization: Yes, it may be scary to be alone. But I am willing to do it if it means waiting for someone that's right for me. Maybe meeting Javier and having all these profound discoveries was really a huge blessing. *What if I'm alone for a long time because no one measures up?* Yes...a long time to learn what it is I really want, to learn how to *be* by myself, to learn how to love *myself*. Maybe that isn't all that bad.

The other realization I had while walking around town? With both Chris and Marcus, I had told myself I wasn't going to have sex... and then did just that. Again, this theme of not just saying no comes up. Ugh, I put it off in Amsterdam, if I'm going to tear up, I might as well cut into one more Thought Onion. Superficial?

- I've chosen *not* to say no to sex three times, even though I knew it wasn't what I needed or wanted.

Half of me wants to scream, "I'm an empowered female, and I can sleep with anyone I want to! Men do it all the time!" but I know that's a load of shit. Alas, what's the authentic thought?

- Ever since my dad died, I've been trying to patch the hole in my heart through my relationships with men.

Yes. I had used all the men in my life to try to mend the brokenness that was left in my heart when I lost my father. That's why I don't want to be alone. But why did I always look for that connection through sex? What's under it all? What's the subconscious thought?

- I know that this will keep them, and therefore I won't be abandoned.

Woah. That's heavy. All my life I have been using this *thing*, this power that I have, to keep myself safe from abandonment. It was a tool that I used to get and keep people close to me. Little did I realize that I was giving up a sacred part of myself in order to...*protect myself.* And just like that, I had uncovered a belief that had been running my life since I was a little girl. No wonder I felt like I had been running forever and getting nowhere. That was going to take some time to process, more time than I had on this trip. But even if I didn't figure it all out right away, I had started, and that's what really mattered. Okay, back to the day...

We found a spot for lunch where we all sat and slowly continued to recover from the night before. Marcus would randomly put his hand on my leg. It was little subtle things like this that would happen throughout the day that were small enough to feel "safe" for a cool guy, but still show sweetness and caring.

After lunch, everyone voted for a relaxing day at the villa with the only thing that could make the already overly American group more American: *football.* Yes, in Mykonos, there were three games being simultaneously streamed on TVs and computers in this gorgeous villa. Honestly, my body welcomed the night off of partying.

Marcus had been telling me how amazing the sunsets were from the villa patio. When it was getting close to setting, he and I headed out, just the two of us. It was absolutely stunning.

"It's being places like this, looking out, that makes you feel so small," I said. There I was again, in front of unimaginable beauty, feeling somewhat insignificant. How do you ever feel big enough in a world like this?

"Yeah, it does," he agreed. We took a picture together with the sunset behind us. It was a pretty perfect photo.

As the boys watched the rest of the games, I caught up with Jess on the phone. She needed to know all the details about this hot guy who was making appearances on my Instagram. I sent her the picture of us with the sunset.

"Oh my God, Gabs," she reacted. It was, for some reason, a rather intimate looking photo. Blame it on the romantic island.

After giving Jess details until she was satisfied, we were catching up on her life when a text came in. It was Javier. It was literally like he had a bell that went "DING DING! Gabrielle is *finally* not thinking about you! Better change that!" Ugh.

Javier: Hey, Gabs, just wanted to say hi. It looks like it's nonstop fun for you with your crew! And definitely not dieting like this poor bastard haha. But that's the way it should be. Take care and keep living it up!

My eyes involuntarily did a major eye roll. Something about it just seemed so...*fake*. Take care? It's almost like he was trying too hard to come off as friendly, whether it was meant like that or not.

Me: Hiiii. Ya, I've fallen in with really great people everywhere I've gone. You guys seem like you're having a great time. Glad you're going out with the guys.

It was not going to be lost that, from his friend's Instagram stories, I knew they had been out and having fun as well.

Javier: Overall how are you feeling?

Really, dude?

Me: That's a loaded question over text.

Javier: True. It was a general question, I guess. Wanna try to video chat? I can't promise great reception.

Me: The Wi-Fi here is awful. I can do a voice call.

Please note I am literally sitting in the living room villa with all the guys watching football. He calls. We caught up on typical bullshit, his diet and workout progress, and my lack of a voice (yes, still). Then he asked...

"So, how are you feeling?"

"Um...I don't know. A lot of stuff has happened, and I haven't really stopped to take time to process it all yet, I guess," I said as honestly as I could.

"Yeah, I get that," he said.

"A lot changed for me in Barcelona." There was a pause.

"Oh." He sounded surprised.

"Yeah," I said after another pause. He asked where I was heading next, and I told him I would be flying to Rome on Tuesday.

"Okay, let's touch base and chat when you get to Rome then," he said.

"Okay, sounds good," I agreed. For whatever reason, the conversation just felt so...*surface.*

I hung up just as the games were ending. We all decided we needed food, so of course we headed to Jimmy's in town. The New York gang was leaving in the morning, so it only felt right to have the epic gyro as their last meal.

"So, you gonna come visit New York?" Marcus asked, smiling.

"Maybe." I smiled back. We talked about where in New York he lived, who he lived with, and the fact that I had only ever been there for work. I had to admit: a proper New York trip had been on my list for a long time and the thought of being taken out in the city by Marcus was definitely enticing.

When we had finished dinner, I told him Jason and I were going to head back to our hotel since they were leaving for the airport early in the morning. I gave all the guys a hug goodbye and took off Marcus's sweatshirt, which I had been in most of the day. I handed it back to him, and he smiled and hugged me.

"So, I'll see you in New York?" he said.

"Possibly." I smiled. We kissed, and Jason and I watched them all head to a cab.

Once we got back to our hotel, Jason sat on his bed and asked, "Will you read me a chapter of the book?" Hmm. I had only read Jess and Emma little sections of it, and I didn't know how I felt about sharing what was only a vomit draft with my new friend. After thinking about it, I figured why not?

With the insanely loud music from the beach club blaring, we sat while I read him one of the Amsterdam chapters. In the middle of it, I stopped.

"What?" Jason asked. I laughed.

"This is my fucking wedding song," I said, referring to the loud music coming from the club. We both busted out laughing.

"You have to put that in the book," he said. And here it is.

Halfway through the *What Was His Name Again* chapter, Jason stopped me.

"Oh my God, you did the party pub crawl?" he asked.

"Yes..." I said warily.

"So, are you talking about the Irish guy who was one of the guides?!" he asked. We both started cracking up.

"Oh, God, yes!" I said.

"I totally hung out with him the whole time on our pub crawl," he laughed. Of course, I would choose the one chapter where he knew my one-night stand. Hilarious.

Before bed, I spoke to Marcus. He said what a great time he had with me and that he was glad we met. I was glad too. And so I said goodbye to the second person who had left an imprint on me—who had brought up things in me that allowed me to add more pieces to my healing puzzle. Later, Mr. Mykonos.

Fuck
Materialism

(All of it means nothing without love.)

DAY TWENTY-TWO

Our last day on the beautiful island, Jason and I rented an ATV and headed into town for a relaxing day of shopping, exploring, and of course, eating. And what better place to start our calorie consumption than Jimmy's.

We walked into the famous restaurant stand and ordered. Jimmy himself was standing at the cash register. He was an older Greek man with a lot of years and character in his face. He had a tough exterior with kind eyes and looked pretty damn good for seventy-five.

Jason and I took our gyro gold into the seating area across the path where, just like in the restaurant, the walls were covered with thousands of pictures of people with Jimmy. Halfway through stuffing our faces, Jimmy came in and took a seat with us.

He asked where we were from and if we were enjoying the island of Mykonos. We chatted about typical stuff for a bit until he began to tell us about his family. He told us about his grandchildren and two sons, both of whom are successful and happy. He told us how well known he is on the island because of the huge success of his business, and that he had more than enough money. But ten years ago, he had lost his beloved wife, Selena, to heart failure. They had been together for fifty years, since Jimmy was only sixteen and she was fourteen. He began to tear up as he spoke about her.

"I have everything. Great business, money, good sons, a good life. But I don't have her. I would give up everything to have her. Without love, none of it matters." As he spoke, you could see his still very broken heart. It was inspiring and scary all at once. This intense love, this thing we all chase and long for can be so wonderful yet so devastating all at the same time. It was a really profound moment to be sitting with this man hearing his words. I was so moved. Then I realized that I was listening to one of my greatest fears. *When I love someone, they die.* On a less literal level, when I truly love someone, they leave. Javier was a perfect example of that. Without knowing it, he had ripped my abandonment wound wide open. But here, listening to this Greek man speak about his grand love for his beloved Selena, I realized something. *It is all worth it.* Yes. It really is all worth it. I wouldn't give up the intense month and a half with Javier for anything. Yes, it had absolutely crushed me. My heart was most definitely broken. But you know what? I now knew without a doubt what love feels like. What not to settle for. So my advice to you is: love may break your heart—*do it anyway.*

Once the conversation ended, Jimmy and I took a photo together and then he walked us to the other side of the restaurant and showed us a huge photo of his beloved Selena. It was a black-and-white picture of a strong and beautiful woman in a long-sleeve knee-length dress, stockings, and flats, her dark hair done perfectly in an old Hollywood-glam style. He smiled up at the picture, thanked us for the conversation, and waved as we headed on our way.

Jason and I walked around the beautiful town, popping in and out of shops, buying things here and there. We stumbled upon a jewelry shop that had absolutely beautiful pieces, and I knew this was where I wanted to get my Mykonos bracelet. The hard part was deciding which one. Each of them was on a card that had the meaning of the bracelet written down. After reading the meanings behind each one, I settled on one called "Explore." It was a small circle with the cut-out markings of a compass. The card read, "Wear this bracelet as a reminder to sail away and dream vividly...Catch the friendly winds in your sails and discover new lands!"

It was perfect, and now added to my collection. Next, we headed to a place that did henna tattoos. While Jason took a power nap on the couch, I had a two-week reminder painted on my forearm: the infinity symbol with "trust" written in it, the om symbol that represented the oneness of all creation, and the words "Que Sera Sera," meaning "What will be will be." It was a good reminder for what the rest of my trip would soon bring.

We took the ATV up to the high points on the island and looked out over incredible views. The endless blue sea and the hundreds of white structures were so beautiful and peaceful. After taking in the gorgeous scenery, we grabbed two beers and parked ourselves on a little bench right on the water.

"So," Jason said, "what do you think you're gonna do about seeing Javier?"

"Right now, I truly don't know," I responded. And honestly, that was the truth. After all that had happened, I just didn't know how I felt anymore. What I did know was that when I got to Rome, I would need to begin to really process everything that had happened and sit with myself after all the nonstop craziness of the last two weeks. That was *scary*.

I tried to Thought Onion it. What was the superficial thought?

• If I see him, I don't know how I will feel.

Well, obviously. That's been the gamble of this entire situation. Every choice I had made on this trip had been taking a chance and not knowing how I would feel on the other end of it. There were some choices (like Ireland back in Amsterdam) that made me feel absolutely awful. Some (like opening up with Chris in Barcelona) that made me feel like I was beginning to heal. But isn't that what life is really made up of? Tons of different choices that direct you in different ways and onto different paths that end up shaping your life. And yet, we have regrets and beat ourselves up if we feel we made a wrong choice, even if that choice helped us learn and grow into who we've become. Okay, what's the authentic thought?

- What if seeing him rips away the little bit of healing I have done, and I'm right back where I started? Heartbroken.

Well to be fair, I still felt heartbroken. So if anything, this fear was that I would be even more heartbroken, if that was possible. But what really ended up being the golden nugget of this onion was the subconscious thought. Isn't it always?

- What if I don't go and I never know.

Whoa. There it is. What if I don't go, and I never find out if anything could have been different? What if I give into what everyone is saying and hate him for what he did to me and never fight to find out if the story is supposed to end a different way? Well...that's just not who I am. But the fear of the superficial and authentic thoughts was intense enough to begin to make me change that.

We sat and watched the sunset which was, again, breathtaking. As I looked out over the infinite sea, I wondered if anyone I was thinking about at that moment was thinking about me, too. Farewell, Mykonos. You were everything I *wasn't* expecting, and more.

Fuck
Processing

(When it's time to...it'll smack you in the face.)

DAY TWENTY-THREE

After a couple of quick flights, I was where it was all *supposed* to have started in the first place: Rome. It was a short five-minute walk to the hostel I was staying at. I had gone back and forth between two different hostels, one which was reviewed as being much more mellow and relaxed and the other which was more of a party hostel. I figured since I hadn't really stopped since Barcelona, it was time to go with the more mellow option and get back to my writing. Besides, so much had gone down in the past two weeks, none of which I had begun to really process at all.

It always was a mix of nervousness, excitement, and loneliness when arriving at a new hostel, especially a more mellow hostel like this one. I noticed that I felt a certain somber weight on my chest, but I wasn't sure what it was. Possibly because I knew I had only booked three nights at this hostel and then it was supposed to be the time Javier and I would be meeting, although none of those details had been discussed since he had told me in Amsterdam that he wanted to meet. At this point, I didn't really believe anything he had decided, nor was I sure of what I even wanted to do anymore. Maybe it was just because Rome was subconsciously tainted for me because I had spent a month daydreaming that this was where our grand romantic adventure would be starting. Or maybe it was all of the above.

It was already around 7 p.m. so I decided on my first night in Rome I was going to take myself to dinner. I had *never* been one to venture to a restaurant alone at home and always felt weird even thinking about it. But by this time, I had gotten a little more comfortable with the whole alone thing and, besides, who the hell else was going to take me?

I walked a short five minutes until I ran into a street of restaurants. I settled on a spot called Mamma Angela Trattoria and was seated at a cute sidewalk patio table for one. Italian food has always been one of my favorites, and I had been saving my pasta and gelato calories for Rome, so I was ready for what everyone raves about. I ordered a bottle of white wine (yes, a bottle...don't judge) and a caprese salad to start. I snapped an Instagram story of my yummy set-up that read "Currently on a dinner date with myself." I quickly got a reply from one of the Torontos.

Toronto: Gabrielle! Where are you going next?! Come meet us in Portugal!

Portugal? Hmm...two glasses of wine in and that didn't sound like a bad idea at all. There was definitely a big part of me that wanted to tell Javier I would see him on our flight home and just go continue on this epic adventure by myself. I just wasn't sure what the other part wanted quite yet. All three of the Torontos started sending me voice messages on WhatsApp.

Toronto: You have to come! We have an Airbnb. It'll be sick! Come meet us!

It was so cool that I had met friends who truly wanted me to come meet them. I had never considered venturing to Portugal on this trip but...why not? I told them it would all depend on the cost because, at this point on my trip, I needed to watch my money. Traveling to Mykonos had definitely not been cheap. I ordered the cacio e pepe pasta for dinner. It was freaking delicious. Jason had also texted me, asking how Rome was, and Emma was asking for updates, too. Even though I was at dinner alone, I didn't really feel alone. I felt like I had met an entire army of people along the way who were all rooting for me now.

I decided to take the last glass and a half of wine back to the hostel with me. I hadn't really had much wine on this trip, and three glasses was more than enough to have me feeling like I could take on the world. After paying, I looked over to see a bunch of people heading out from a much more energetic hostel. I looked up at the door and realized it was the other hostel I had been considering. Part of me wondered if I had made the right decision or if it was good that I was having "me" time. The problem with "me" time? Sometimes you get *way* too in your head.

I went back to my hostel to get some rest for the night because I had a big day of typical tourist shit planned for the next day. By the time I was lying in my bunk, I was pretty sure about my decision. Why go meet Javier? What was it going to do, rip my heart open all over again? *You have friends begging you to go on an epic adventure in Portugal, Gabrielle. Fuck him, GO,* I thought. Honestly, 95 percent of me was on board. But damn, that stubborn little 5 percent would not go away. After thirty minutes of drunken research and going back and forth with the Torontos, I found it was way too expensive and would take way too much travel time. We promised we would all catch up either in LA or Toronto and stay in touch. But still, that 95 percent was really adamant that I listen to this feeling of not going to see him. So, I started looking up different hostel options in Cinque Terre and towns along the Amalfi Coast, such as Positano, all of which I had always dreamed of visiting. I bookmarked a few that looked promising and slowly began to switch my brain to the fact that I would end my trip alone. Then? Time for a drunk Thought Onion. Superficial thought...

- Do not let him dictate your trip. Go be a badass.

I mean, seriously, though. Javier had convinced me to go on this trip in the first place, bailed on me forty-eight hours before getting on a plane, told me we *would* be meeting at the end, decided it wasn't the best idea and that we *shouldn't* meet, and then decided twenty minutes later that we *would* in fact be meeting. Yet, since that last decision, he hadn't brought it up, nor made any plans, or shown any type of follow-through on that decision. So, why the hell am I even waiting for this to happen? Well, what's the authentic thought?

- I can't let go of the possibility of seeing him.

WHY Gabrielle, WHY? What is it about this man that has you under such a stupid fucking spell? I had been in a dozen relationships before, ones *much* longer than this, and I had never had such an issue letting go of someone. So then, what the hell is the subconscious thought?

- If we see each other, maybe his feelings will change.

Fuck. Really? I thought I had decided that could not even exist in my mind when I was back in London, for Christ's sake. How am I letting that still be a thought, much less an option? It can't be, and it is the reason that my heart isn't healing. I need to somehow figure out a way to move on. If only I had a switch, like it seemed he had, that was easy to flip. If I had a choice, I would flip that shit from "head over heels" to "nothing but a friend" *so* goddamned fast. Sigh. I'm human and don't have a fucking off switch. Goodnight.

Fuck Speaking Your Mind

(You're always allowed to...but there's always a consequence.)

DAY TWENTY-FOUR

didn't sleep well at all. I would wake up and not be able to go back to sleep, answer messages on my phone from people in different time zones, browse social media, and fail at trying to go back to sleep. By 6 a.m., I gave up. I got up and got ready for the day and figured I might as well see the sun come up my first day in Rome.

I headed out for the two mile walk down to the Colosseum. I stopped into a café to get a cappuccino and two pastries. I sat and wrote a little bit more of my final Barcelona chapter. I had been putting a lot of the book progress on my Instagram story, and all my new friends that were now following me would message me about how excited they were about it. It was a pretty cool feeling that everyone I met would be in this book, and they were all stoked for it. I snapped a picture of the chapter I was writing: "FUCK Your Plans – Because someone will cross your path and change them." I tagged Mallory, Jacob, and Chris. A few moments later, Chris replied in a message.

Chris: What a title. That made me smile.

Me: What can I say. You did.

I smiled as I enjoyed my breakfast before heading over to my first stop. Yes, the Colosseum really is as unbelievable in person as people say. It was another structure I stood next to that made me realize how small I am. There were so many different archways and steps, with light coming in through various openings all around. Even the texture of the stone was filled with history. It was really something, standing in the middle of it all. When I had finished exploring the Colosseum to my heart's content, I walked back to the higher point where I had first started.

There were two younger guys there shooting some type of video blog who looked like they knew what they were doing, so I asked them to snap a photo of me.

I hopped up on the ledge, with the giant Colosseum towering behind me. I opened my journal to the first page where I had written the title, *"Eat, Pray, Fuck My Life."* I smiled, stuck my middle finger up, and got one of the most epic pictures on my trip. I posted it with the caption: "Questo é solo l'inizio #EatPrayFML" which is Italian for "This is only the beginning."

Next, I walked for what seemed like forever through the streets of the city. I grabbed my first gelato in Rome. It's seriously no joke, what they say. However they make it differently there, it really does make an insane difference. It was delicious. As I devoured my midday dessert, I walked through the Imperial Forum with tons of beautiful ruins that looked like they had been pulled out of a movie. There were musicians playing live music on the sidewalk, and as I walked by, I recognized the song I was hearing. "Despacito." Of course it was. That song had been following me all over Europe. I walked past the giant Altar of the Fatherland and stood on the steps looking up at another grand structure. It was so beautiful, and all of Rome was unlike anywhere else I had ever visited. There were huge statues of lions with wings, gigantic horses, and more solid stone than I had ever laid eyes on.

I walked for another few hours all around the city, across a bridge and along the water, until I stumbled into a cute little restaurant. I had walked off a lot of my food and hadn't really had a substantial meal yet. I sat down on the open-air patio to write for a while. It was good to finally get back to my writing. For whatever reason, Rome was making me feel emotional, and when I was emotional, I didn't necessarily want to see all the tourist sites. I just wanted to write.

A very, *very* good-looking Italian waiter came over to my table to ask what he could get me. Seriously, I definitely have a weakness for men with accents. Then again, don't we all? I ordered a glass of white wine, and he brought me a complimentary bruschetta piece. After I had sipped and written for a while, he came back to tell me about his favorite pasta. Whatever it was, that's what I got. Good Lord, Rome really does do pasta the right way.

I spent two hours there enjoying my wine and super unhealthy pasta while writing about Barcelona. Reminiscing on the time I had spent with the people there made my heart happy. After I paid my bill, I headed toward the exit.

"How long are you in Rome for?" my waiter asked in his adorable accent.

"Two more days." I smiled.

"How are you enjoying it so far?"

"It's beautiful," I replied.

"What is your name?" he asked.

"Gabrielle."

"You're beautiful. It's nice to meet you." He smiled.

"Thank you." I smiled back as I turned to head out. After Amsterdam, Chris, and Marcus, I didn't want to add a hot Italian in Rome. Well...I didn't *need* to.

That night I headed off to Trastevere. I started off solo at a bar a block away from the restaurant. I sat down, ordered a glass of white wine, and hopped on Wi-Fi. I immediately got a message from Jess asking me to fill her in on what was going on in Rome. I told her I was currently at a bar, drinking, before taking myself to dinner. We chatted for a little bit about the past few days and, by this time, I had ordered my second glass of wine.

Me: Slightly nervous I'm going to get drunk by myself tonight and text Javier, Chris, and Marcus all different inappropriate or offensive things.

Jess: Hahahahahahahahahahaha.

Me: Like "Hey, Javier, I'm so fucking done with this shit. Just thought I'd let you know that THIS IS A JOKE."

Jess: I wish I was there eating and drinking with you!

Me: Hi, Chris, when are you coming to LA? I'm currently writing about our Barcelona romance. Come fly back.

Jess: Hahahahahaha. Oh, my gosh, I'm dying!

Me: Hey, Marcus, why are you so fucking hot? Lol.

I laughed at the exchange my girlfriend and I were having. I seriously missed my close girlfriends so much. The bartender chuckled as he witnessed me laughing at my text conversation. Although I was kidding at the time, all I needed to add to that hypothetical scenario was a little more wine for it to end up coming to fruition.

After two glasses of delicious sauvignon blanc, I headed over to Taverna Trilussa for dinner. I was seated by yet another good-looking Italian waiter (I guess this is a theme in Rome) and ordered a glass of red.

I started with whatever appetizer my waiter recommended and enjoyed my wine as I sat and people watched. A text from Jason came in.

Jason: You inspired me to write a little bit. Obviously not a book, haha.

Me: Yesssss! Are you in London yet?

Jason: Unfortunately, no. My flight isn't for another four hours. I'm doing like each lesson learned, anecdote behind it, then later I'll come back and write how it applies to the bigger picture.

Me: Dude, yes. That's so good. Writing is the best way to check yourself and get on top of shit.

How cool that I had inspired my new young friend to start writing.

Jason: So how's everything going in Rome?

Me: Well…I'm currently drunk on a dinner date with myself. So there's that.

Jason: Haha good! As you should be. Any word from Javier?

Me: Nope. Not a damn thing.

Jason: Damn. Aren't you supposed to be leaving in like a day?

Me: Yep. Surprise, surprise.

Good, it wasn't just me thinking it was ridiculous.

I continued to chat with Jason and had ordered my fourth glass of wine when I decided to text Marcus.

Me: About to start the Mykonos chapter. What would you like your name to be? Also, I am absolutely tipsy at a really fancy dinner by myself.

Marcus laughed and said he was jealous of my location and alcohol intake. I sent him a picture of my gigantic pasta dish that had just arrived. It was cooked and served in a tin pan and was one of the best pastas I have ever had, though the wine may have influenced that opinion. He asked why I wasn't with any travel friends at my dinner. I explained I needed some time to process everything and continue writing.

I was now in two conversations while also in heaven with this giant pan of pasta and my giant fourth glass of wine. To be honest, I was drunk. Of course, then a message came in from Chris.

Chris: How's Rome?!

Me: Amazing. Insane food, lots of wine.

Chris: Fuck, I'm so jealous.

Me: You could always hop on a plane.

Chris: You have no idea how quick I would if I could.

I was now in *three* conversations trying to not drunkenly text the wrong thing to the wrong person. Of course, I told Jason all of this, and he was dying of laughter on the other end. Then...the wine decided to take control of my better judgment. I'm sure you all know what's coming. I texted Javier.

Me: Javier.

Javier: Hey, Gabs.

Me: Ugh. Fuck.

Javier: What? You okay?

Me: Yeah. Aren't I always?

He FaceTimed me. I declined it.

Me: I'm at dinner.

Javier: Me too. You sure you're alright?

Me: Yeah.

Javier: So why fuck?

Me: Never mind. I shouldn't have even said anything. I've had too much wine.

Then a voice message came in. I put my headphones in and listened to it:

"Please be careful, Gabs, okay? I know it's a safe place and you're not dumb, just be careful. Don't walk back too drunk and keep an eye out, okay? Please. Anything happens...no not if anything happens nothing is gonna happen but call me or text me for anything, okay."

I don't know if it was the wine or just the straw that broke the camel's back but whatever it was...happened right then. I got pissed, the fuck, off. Like...*now* you decide to care about my well-being? *Now* you decide to act how you should have been acting this entire fucking trip? No. You are not allowed to suddenly decide to be my knight in shining armor, dude.

Me: Veto, Jesus, I'm fine. I have been by myself this entire time without you. I'm fine.

And then? In true Javier fashion...silence. No response. Of course, my drunk brain then goes, *Oh shit, that was mean.*

Me: Sorry, that was mean.

But was it really? After all the things I had been put through emotionally, did I really not have the right to react that way? No, I most certainly did. Drunk or not, that was a valid thing to say, and probably long overdue.

Me: You know, it may have been a little mean, but it's true. I don't know how you're gonna be mad at me for saying that.

Cool. I'm now in a conversation with myself. And just like that, my epic drunken dinner was ruined by someone who wasn't even there...and hadn't been for a while.

By the time I was back at my hostel (yes, safe and sound, all by my big-girl self), it was almost midnight. I realized that being in all the different conversations at dinner meant I really wasn't being with *myself*. I was definitely afraid to start processing all the emotions... especially alone. I went downstairs to the little common area to hop on Wi-Fi and attempt to get slightly less drunk before bed. I messaged Jacob on Facebook.

Me: I'm drunk at my hostel right now. I finished the last Barcelona chapter today. So epic.

Jacob: Haha, yesss. I can't wait. Also, I know you're deciding how to spend the last part of your trip. In my opinion, don't go see Javier. You deserve better, and he hasn't treated you properly.

Dude. Join the club. Everyone has that opinion.

Me: Fml. I know. Ugh.

Jacob: Seems like he's doing everything he wants and on his terms without considering what you want or need.

Yep. Pretty accurate fucking statement.

Me: I'm drunk. So keep that in mind when I start saying this. Why the fuck can I not stop thinking about Chris? It's cause I'm writing about it all, right? Fml.

Jacob: Seems like you two really had a connection.

Me: Yeah, but I'm sure a lot of that, for him, was the travel and whatnot.

Jacob: Why do you think that? I think he genuinely cares about you. Chris is a real quality guy.

Me: Yeah, I know, which is why I'm saying fml. He's twenty-three. I'm not. And I'm not even legally divorced. LOL.

Jacob: LOL, I forgot about the divorce not being finalized yet.

Me: Our conversation on the beach that last night was like...I don't even know.

Jacob: Why does him being twenty-three matter that much? I feel like once you cross into your twenties age doesn't really matter. I'm assuming the conversation was really good?

That is a hugely incorrect statement. Twenties are when people change...a lot.

Me: Because my ex-husband proposed to me at twenty-three and was younger than me. Look how that turned out. The conversation was just really...deep. Like out of my whole trip, Barcelona and the group we had really was the first place I felt I healed, and a lot of it was because of him.

Jacob: Just because Chris is almost twenty-four doesn't mean he will be like your husband or Javier. I've known him for five years and every year he continues to become a better person. It says something that you two were able to connect on that deep of a level having not known each other for a long time. I'm glad you feel like he helped you heal. I think you were good for him too.

Me: In what way?

Jacob: I've known him for so long, and I haven't seen him that happy in a long time. Have you followed up with him? Because, just like you're hesitating, I'm sure he's in the same boat.

Me: I mean, we've talked briefly. I feel like he doesn't wanna intrude on my travels. But, then again, that's me, assuming.

Jacob: I think your assumptions are pretty accurate. I think he's trying to be considerate, because he knows how therapeutic this trip is for you. He only talks about how much he enjoyed talking and spending time with you.

Me: I told him on the beach, I may seem okay, but I know how messed up the past three months have made me, and I honestly don't understand what I feel, or want, from him, and I was super honest about that.

Jacob: Well, I'm sure he appreciated you being open with him. From watching you two, I think there was definitely something between you guys. But, that's just my opinion.

Me: Yeah, I know. I'm just trying to fight that because it all seems ridiculous. Also, I just went off on Javier.

Jacob: What happened?

I explained the short exchange that ended with silence.

Jacob: Oh my. That voice message must have been intense. Stop talking to him. You can rant on him when you're sober.

Me: I know lol. It was more or less like 'be safe, don't walk alone,' like I'm a fucking child. Because if anything happened to me, he would feel responsible.

God forbid he ever be responsible for anything. That isn't part of *The Four Agreements*, after all.

Jacob: Kind of true, to be honest. I feel like he's being a son of a bitch. In the end, it's his loss. You deserve better.

Isn't that every woman's issue? We fall for the men who don't treat us how we should be treated instead of the ones who want to put us on a pedestal and give us the world. Why does it always work out that way?

Jacob: Hey, but you're traveling and healing! You're focusing on yourself for once and that's amazing.

Me: Yeah. Been trying to. It's been a long time coming.

Jacob: Well, better now than never. Plus, you're getting a number one bestseller book out of this experience lol.

Me: This is true, dude.

As I sat there talking to my new friend from across the world, I started to think. Literally everyone was telling me the same thing. It's a cop-out, he's not treating you right, you deserve so much more. Why was I the only person who was still fighting for him? Still defending him? I looked at my text to him on WhatsApp. He had read it. It wasn't like he suddenly got busy and didn't respond. He was intentionally not responding, and that seriously angered me. I had been on his side from the moment he told me he had to do this trip by himself. I had supported him, loved him, and given him as much of me as I could. Yet he couldn't allow me to be upset for *one* damn second? No. I'm sorry, just...no. Apparently, it's not okay to speak your mind if what is being said doesn't sit well with the other person. Yes, you're always allowed to, but you'll have to deal with the consequences. Well, you know what consequences? Fuck you.

Fuck The Bullshit

(Sometimes you just have to say…"I'm fucking done.")

DAY TWENTY-FIVE

It is only 11 a.m. and I am sitting in a café by the Trevi Fountain in Rome. For the first time in two weeks, I feel anxious. I feel frustrated. I feel like crying. But if I am to practice what I preach, I need to meet myself exactly and authentically where I am so that I can begin to understand and deal with my feelings. I just wish they didn't feel like *this*.

So far, to be honest, Rome hasn't been so incredible. Maybe I stayed at the wrong hostel and would have enjoyed it more having met people. But, then again, isn't being alone, and being okay with that, part of this journey I'm supposed to be on? Maybe the feeling is because this was the place Javier and I were meant to start our romantic adventure together. What I did know was that I felt pressured to love the city and do all the "must sees." Maybe because it was one of my mom's favorites…I don't know. But in this city, I felt most content sitting at a café, eating ridiculously amazing food, and writing, so that is what I was going to do.

I was so fucking frustrated with Javier. That's not even the right word. Irritated. Livid. Even Jason had texted me that morning asking if I was okay. Not a damn word from Javier. I was done playing the bullshit non-communication waiting game. I was over it. So *I* took the initiative (which had become a pattern) and sent him a message.

Me: We need to have a conversation today if you have time.

I wasn't holding my breath for a response. I started to try and talk myself through what all of it was really about. When you strip away the grief—the reasons, the circumstances, and the backstory—and just look at the facts of what happened, it looks something like this:
Woman gets cheated on and lied to for six months
Woman goes through shocking divorce
Woman meets Man
Man and Woman fall madly in love
Man convinces Woman to go on a romantic trip together
Man bails forty-eight hours before trip
Man breaks Woman's heart
Man doesn't handle the aftermath particularly well

Okay the final one is technically an opinion, not a fact, but everyone, including his mother, is in agreement about it, so I figured it was worth including. Now, during *all* of this, still, I have been supportive, loving, and compassionate. All I said last night was yet another fact:

Me: Veto, Jesus, I'm fine. I have been by myself this entire time without you. I'm fine.

He had the audacity to think he could be mad at that? Are you fucking kidding me? Cut me some fucking slack. I have handled this entire situation 99 percent better than any other female I know would have. To be honest, I've been like Mother fucking Teresa toward him this whole time. That was a true statement. You can't even give me the decency of a response? No. Not okay.

Then, of course, all of the emotions and pointless assumptions start.

Emotions:
Fear. What, that he's angry at *me*? After all of this?
Ridiculous.
Anger. For being treated in a way that I do not deserve.
Annoyance. Fucking self-explanatory.

Assumptions:
Maybe it hurt him a lot to hear that. And he feels guilty.
Then why make it worse by not responding?
Maybe it genuinely pissed him off...In which case, we
have *way* bigger problems at hand.
Maybe he was looking for an excuse to not have to see
me, and this was it.

Either which way, it was bullshit. For the first time, it was impossible to defend him. And you know what? I no longer wanted to. Because now, when Emma said, "He pisses me off," I agreed. And when Jess said, "That wasn't even that mean and it was true," I knew she was right. And because when Jacob said, "I feel that he's being a son of a bitch. In the end it's his loss and you deserve better," I agreed. And lastly, when his mom said she didn't feel he'd handled the situation right, I knew she was correct. So, with all that...what was at the core of it? Trusty old Thought Onion time. Superficial thought.

• You're being a fucking jerk.

Well...yeah. That was pretty much it on that level. Authentic thought?

• Why are you suddenly acting concerned when you've shown so little of that this entire time?

It was so upsetting that he couldn't care less to check in on me when I had been in Barcelona or Mykonos. If I heard from him it was either because I contacted him or he was commenting on something insignificant that he had seen on my Instagram. Apart from him asking, "Overall, how are you feeling" in Mykonos, he had never called to *really* see how I was doing or if I was okay. Now suddenly he was telling me to be careful and saying "...if anything ever happened to you..." Why now? So, what's the subconscious thought?

• Maybe you're just not as good of a man as I thought you were.

That is going to hurt him to read. It was a revelation even for me. Here was this man who I so clearly loved, who I had been constantly protecting and defending...and now I wasn't sure he was all I had thought he was. Wow. In the last twenty-four hours, I had really started to question everything, including how we were ever going to work as friends. Now, the ever-tiring waiting game. I was *so* fucking over this.

I finished my pizza (yes, my entire and delicious pizza) and went off to try and find the gelato place all my friends had raved about. It was a six-minute walk away and although I had screenshotted directions from Google Maps, I still managed to get lost. I'm convinced Google Maps is only half-accurate abroad. I turned on my data so I could get updated directions and a message came in. It was Javier.

Javier: Okay. I can in the next hour cause we are going to a wedding afterwards, and I won't have Wi-Fi.

Even the casual manner of that text bothered me.

Me: Yeah, whenever, just let me know. I'll be in Wi-Fi in like five minutes.

Javier: Okay, call you in five.

I stood in the famous gelato shop (that I had successfully found... finally), put my headphones in, and answered the call that would ultimately, one way or another, decide the last location of this trip.

"Hello?" I answered.

"Hey," he said on the other end. Long pause.

"Uh, how are you?" I tried to not sound like I had been fuming for the past twelve hours.

"I'm okay, I'm good," he responded in an unsure tone. We bull-shitted around the subject for a few minutes.

"So, why did what I said last night upset you so much?" I finally asked.

"It didn't upset me. I just knew you were drunk and whatever I had said clearly upset you, and I didn't want to engage," he said calmly.

Welcome to the perfect example of why trying to analyze this human is a complete waste of fucking time. We continued to awkwardly dance around this conversation until I let out a big sigh.

"What, what it is? Talk to me," he said, sounding genuinely concerned.

"I just think our communication has been nonexistent," I answered. He agreed. Then I felt the surge, which was promptly followed by tears coming up. At that moment, in the middle of the gelato shop, I decided that there was no reason to be indirect or subtle any longer. At this point, who the fuck cares? At this stage, we were out of time.

"Quite frankly, the past two weeks have changed so much. I've been going back and forth on if I wanted to see you or not. But there are things that need to be said that I refuse to say on the phone and conversations that need to be had face-to-face. You have made no effort to show me you care or want to see me. I've had to take the first step on *every* front. All I wanted you to do was step up and say, "I want to see you," and you couldn't even do that." Another long pause as I wiped tears away, hoping ice cream shoppers weren't watching me.

"You're right. I was just seeing you with all your new friends in Barcelona and Mykonos, and you looked like you were having such a good time, and it made me really happy. But I get that you've had to be the one to pull things out of me, initiate things, and make me be clear about things, and that must be exhausting. I'm sorry," he said.

"You have no idea," I answered.

"I want to see you, Gabs. What do you want to do? I'll meet you anywhere. Tell me."

"I just don't know," I responded.

"Do you want to come here?"

Here? As in San Vito? Up until now I was planning on going to the Amalfi Coast even if by myself. I'd never even considered going to San Vito where all his friends were.

"Ugh. I don't know," I said.

"Why?"

"Because all your friends are there, and I'm still not sure if it's even the right decision," I responded.

"Why does it matter if they're here? They all work and I'm by myself a lot of the time."

"I don't know. I just feel weird going after I was supposed to go on the trip with you in the first place and then didn't." I mean come on...slightly awkward, no?

"Listen, it's not even like that. I don't talk to everyone about all of this. To me, this is our thing between us. I don't talk to everyone about it like you do," he said.

"Okay, excuse me, I don't talk to everyone about everything," I snapped at him. Which of course I did, but how the hell else was I supposed to navigate this epic roadmap of bullshit he'd sent me on? Besides, he didn't talk to people about it because, when he did, they didn't agree with him.

"Okay, well anyway, they don't even know anything. It would be more than fine and it's amazing here," he said. We continued to discuss the details while I groaned, sighed, and fought tears between every sentence. "So you can fly here tomorrow and we can head to Palermo for our flight on Tuesday." Well...decision time.

"Okay," I said.

"Or tell me what you want to do. Do you want to go somewhere else? I'll come meet you wherever you want to go," he said. Geez, finally, some initiative.

"No, it's fine. I just...that's a lot of days to come for," I said, realizing the amount of time that would put he and I together. It would be six days including the travel day home, and that worried me a little bit.

"I'm sorry that you've had to be the one doing things. You're right, that's not okay. I'm going to start doing more," he said. I scoffed. "What?" he asked.

"Sorry, it's just...I don't mean this in a mean way but even your sister was like, "I don't know how you believe anything he says right now." So it's kind of like, I'll just believe it when I see it at this point." There was an extra-long pause.

"Yeah, okay, I understand," he said, sounding like he'd just gotten punched in the gut.

"Okay."

"Okay, I'll look up flights," he said.

And that was it. It was decided. After three weeks of limbo, of back-and-forth thinking, of flip-flopping decisions, of being on this fucking roller coaster, we were going to see each other. I stood in the gelato shop and felt the overwhelming need to burst into tears. Then, I felt a giant sense of relief, because regardless of whether it was the right or the wrong decision, a decision had been made.

I got an epic gelato that didn't disappoint and enjoyed it while I headed over to the famous Spanish Steps. Although they were beautiful, all the emotion that I was experiencing, mixed with the fact that I had originally imagined kissing my boyfriend on these steps, was just making me feel kind of...*off*. A girl asked me if I would take her picture, and I of course did. She then offered to return the favor and take one of me. I sat on the steps, looked up toward the warm sun, and shut my eyes. I thought about all the people who had messaged me and asked me to share my journey. I had been posting so many happy photos the past two weeks between Barcelona and Mykonos, so I decided to post this one with a very honest quote from C.G. Jung that was exactly where I currently was on this journey: "Until you make the unconscious conscious, it will direct your life and you will call it fate. Even on the down days...choose." What an incredibly informative quote. When you aren't aware of what the subconscious thoughts and beliefs are, they drive your life like someone who has highjacked your power steering without you knowing. We blame it on bad luck or circumstances or fate. But once we realize those subconscious thoughts and beliefs, we can start taking back the steering wheel—taking back our power. I was slowly learning how to get better at this over the course of my trip. Even on the days when you want to burst into tears, you have to choose. Choose to look deeper, to search further, and to be happy. Sometimes, it's the hardest thing you will do that day—but you have to *choose*.

As I was walking back toward my hostel, a text from Javier came in about flights. After deciding on what day I would come:

Me: I might take a day to myself at some point in San Vito.

Javier: Absolutely. This place is amazing and healing.

Good. I fucking hope so.

Javier: Besides, between my lack of emotional comprehension and my diet, you might need two days alone.

Lack of emotional comprehension? Understatement of the century.

Me: That is a very true statement.

Javier: Okay, I'll let you know when we buy it.

Me: Okay, I'll just bring cash with me. Let me know how much.

Javier: This is my treat. Early Christmas present and "sorry" present as well. Let me do it, please. No arguments.

Me: I won't argue but it doesn't even begin to cover a sorry present.

Javier: I'm sure I'll be poor by the time you forgive me.

Me: I don't even know what you're apologizing for anymore. Lol.

Javier: Let's start with ruining the month of September. Check that off the list.

Me: Check.

At least I was finally getting *some* type of ownership and apology. Better late than never, I suppose. Then, suddenly, the sense of relief I had felt in making a decision turned into complete and utter panic because this was actually happening. *Tomorrow.* Okay, Gabrielle, what the hell is this about? Onion. Superficial thought?

• I can't fucking do this. Is this the right decision?

Self-explanatory. Authentic thought...

• I am letting everyone down.

Whoa. Interesting. This is *my* journey, and I need clarity and closure, and no one else's opinions should matter at all. So then why could I only suddenly hear, "He doesn't deserve you," "This is a cop-out," "Don't go see him," "Finish the trip by yourself." Why could I only think of my mom, Jess, Emma, everyone I had met along the way? I felt like this one decision was about to disappoint all of them. I thought about *The Four Agreements*: "What others say and do is a projection of their own reality, their own dream." Interesting. What I was once judging, I was now attempting to put into practice. This should be *my* decision. What others may feel or say about it isn't my responsibility. Maybe Javier's grief, which led him to choose to go alone, wasn't so different. Then the subconscious thought dropped one on me like the house dropped on the witch in the *Wizard of Oz*.

• I am letting *myself* down.

Wait, what? What does that even mean and why am I feeling that way? I sat there with this for a few minutes, trying to understand what my emotions were attempting to communicate. I was afraid that in making this decision, I was giving up, surrendering where I shouldn't. Then it hit me. Maybe it was the travel, or what I had emotionally been through, or the growth that had happened as a result of it all. But I wanted to make sure, without a doubt, that I was 100 percent doing what was best for *me*, and only me. Part of me wanted to be strong and badass and say fuck him and everyone and go finish this insane journey in some epic place by my damn self. But that wasn't what I *needed*. The old me would have gone to meet Javier in the hopes of having some type of fairy-tale ending and living happily ever after. That wasn't what I needed either. What *I* needed was to go see this person who had made me realize what being in love really is—this person who drastically changed me. I needed to see him to ask every unanswered question, tell every unspoken feeling, and get the closure my heart so badly needed. Ultimately, I needed to finish this crazy roller coaster of a journey how it all started. *With him.*

So, with the fear of judgment, the possibility of more heartache, and the hope of some clarity...I decided. *This* is how the story will go.

Fuck
Closure

(What the fuck does that really even mean?)

DAY TWENTY-SIX

I sat on the plane looking out the window as Rome became smaller and smaller below me. Holy shit. It was officially too late to turn back or change my mind. I was going to San Vito. The amount of mixed feelings swirling around inside me were like fucking Costco-sized proportions. What the hell was I doing? Was I about to ruin my trip? Would we even be capable of enjoying the time there together with everything that had gone down? Are my feelings going to rush back the second I see him, like the water behind the Hoover Dam if it gave way? What if I feel nothing? What the fuck am I about to walk into?

As all these thoughts plagued my brain, I realized this would be the last flight I would be taking by myself on this journey. It really made me kind of sad. The fact that it made me sad made me smile, because I knew I would be traveling alone again sooner rather than later. I had found a new courage inside of myself that I never knew existed, and it wasn't fucking going anywhere now that I had discovered it.

The wheels touched down, and I realized how real this all was. I wouldn't say I was nervous...that wasn't the right word. I felt like I was walking into a giant paintball arena, not knowing if I needed to prepare for battle or if I should duck and fucking run for cover. I grabbed my backpack from the small baggage claim area and headed out the front doors.

Right there waiting for me was a much shaggier, slightly thinner, and still obnoxiously handsome Javier. Jesus Christ, here we go.

We hugged and did the casual small talk of "how was the flight" and "did you get some sleep?"

"Let me take your pack," he offered.

"It's fine, I've got it."

"Stop, let me take it," he persisted.

"Really, I'm used to it."

He led the way over to the car he had borrowed from his friend. We loaded my pack in and hopped in the car. It was a beautiful day, and San Vito was the warmest city I had been in thus far. Rolling the windows down, we headed out of the airport parking area and onto the open road.

"You're going to love it here, Gabs. It's one of the most healing places. It's amazing," he said.

"It looks beautiful."

"Oh, just wait until we get into the city," he added. "So what place has been your favorite so far?" he asked.

"I think Barcelona. Mykonos was a close second. But I think it had a lot to do with the people I was with."

"Yeah, you mentioned that. All your pictures have been incredible," he said.

"I think Paris was my least favorite," I continued.

"Really! Why?"

"I don't know. I just feel like people romanticize it so much and it just kind of felt...dirty. Although, my hostel wasn't in the best part of the city. Don't get me wrong, I loved the Eiffel Tower and stuff. It's just, out of everywhere I've been, I think it was my least favorite," I said.

"Yeah, I've heard that about Paris. Makes sense your two favorite places were beach cities, too," he pointed out.

"Yeah, of course," I agreed. There was a lull in the conversation, and I gazed out the window at all the beautiful land we were passing. It was very picturesque. After a few long moments...

"So, what changed in Barcelona?" he asked. Oh, I was so not planning on having this conversation this quickly.

"Um. I don't think this is the time for that conversation."

"Okay," he said.

We continued to drive and discuss things that had happened on his trip and different things I had done on mine. We drove past the coastline, where crystal blue water washed up on beautiful stretches of beach.

"I'm really glad you're here, Gabs," he said. I just forced a smile and continued looking out the window. I wasn't sure if *I* was glad to be there yet. Giant mountains surrounded the city with blue skies for miles. After about thirty minutes, we pulled into town, which was made up of only a few main streets and the beach. It was really a mom-and-pop place, where everyone seemed to know each other. Javier parked the car and we hopped out.

"The apartment is right here, and the hotel that Gio works at is right next door. Here, come say hi, then I'll show you the place," he said. I followed him through the little hotel entrance.

"Gio!" he yelled in Italian. "Come say hi, Gabrielle is here." God, why is it so sexy when men can speak other languages? Much less five. Ugh.

A tall, good-looking Italian came around the corner with a smile. He came over and gave me a kiss on each cheek.

"Nice to meet you," he said in English with a ridiculously heavy accent.

"You too." I smiled.

"I'm gonna take her to drop her stuff, then we'll probably head to the beach," Javier told him.

"Okay, I'll let you know when I'm done here," Gio said.

"Perfecto," Javier replied. They gave each other a kiss on the cheek (yes, this is super normal in Italian culture).

"See you soon," Gio said to me with a smile. I smiled back as Javier and I headed back to the street.

The apartment was literally right next door. We headed up two flights of stairs to where Javier had been living for the past ten days.

"So, here's the kitchen, where I've been cooking all the boring meals for my diet," he said, showing me around. Seriously, I knew he was doing this for a role, but I think he is the only person in history that has gone to Italy for a month and *lost* weight. How depressing. "Here's the bathroom, shower, everything. You can have the room that I've been staying in with the big bed," he continued.

"No, that's fine, I can sleep in the other one. I don't care," I replied.

"Gabs, come on, you've been sleeping in bunk beds in all the hostels. It's fine. I'm happy to give you the good room."

"It's really not a big deal," I repeated.

"Don't argue," he said. It was so weird. We had gone from sleeping together night after night to needing to be in different rooms. What a freaking adjustment in a mere thirty days. He grabbed a bunch of his stuff out of the room and walked it into the room next door. I set my pack down, unloaded my toiletries, and threw some of my clothes in the dresser. It was nice having some space after living out of my backpack for so long. Every time I needed something, I would have to dig and unpack half of it, so having my own room with storage space was a welcomed change this far into the trip.

"Are you hungry?" he asked from the kitchen.

"No, I can wait a while. I ate at the airport," I said.

"Okay, do you want to head to see the beach in a little bit? I need to work out but can do my circuit while you're lounging," he said. At this point I felt so fat that hearing the words *work out* literally made me angry. Ew.

"Sure," I said, heading in to meet him in the kitchen.

"Okay. So sit down, let's talk," he said. Oh Lord, really? I was so not mentally prepared for this. I walked over and took a seat next to him at the table. "So what happened in Barcelona?" he asked again. I took a pause. A *long* pause. Not because I didn't have the answer, I did. But because I could feel the tears wanting to come up, and I knew that we were about to have *the* conversation. It was time to get some fucking closure. Whatever the hell that means.

"Well...," I said, not sure how in depth I wanted this answer to be. "I met a group of really amazing people...one in particular, who really made me see some things differently, I guess," I said.

"Okay, like what?" he asked.

"This whole time everyone has been saying that this is a cop-out," I started.

"What do you mean, a cop-out?" he cut me off.

"Like...a cop-out. Like you just didn't want to be with me anymore and couldn't just say it, so you created all these reasons and excuses instead of just telling me you didn't want to be with me," I explained.

"That's ridiculous. That's not true at all," he said with frustrated emotion in his eyes.

"Anyway, everyone, since this all happened, has been saying that, and I have fiercely defended you and protected you to everyone." I paused, still not letting the tears come. "In Barcelona, this person also agreed it was all a cop-out. But he also said that, regardless of whether it was or wasn't, that I was incredible and didn't deserve to be treated like this. And for the first time, I didn't defend you. I actually kind of agreed," I finished. He looked at me with sad eyes, like someone had just punched him in the chest.

"I agree with that. I don't want to hurt you anymore. I never wanted to. You don't deserve the way Daniel treated you. You don't deserve the way I've treated you," he said. Wow, what a concept.

"There have been so many things handled the wrong way on your end, Javier," I said.

"I know," he agreed.

"Like, why would you tell me you loved me when I was in Amsterdam?" I asked point-blank.

"What do you mean? I do love you," he said, confused. I paused and gave him a look. "What?"

"You don't think with the circumstances and where we were at with everything, that telling me 'I love you' wouldn't be taken in a certain way?" His face literally looked like someone had told him Santa Claus didn't exist.

"Oh," he said. It was shocking to me. This thirty-five-year-old man literally did not understand that saying he loved me was confusing to me. And believe me, I know how ridiculous it sounds, but I watched his face genuinely fall and saw how badly he felt for such an epic mistake.

"You get what I'm saying, right?" I asked.

"No, of course. I just...I do love you as a person. You're so important to me, and I care about you so much. You changed my life," he said. "But you thought I meant like...in love with you." He nodded as if it was all finally making sense in that moment. "I just don't understand why you think it's a cop-out. Believe me, I wish I knew what the hell was wrong with me," he continued.

"Javier. If you take away all the grief, all the love and compassion and understanding around the situation, and just look at the facts...it is man meets woman, man and woman fall madly in love, man convinces woman to go on a romantic trip together, then man bails forty-eight hours before the trip. Regardless of the circumstances, that is what happened," I said sternly.

"You're right," he said.

"And then, on top of all that, you don't even do a good job of making sure I'm okay throughout this entire fiasco that you created," I continued.

"You're right. I have not handled this well, and you deserve way better than that," he confessed. It's so funny how hearing someone finally admit to something so huge never makes you feel quite as resolved as you initially hoped it would. It still left me in the same position. "I just didn't want to interfere with your trip and make things worse. I was always seeing your Instagram stories and watching what you were doing. I knew you were okay," he said.

"That's irrelevant. You should have been reaching out, asking if I was okay or if I needed anything. Regardless of if I wanted you to or not, you didn't even try. You just sent me off on this insane trip that I didn't ask for and expected me to be fine." I started feeling the tears fight their way up even more. Still, I held them back. "I may seem like this strong woman that has it all together but I'm not you, Javier. I don't go off on random adventurous trips by myself with nothing planned. This was terrifying for me and a huge deal," I said, getting slightly more worked up.

"You're right. I get it. I should have been there for you," he agreed solemnly.

"Yeah. *Especially* as a friend," I added. "You're telling me you want me in your life forever, and you want me to be your best friend, but you don't even treat me how a friend deserves to be treated." I could see *he* was now the one holding back tears. Was this the first time he had sat down to really think about the entire situation? Or did he really just not realize half the things he was doing or the effect they were having. I looked at him and began to say something, but then stopped.

"What?" he asked, as he looked at me concerned.

"Nothing," I said. The tears were about to win.

"No, tell me," he persisted. Then my tears won.

"You broke my fucking heart," I said, as my voice cracked and tears fell down my cheeks. We sat there for a minute in silence. He didn't know what to say. I didn't know what to do. We both just recognized what a mess it all was. After pulling the tears back, I continued, "I have been the one that had to initiate and fix everything. I was the one who said we had to talk after the three days in London. I was the one who said I wanted to see you. I am the only reason I am sitting here talking to you right now. You didn't do *anything* to make any of this happen or show any type of effort," I said.

"I know. I'm sorry. I just get so in my head and...it's like I always think I'm making the right choice for the other person and then it just blows up in my face and ends up being the complete opposite. I never intend for it to be that way," he replied. I was watching what a struggle this was for him.

"I know that you didn't intentionally do any of this. I know you're not a malicious person, and you didn't plan on all of this happening. But you kept everything so open-ended when you should have just been honest and direct with me, Javier," I said.

"What do you mean?" he said, clearly struck by this statement. "I haven't ever fallen for someone and then woken up and had all those feelings be gone! I didn't know if they were going to come back! I was hoping they would. This was all new for me, too," he said defensively.

"Yes, but when you told me 'I don't feel anything for my parents, my sister, or you,' that wasn't true," I said.

"What do you mean!?" he asked.

"You still loved your parents and Sophia."

"Of course," he answered.

"So you did still feel for them. You just didn't feel anything for me." He paused.

"Right," he reluctantly agreed.

"You kept me in this gray area of not knowing what was going to happen in the future instead of just telling me that we were done and not to keep that option open," I continued.

"Because I was hoping the feelings would come back. I didn't want to close the door on it," he said.

"BUT THAT'S NOT FAIR TO ME," I raised my voice at him. Another pause.

"You're right," he finally said. We sat in silence for a few moments. I took a deep breath.

"It's just really difficult to switch my feelings for you to friendship feelings," I said.

"Yeah, me too. I don't know how to do this either," he responded.

"See, no. You can't say that. That makes it sound like it's hard for you, too, like you have other feelings for me still. It's not hard for you. You say you only feel friendship feelings toward me, then that's what it is for you." It was like having to explain to a child how to clearly communicate what you mean.

"Right," he said. "I'm just so sick of this. Like, when is it going to finally work for me?" I could tell his hurt was turning into anger.

"It will work when you find the right woman. It just wasn't me," I said, even though it made my heart ache.

"That's bullshit. You are the perfect woman, and everything was amazing. I don't know what the hell is wrong with me. I feel like I'm just going to be alone forever," he said. We sat for another few minutes in silence. We had said everything we needed to say. I hadn't gotten any of the answers I wanted, but in some weird way, I got an answer: he just went to bed in love with me and woke up...*not*. Ridiculous? Maybe. Impossible? Some may say. Heartbreaking? Definitely. Infuriating? Yes. Confusing? Fucking hell yes. Regardless of whether it was a satisfying enough answer for me, his mother, Sophia, his friends, my friends, or himself even, it didn't matter, because it was the only answer there was. That was what my closure would have to be. *Closure.* What the fuck does that even mean?

* * * * *

We headed out of the apartment and down to the beach. Javier pointed out things in the town along the way as we walked. He would stop and talk to people as if he had been living there for months. I walked alongside him with my thoughts. It was so interesting. From the conversation in his truck when he'd told me he had to go alone, to the ten-hour plane ride together, to the long FaceTime calls, and in the heavy conversation we had just had, we were always somehow... *okay*. We would always have moments of laughter between the tears. We were always still connected, no matter what was going on. It was something I had never experienced with another human being before, male or female.

We arrived at the beach after a short walk from the apartment. It was a beautiful day. The sand was lined with lounge chairs and umbrellas that the public could use at their leisure. I sat on one of the many chairs and put my stuff down.

"I'm going to go on a quick run and do my circuit. Should only take me thirty minutes or so," Javier said as he pulled off his shirt. His sexy dad bod had definitely become less dad-ish over the past month.

"Have fun!" I said sarcastically, knowing that there was no fucking way I would be working out until I got back home.

"I hate you," he joked back and headed off down the beach. I lay back on the lounge chair and opened my journal to start writing. The conversation we'd just had was so heavy and so long, I knew if I didn't write down some of it, I wouldn't be able to remember it all. There's something about important and heavy conversations that make you almost...*leave* your body. It's like you're present, but afterward it feels like you were watching a movie. That was exactly how this all felt.

After writing a bit, I headed down to the water. I stood by myself, looking down through the crystal-clear water at my feet squished in the sand. To my left, there was a long stretch of beach that curved into a marina with boats and a lighthouse. To my right was more beach with giant mountains at the end, creating this perfect little half circle of heaven. It was truly beautiful, and I could see why Javier had fallen in love with this place.

Once Javier returned, we lay on the chairs for a while soaking up the sun.

"You hungry?" Javier asked.

"I could eat," I replied. We headed a few hundred feet away to a little restaurant. Sitting at one of the outside tables, I ate as Javier sipped a cappuccino.

"So the person I met in Barcelona that really helped me," I said starting to smile, "guess what his name was?" I asked.

"Daniel," Javier guessed.

"Ha! No," I said with a laugh. "Chris." His face froze and his eyes widened.

"You're kidding."

"Nope," I responded. It really was crazy how many things had happened to each of us on this trip with that significant name.

"Wow," he said.

We grabbed two bikes and rode around the town. He took me down the main street where all the shops and restaurants were, and then we headed out toward the marina and lighthouse. It was one of the most beautiful spots I had ever been. Sitting on the edge of this stretch of land with boats to my right, the turquoise water surrounding us, and the giant mountains in the near distance was magical. We had a man passing by snap a photo of us, and then I asked Javier to take one of just me. I sat on the edge of the rocks, looking out at this gorgeous slice of heaven. It was the perfect photo to start my San Vito posts. I uploaded it with the caption: "Know your worth and love yourself enough to heal." *Sigh.* If only I could take my own brilliant advice.

We headed back to the apartment to relax for a while. I unpacked a little bit and wrote some more in my new room. There was a big window that opened outward to overlook the street below, with a little ledge just big enough to sit on if you were careful. It reminded me of something out of the town in *Beauty and the Beast*.

"I'm going to head over to the library and check in with Alvaro. You good?" Javier asked.

"Yep," I replied. Alvaro owned the main library/bookstore in town. He was one of Javier's closest friends, even though they didn't get to see each other that often. When Javier's brother died, Alvaro flew out from Italy to be with him and his family. He had always been an unwavering source of support for him, and he was the only friend in the group of Italians that really knew the backstory of what was going on with me and Javier.

After writing and relaxing for a while, I hopped in the shower to get ready for the night. Javier had been raving about a restaurant right next door that he wanted to take me to before meeting up with some of the Italians. During the day, it had been in the back of my mind that it was September 29th. Javier's brother's birthday was September 30th, and I had known since the early stages of discussing the trip that his birthday fell during Javier's time here. We had even talked about what he might want to do to celebrate it, but since everything had changed, I had no idea where he was at with all of it. The whole day I had been wondering how it would play out.

Later that night, we headed a few doors down to an adorable restaurant that had twinkle lights and beautiful trees sprinkled throughout the open-air patio. The owner came over and spoke to Javier in Italian for a few minutes. They laughed and joked as if they had known each other for years. He had been here ten days and literally knew everyone. Shocker.

We started with a bottle of wine—well, I started with a bottle of wine; he had half a glass—and then got an appetizer of various fish. It was delicious. He ordered some giant fish with grilled veggies, and I got a giant plate of gluttonous pasta. The pasta that was popular in San Vito was special because it was made only in San Vito. They used a particular plant leaf to roll the pasta into the specific shape. Javier had been raving about it and I must say, it was pretty unbelievable. For the record, I regret nothing.

"So...your mother," I said.

"What about her?" he asked.

"She's incredible."

"Yes, she definitely is. But why?" he questioned.

"She has just been such a huge support to me on this entire journey. I honestly don't know what I would have done without her."

"Yeah, she really loves you. I haven't really talked to her about you or the situation a whole lot, because I know she thinks I didn't handle it well," he admitted.

"Yeah...well..." I agreed with a smile to keep the mood light.

After an amazing dinner, which Javier insisted on paying for, we headed over to the main street of the town. There were a few bars that were playing music, and people were in the streets dancing. It was such a different vibe than anywhere I had been thus far on my trip. We met Gio and his summer fling Mariella, a spunky Italian in his forties named Vincenzo, and Alvaro.

"Alvaro, this is Gabrielle," Javier introduced us. We both smiled and gave each other a big hug. I felt instantly connected to him. He had such a great energy about him, and I could tell he was compassionate about what was going on with Javier and me.

"So nice to finally meet you," he said with a smile in his Italian accent.

"You too. I've heard so much about you." I smiled back.

We all danced and joked for a while, and Vincenzo (who I instantly fell in love with) got me another glass of wine. After about twenty minutes, I felt Javier grab my hand.

"Come with me," he said rather intensely. I took his hand and followed him to the beach that was just past the bars on the end of the strip. At first, I thought he just wanted to show me the beach at night. He let go of my hand and continued to walk forward a few steps. Then he took a deep breath in and let out what I soon realized was a sob.

"My brother would have been twenty-one today," he managed to get out through panicked breath. It was midnight and officially September 30th. I put my cup down, walked over to him, and put my arms around him. His head fell into me like he was hiding from the world, and I held him as he continued to cry.

"You're okay. I've got you," I said. And I did. Through all the ups and downs, the insane roller coaster, the never-ending saga that this whole situation had become, that had never changed. I had taken care of this man since the moment I walked into his life. I felt such a love, such a protective nature, such a divine connection with him. So, I stood there for what seemed like minutes and just held him.

"It's just so unfair. He should be here. Why am I here and he isn't?" he said, trying to slow his breathing down. I put my hands on each side of his face to get him to focus and calm down.

"You can't keep focusing on that. He's free and in such a better place, and he would not want you to be in pain and stuck in this grief for him. He would want you to celebrate him and be happy," I answered.

"I know," he said through tears. "We should be celebrating him."

"Yes. He would want nothing but for you to feel all the happiness in the world. You know that," I replied.

"You're right. Thank you. I'm so glad you're here," he said, the tears subsiding. "Come on, let's go dance." He grabbed my hand and we headed back to the street where everyone was dancing under the night sky.

We danced for the next hour and celebrated in his brother's honor. I was really happy I was there that night. When I saw him break down on the beach, I knew it could have been bad if I hadn't had been there.

After saying goodnight to the Italians, we walked back to the apartment. It was still beautiful out and we strolled slowly through the streets of the quaint town. Once we arrived back at the apartment, I got ready for bed and sent his mother a text.

Me: Sending you lots of love today and celebrating who I know was such an amazing human. I'm sure he's smiling down, feeling all the love everyone has for him.

I went to the kitchen and grabbed a bottle of water to yet again try and offset the amount of wine I had consumed.

"Do you have everything you need?" Javier asked. I don't know if it was the wine, the amount of emotions that had come to the surface in our heavy conversation earlier that day, or the fact that this man had just wept into my arms as I held him, but regardless, this is what came out:

"Will you sleep with me?" I said. His face froze. "Not like *sleep* with me just like...sleep with me," I badly clarified.

"Gabs, I..." he trailed off.

"Not if it's gonna be weird. I just...I don't know, I just feel like I need to be held," I admitted.

"Yes, but I'm still a man."

"So you can't sleep with me without having sex with me?" I laughed.

"No, I just...I don't know. I don't want to hurt you anymore," he said with a genuine sincerity.

"Okay. You're right, it's probably best," I said. We stared at each other, both of us knowing that we wanted to be in the same bed. But he was trying to do the right thing, and I did acknowledge and respect that. He walked forward and gave me a hug. We stood there for a moment. "Goodnight," I said.

"Goodnight, Gabs," he responded.

I turned around and went into my room, shutting the door behind me. As I lay in bed, I thought, *good*. We chose to be smart about the situation and keep everything in this new black-and-white friend zone that he had decided we were now in. The million-dollar question: Would we be able to stay there?

Fuck
Conflicts Of Interest

(Welcome to the fucking real world.)

DAY TWENTY-SEVEN

I opened my eyes to a still-dark room to get up to pee. It was 3:23 a.m. I walked from my bedroom to the bathroom and glanced over at Javier's room. It was so weird to be staying in the same apartment in separate rooms. All I had ever known with him was sleeping together—from the first night we went out dancing and back to the hotel room, to camping on the beach, to Santa Barbara, to Las Vegas. Now, in this romantic town across the world, I was starfished out on the queen bed while he was cramped on a bunk bed in the room next door. Oh, the irony.

I hopped back in bed and looked at my phone. There was a message from Chris.

Chris: How's Sicily? It looks freaking gorgeous.

I smiled. We talked about how beautiful the town was and the incredible beaches.

Me: I'm with Javier. Getting some much-needed closure and realizations. Got here today.

Chris: Oh, damn, that sounds pretty real. How do you feel about it?

It was so strange. From just knowing him for a few days in Barcelona, I knew that he wasn't asking from a place of jealousy. He was genuinely asking to see how I was doing, and that said a lot about him.

Me: It's really real…and lots of emotions. But definitely have some clarity about a lot of stuff. I had mentioned that a lot changed in Barcelona. So when I got here, he immediately asked about it, and we had a really long and intense talk.

Chris: I'm glad things are more clear for you. To add some more (or less?), I definitely have feelings for you.

And the twenty-three-year-old boldly surprises me yet again.

Me: I have feelings for you too. I just don't know what any of it means right now in the middle of everything.

Chris: You've been through a lot of shit the past few months. And we did meet while traveling, so you have to think about that… Would you know if your feelings stemmed from us being in the paradise that was Barcelona? I know mine aren't, but I totally wanna respect everything you've been going through.

Me: Um…I know that the feelings weren't because of Barcelona, they were…are…because of you and how I feel we bonded the whole time, especially that last night. But I'm not stupid, and I know how many different things are happening to me and my emotions right now so, although I know what I'm feeling on some level, I don't really know what to make of it right now, if that makes sense. I do know that after all this, I am terrified of ever making someone feel the way Javier made me feel. So, if anything, I would say the feelings I'm experiencing toward you are making me cautious and trepidatious right now. Like, I don't ever want to not be upfront about where I'm at, and I can't say I'm emotionally in a place to decipher the feelings I'm having. But I'm definitely able to recognize the fact that they are there and legitimate in some way. Sorry, I know that's not really any type of answer, but it's the best I can articulate, even for myself, right now.

Damn, Gabrielle. This is progress. Why? Because the old me would have entertained the notion of starting something full on with this person if only to take my mind off of Javier. In the past, I had never been cautious or super careful with other people's feelings when it came to new relationships. But everything that had gone down with Javier had seriously changed me. I didn't *ever* want to make someone feel the way he had made me feel, and if that meant being super blunt and honest about everything, so be it. We continued texting for a bit before I fell back to sleep. Seriously, is my life ever uneventful? Even when I'm sleeping there are new developments.

The sunlight poured into my room, and I stirred awake for a second time. Javier had just gotten up as well, and we decided to head down to get some breakfast. Well, I got some breakfast. He had some healthy crap at the apartment before we left that looked oh so exciting. We walked down the street to a little café where he, of course, knew the owner. They greeted each other in Italian and exchanged the traditional cheek kisses. I got a chocolate croissant (which was literally like an orgasm on a plate) and a latté. Javier got a cappuccino and we sat outside and discussed plans for the day.

"We're going to go with all the guys to this awesome spot with cliff jumping and snorkeling," he told me.

"Awesome, that sounds amazing."

"We'll head back to the apartment to get ready. I'm gonna run by the library to get Alvaro, and then we'll pick up sandwiches for lunch and go," he said.

"Sounds good," I replied as we finished up our breakfast. When we got back to the apartment, Javier hopped on a bike to head to Alvaro. I got ready and checked my email. Big mistake.

An email from my lawyer had come in. Included in it was a very rude, very nasty email from Daniel's lawyer claiming that I was responsible for half of Daniel's debt, which he had irresponsibly racked up at his former sports club. I immediately reacted. My lawyer had told me that I didn't need to worry about any of this, but reading his lawyer's crude words, which were written in an inappropriate and childish tone, reminded me that I would soon be going back to reality to deal with *this*...and I did not fucking want to. I burst into tears as I sat in my room by myself. A few minutes later, Javier returned to the apartment.

"You ready to..." His voice trailed off as he walked into my room. "Gabs, what's wrong?" he immediately asked as he came over to me. I showed him the email and explained how I just did not want to go home. He put his arms around me, which, for whatever reason, made me sob harder.

"It's okay. You're going to be fine. This is all going to be over and you will be fine," he told me. *Yep*, I thought to myself, *of course I will be. I'm always fine, aren't I?* My husband slept with a nineteen-year-old for six months and I was fine. I filed for divorce and I was fine. Javier broke my heart and I was somehow still standing. But at this moment, in this room, I was not fine. I was done. I was finally at my breaking point.

"I don't want to go home," I said.

"Why?" he asked. "Because you have to deal with all of this?"

"No. For so many reasons. I just don't want to go home," I repeated.

I didn't really know why. Which, of course, meant I needed to bust out the Thought Onion. First, the superficial thoughts.

- I don't want to go home and deal with the legal divorce bullshit.
- After I've been to these incredible places...fuck LA.
- How is anything at home going to measure up to what I've done this past month?

Yep. Those were all pretty accurate statements. Now, to dig a little deeper and find the authentic thoughts.

- I don't want to keep getting plugged into the drama.
- What if home doesn't feel like home anymore?
- What if I have major travel withdrawals?

That all made sense to me. So now, what is at the root of all those thoughts? What is the main subconscious thought?

- What if I'm not healed?

Boom. There it was. The giant fucking fear that had been slowly creeping its way to the surface the closer it got to the trip coming to an end. What if I went home and I wasn't okay? What if I was still heartbroken and feeling like a huge mess? What if this journey that I was on to learn how to be by myself and love myself...*didn't work?* That, to me, was absolutely terrifying.

After some crying and some failed attempts by Javier to cheer me up, I decided fifteen minutes was already too much time wasted on the immaturity of my soon-to-be ex-husband and his so-called attorney. We grabbed our stuff and headed down to meet Alvaro, Gio, Mariella, Vincenzo, and two other Italians from their group. We stopped to grab sandwiches from a deli and then headed off to a special spot they knew about. Let me tell you, special was an understatement.

We took a steep mountain road down to the water, where we were surrounded by cliffs, caves, rock formations, and the ocean. There were also dozens of wild cattle running around. Each way you looked, all you could see was nature and ocean. It was beautiful. We hiked down to one of the clearings by the water and set up our little spot for the day. Alvaro and I hopped up on one of the higher rocks, and Javier snapped a photo of us. Alvaro had such a genuine energy about him, I felt as if I had known him for years. Javier and Alvaro immediately jumped in and started swimming around. The sun was shining down on us as we listened to the waves crash on the rocks.

We swam around for a while and then hopped out to warm up and eat our sandwiches. Good Lord, it was one of the best sandwiches I had ever had. It was literally just bread, cheese, and bresaola, which is an aged beef, but it was *so* freaking good. Once we had warmed up and our food had digested, we headed over to a higher point where the cliff jumping was.

"This is the spot I jumped from the other day," Javier said. I looked down over the edge of the fifty-foot drop. It suddenly seemed so much higher. I knew I was going to jump, there wasn't a question in my mind. How long it would take me? That was a different story.

Javier stood on another rock with my phone, ready to film this giant leap of faith.

"You're sure I won't, like, hit a rock and die?" I shouted over to him. I mean, with my luck the last three months, would it really fucking shock you?

"You'll be fine, Gabs! I did it and I'm alive," he answered.

"Yeah, I'll make sure to tell my mother that. She already wants to kill you," I joked...sort of. There was ten minutes of me freaking out while Javier heckled me and two Italian men who were sunbathing naked a few rocks over cheered me on.

"Okay, I'm gonna go!" I yelled.

"I'll count for you!" he shouted back.

"No! Just let me go!" I laughed. I bent my knees (like getting a few inches lower was going to make a difference) and jumped. I let out a scream and fell all the way down to the water below. It was terrifying, exhilarating, and liberating all at the same time. Jumping off this cliff was literally a metaphor for my life at the current moment. It was terrifying to love someone as deeply as I loved Javier. It had been terrifying to go on this trip. Both had proven to be exhilarating, liberating, and most importantly, had taught me so much about myself. The biggest take away from it all? *I survived.*

We headed back to our lounging area, and I laid out on my towel to dry off. Javier and Alvaro decided to hike up to the top of one of the giant mountains that stood to our right. I closed my eyes and listened to the sound of waves mixed with the Italian and Portuguese that our group was chatting in. I drifted off for about forty-five minutes in this little slice of paradise.

When Javier and Alvaro returned, they pointed out a rock formation they had made on top of the mountain. They had made it in honor of Chris's birthday, and it made me smile to see Javier filled with such happiness around the subject.

"What a perfect thing to do for his birthday. This is perfect," he said. And it was. We all sat together and took a group picture on my phone. It turned out looking like a vintage postcard from old Italy. I posted it with the caption "*Siate felici,*" which is Italian for "Be happy."

After a full day in the sun, we headed back to the apartment to relax, shower, and freshen up for the night. Javier and I were going to a restaurant where one of the Italians worked, and then we would be meeting everyone to celebrate Mariella's birthday at the bar that we had danced at the night before. As I was getting ready, Javier came in from talking with Gio next door.

"So, uh...one of Mariella's friends is coming into town tonight and is going to stay here in the second bedroom," he said.

"Okay...Oh," I responded.

"If that's weird, I can sleep on whatever bunk he's not on," he offered. I thought for a moment.

"No, don't be ridiculous, it's fine."

"You sure?"

"Veto, it's just sleeping. It's not like we haven't done it before," I said.

"Okay," he agreed. He started to move some of his stuff back into the big bedroom I was in.

Seriously, universe? Could you make this already difficult situation *any* more fucking difficult? Jesus.

We headed out to walk over to the restaurant for dinner. It was another beautiful outdoor patio, with twinkle lights hanging delicately around for ambiance. We ordered a bottle of wine, which of course meant three glasses for me and one for him. I had to hand it to him, he was really being diligent on this whole diet thing. I mean, I get it, I'm an actor too, but...pasta.

We sat, ate, and talked. It was weird how normal everything felt. Nothing had changed as far as how we laughed, joked, bantered back and forth, or spoke about intimate things. The only thing that was different was that we weren't holding hands and kissing all the time.

In any normal real-world situation, it would be completely weird and awkward to sit with your newly ex-boyfriend in a romantic setting when you're still in love with him. But it just...wasn't. When the bill came, I again fought him on it and he again won.

"Please, just let me do this. It's my treat," he said.

"You treated last night," I argued.

"Yeah, and it's not a big deal. Don't argue." I didn't. I had spent a ton of money by this point and I must admit there was definitely a part of me that was saying, "Yes, you most definitely can buy me dinner. And a new heart while you're at it."

We headed over to meet everyone at the bar, where we all continued to drink, laugh, and celebrate Mariella's birthday. Her friend from Brazil had arrived, and we all greeted him. We hopped around to the few good spots that were all clustered at the end of the main street and danced. Around 12:30 a.m., Javier looked at me.

"You ready to head back?" he asked.

"Yeah, I'm exhausted," I replied, five glasses of wine in at this point. We said goodbye to everyone that was still dancing the night away. We strolled back toward the apartment in the crisp outside air. We talked and laughed but it wasn't lost on me that we were on our way back to an apartment where we would be getting into the same bed. *So* many thoughts were flying through my head.

Once we were back in the apartment, I changed into a shirt and some shorts to sleep in and brushed my teeth. Javier was already in bed, and I flopped down on my side and lay there for a minute in the darkness. A minute of silence was all I could take.

"Yeah, I'm not gonna be able to do this," I said.

"Do what?"

"Sleep next to you," I answered. He quickly sat up.

"Do you want me to go next door?" he offered.

"No. I mean I'm not going to be able to just *sleep* next to you." Luckily, the wine was assisting in my feeling sharing.

"Gabs, I don't want to do anything else that is going to hurt you," he said. I could hear in his voice how much he really meant it.

"I know you don't. I'm trying to decide if I can do just...sex. Like, not emotional sex." HA, okay, Gabrielle. Go ahead and try and convince yourself of *that* joke. We lay there for a few minutes in silence and all I could do was restlessly sigh. "Yeah, I can't just lie here," I confirmed.

"I just...Ugh, I don't know," he said. At this point he was wrestling with himself, too.

"Okay. It's fine. I'm aware that it doesn't mean anything in that way," I stated. Thank you, wine, for that liquid load of bullshit. I leaned over onto him and ran my hand through his hair.

"Fuck, Gabs," he said, letting out one last sigh, knowing that he was about to lose the battle of intending to be gentlemanly and respectful. In his defense, if it wasn't for me, we would have just gone to sleep. After we'd stared at each other for a moment, he kissed me. Let me tell you, there was no turning back after that. We had always had incredible sex so that was a given. But something about this was just...different. Maybe it was because we both knew we shouldn't be doing it. Maybe it was because we were in one of the most romantic places on earth. Or maybe it was because we had been strictly religious about using protection and for whatever reason at this moment in time that was the last thing on either of our minds. There had never been more passion, we had never been so connected, and we were absolutely spent by the time he collapsed on top of me.

Like I said, I wish I could say I had made a good decision and kept things in the new black-and-white friend zone instead of turning *Fifty Shades of Grey*. Alas, it would make things way too easy without a massive conflict of interest. Welcome to the fucking real world, Gabrielle. At least the sex was worth it.

Fuck The Gray Area

(It's a shitty color for a reason.)

DAY TWENTY-EIGHT

I woke up the next morning beside a still-sleeping Javier. I looked out the window and saw gray. The sky was still looming as the morning clouds came in from the ocean. What an appropriate color to wake up to that morning. I had very clearly walked my ass out of the newly decided black-and-white friend zone and plopped it down into the gray area. However, I can't say I woke up with any regrets. I will state that for those reading this, I don't suggest or promote unprotected sex. While I was on birth control, this happened solely because it was with someone I trusted not only with my body but with my safety. Maybe it was because my brain wasn't letting me think about what all this would mean once we went home, but regardless, it wasn't making me uneasy. As I lay next to him in bed, I allowed my thoughts to attempt to work themselves out silently. The superficial thought?

- I'm going to wake him up and not leave this bed all fucking day.

Kidding. Kind of. But the type of passion we had in bed was different. I'd never had that with Daniel. Unfortunately, now that I had experienced it, I was going to compare everything in the future to that. Lovely. Now, what's the authentic thought?

- How is it possible to have that type of passionate intimacy with someone you only have friendship feelings toward?

I mean, really. I understand he's a man, and they have a reputation for fucking anything that walks. Even as a woman, I'd experienced having sex with someone I wasn't necessarily *that* interested in or just had a good friendship with. *But,* when that type of sex happens, it's usually lackluster and unsatisfying, which definitely didn't describe what had taken place in this bed the night before. So, what's the subconscious thought at the root of all of this?

- That wasn't friendship sex.

It wasn't the sex itself that was emotionally confusing, it was the level of everything it encapsulated. I'm smart enough to know when people are or are not interested in me. I'm the first person to tell my girlfriends, "Girl, he's just not into it. Move on." But the things that had just happened between us were such a strange contradiction to what he'd said in our conversation the day before. Maybe I just wanted to hold on to some part of our relationship. Still, I forced myself to latch onto his statement: "I haven't ever fallen for someone and then woken up and had all those feelings be gone." Really, that was my "answer." He just went to bed in love with me and woke up...*not*. I had to keep reminding myself to remember that.

I hopped up to rinse off and brush my teeth. When I came back in to get dressed, Javier was awake.

"Morning," I said.

"Morning," he answered. "You okay?" he asked, clearly referring to the decision I had made the night before.

"Fine. What's the plan for today?" I replied with a smile. I had gotten my fill of long emotional conversations for a while and wasn't about to have another one this early. He took the hint.

"We're gonna head to a cove with Vincenzo and spearfish, then go to another cool cliff spot with Alvaro once he's off work," he answered.

"Sounds good," I said. We both finished getting ready and headed to a little café to grab some breakfast. I ordered a crepe, which was by far one of the best things I had consumed on this entire trip. Yes, I realize that is how I describe half the stuff I ate, but it really just kept getting better and better. It was filled with Nutella and had crushed macadamia nuts sprinkled on top. It was then finished with powdered sugar and chocolate sauce. It was heaven on a plate. Javier whined as he watched me eat every last bite.

"I'm proud of the way you're eating. It's the only way to travel. I'm living vicariously through you," he said.

Vincenzo arrived to pick us up, and we headed to another hidden spot on the coast. They busted out full-on spear guns (like I said... Bear Grylls), and I found a beautiful spot to stretch out and soak up the sun. I dozed off on the rocks, hearing faint Italian conversations between the few people that were hanging out around us. God, I didn't want to go home.

It was such a beautiful day out. The gray had burned off and the sun was shining. All three of us lay on the rocks and fell asleep in the warm sun. Life was so much simpler in this place. It made me question why I lived in Los Angeles. The only reason I could come up with was my career.

Once we had gotten more than enough sun, we headed back to town. We walked around the main street for a while, where everyone was out and about.

"We have to get you a cannoli," Javier said.

"You're just trying to fatten me up at this point," I joked.

"I told you, I'm living vicariously though you." He laughed. "Besides, they're the best in town. This woman makes them from scratch."

We headed into a little shop and he ordered one from the woman in Italian. I've had cannoli in the past in LA, and I can't say I was ever a huge fan. Well, this was not LA, and this was *not* a normal cannoli. Jesus. Christ. First of all, it was absolutely gigantic. It was stuffed with the best ricotta cheese I had ever tasted and had incredible chocolate chips sprinkled throughout. It was all stuffed into a flaky, delicious dough that you could tell had been made from scratch. It was amazing. We walked along the street as I ate it.

"You're struggling right now, aren't you?" I laughed, knowing he was miserable on his diet.

"You have no idea," he said. I took out my phone and took an Instagram video.

"This is so good, Javier," I said, taking a bite of the cannoli. His face looked pained in the background as he watched. "You want a bite?" I asked.

"Yeah," he said as he leaned in toward the desert, opening his mouth.

"Oh, wait, you can't have one cause you're fucking fat," I replied as I pulled it away from him. We both started hysterically laughing. I posted it with the appropriate title *#ActorLife*.

"You have to send that to my mom," he said, still laughing. I did. She appreciated it just as much as we did.

After showering and relaxing at the apartment for a little bit, we headed out for dinner. That night, one of the Italian's brothers, who ran the one and only hostel in town, was having everyone over to hang out, and we were planning on heading there after grabbing a bite to eat. We went to yet another super delicious restaurant, right on one of the main streets in town, that had a beautiful outdoor patio. We sat and ordered a yummy cocktail in the warm summer air.

"So, when do you leave for Mexico?" I asked. In case you forgot, he was dieting because he was about to shoot the lead in a new TV show for four months. Hence the need to get closure on this trip and not once we were home.

"October 11th," he said.

"Wait, I thought you were leaving like the day after we got home?" I asked.

"Yeah, they switched it because I have to get my work visa and a bunch of stuff straightened out before I go," he answered. So much for not having the option of LA closure.

"Gotcha. Well, that's good. You'll be able to spend some time with your parents and the pup," I said.

"Yes, definitely. I want to see you, too, before I leave." Ah, yes, welcome back to that good old gray zone.

"Well, I want to see your mother. So maybe if it's like a BBQ night," I said with a laugh.

"Great, don't care about seeing me before I leave for four months but you want to see Mom. I get it." He laughed back. "We can definitely do a BBQ night," he agreed.

We ate and talked about a million different things.

"How's the book coming along?" he asked.

"It's coming. Definitely still have a lot to work on once I get home." I paused for a second. "You know a lot of it is about us. And about *you*," I said.

"I know. I figured."

"Just so you know, I'm very...conscious of the way I portray you, and everything really."

"Other people are always going to have their opinions, and I can't do anything about that," he answered.

"I know. But I just want you to know it's all written with...I don't know, care and respect."

"Okay. I'm sure when it's a bestseller they'll say, 'It's rumored to be about actor Javier Alvarez!'" We both cracked up. He paused.

"I'm really glad you came," he said. I nodded. "It's really good to have you here." We finished up the rest of dinner and he tried to pay yet again.

"No," I said.

"Gabs, seriously, it's fine. You've spent so much money on this trip already." His tone was firm.

"I don't care. You've paid for dinner the last two nights. We can split it," I said just as firmly back.

"You really do have a thing with money after Daniel, don't you?"

"I do," I agreed. Quite frankly, this pattern was a little too close to home for me. Daniel had always fixed things with money. Every time he would make me miserable while I was on set or ruin something in some way, he would fix it with a shopping spree, a vacation, or a fancy dinner. Even when he was having the affair, he would feel so guilty he would offer to send me to the spa for a day. It was sick, and I had let it happen for way too long, making all the things he ruined okay, in a way. Even though I didn't think Javier was intentionally trying to pay for things to make up for breaking my heart and bailing on the trip, the pattern was still a little too similar for me to be comfortable with.

In no way, shape, or form did I think any of it was okay, so I was not about to let him feel like it was. We split dinner that night.

We arrived at the hostel which had, by far, one of the coolest designs for a hostel I had seen thus far. It had unique and eclectic touches everywhere—an awesome back porch with a ping pong table, an outside bar, and colorful hammocks. The rooms were something you would see at a really hip summer camp, and it was definitely a place you'd want to spend your vacation. We all sat outside drinking and chatting. There was the core group of Italians that we had been with the last few days—Gio, Mariella, Vincenzo, and Alvaro—a few other friends who lived in the area, and some people who were staying at the hostel on vacation.

I still needed my bracelet from San Vito. I had eight so far (I had bought two in Barcelona and two in Mykonos), and needed my final one. Mariella made jewelry and had some incredible handmade pieces. Since she spoke literally no English, I asked Javier to ask her in Portuguese if she could show me some of the things she had. She brought out a bunch of beautiful earring sets, necklaces, and bracelets. I zeroed in on one with a brown leather strap and a brass feather. It immediately called to me in some way, and that was that. I had found my ninth, and final, bracelet.

The guys had a ping pong tournament that was one of the funniest things I had ever witnessed. Javier sat on the side pretending to be an announcer and commentating on everything that was happening in both English and Italian in a hysterical broadcaster voice. Vincenzo would act out replays in slow motion and all of us laughed so hard we cried.

About an hour into the gathering, I received a text from Javier's mom.

Ana: Are you enjoying Sicily?

Me: I am. It's really beautiful here and we've had a great time with all the guys.

Ana: Did it help to go there?

Fuck, I don't know...did it?

Me: In some ways. At least I got a final answer on what he wants.

Ana: Which is?

Bullshit. I mean, the answer none of us wanted.

Me: That we can only be friends. And that as much as it doesn't make sense to me or you or Sophia, there's no real answer. He just went to sleep one night feeling one way and woke up and it was gone. So I have to accept that.

Jesus. Even writing it sounds ridiculous.

Ana: I can't understand how he feels and what he wants, but I know for sure that you are the daughter-in-law I have dreamed of. Again, I don't really know you, but I have good instincts and I care for you very deeply. You are likable, kind, respectful, funny, and especially a good person. I promise you that there is someone in this world who is waiting to find you, and that will be crazy about you, and that will love you the way you are.

God. What was it about this woman that made both of us feel like we were already family? I mean seriously. We had only spent a total of what...twelve hours together? And we literally were like old friends.

Me: And I love you for that. I appreciate you so much, you truly have no idea. I was telling Javier the other day that I don't know what I would have done without you on this trip. Because my mom was so hurt and so angry at him, she didn't know how to help me the way she normally does and having you was truly invaluable. He said today, if there's time, he wants to see me before he goes to Mexico, and I said only if it's a BBQ or dinner with you and the family lol. I do love you.

Ana: BBQ it is then!!!! Love you, too.

After hanging at the hostel for a while, Javier and I decided to call it a night. We rode bikes back to the apartment and got ready for bed. As we were lying there, I could feel both of us thinking about what was going to come next. Normally, I hate having to be the one to always initiate things sexually but, let's be honest, I had to initiate literally *everything* with Javier on this trip, so it was nothing new to me. In this specific area, however, I knew it was because he was trying to be respectful of all the harm he had already caused and in no way wanted to take advantage of me or where I was at emotionally. I truly did see that.

However, whatever damage the gray area caused had already been done. So...was I just supposed to *not* have great sex in this little romantic apartment in Italy? I leaned over to him, and I could feel something I hadn't felt from him before. Nervousness.

"Look, I know you don't want to hurt me. I can see you're trying to make sure this isn't making things worse, and I appreciate it. I'm fine. I don't want you to be hesitant with me. You're fine. I want you to," I said in the dark room that had moonlight coming in from the street window.

"Okay," he said.

"Okay," I repeated.

That was all it took to initiate night number two of passionate, intense, incredibly intimate sex. As we lay there after, I thought about how truly gray this area really was. But even more so I wondered... what the fuck was I going to do once we went home?

Fuck Reality

(It's always still there no matter how far you run.)

DAY TWENTY-NINE

We woke up the next morning with the sound of heavy rain outside our window. After three days of sunshine and warmth, it was absolutely pouring. I had to admit, it was kind of nice looking out the bedroom window to see the town being showered with beautiful rainfall. It was cleansing and very metaphorical for our final full day in San Vito. Tomorrow, we would have a few hours in town before heading down to Palermo to catch a flight to Rome for the night. Then, the following day, it was back on a plane to the USA. I was *so* not ready to go home.

The town had literally closed up shop to wait out the rain. The streets were rushing with water, and it looked like you could canoe from place to place. There was loud thunder booming in the distance like a warning, saying, "Gabrielle, what the fuck are you doing having sex with him?" Obviously, I'm kidding. That's so overly dramatic. To be honest, it really wasn't all that complicated in that moment. We didn't act like a couple during the day, and we didn't kiss or hold hands. We were like best friends hanging out...who then went home and had wildly passionate sex. Totally normal, right?

Once the rain stopped, we headed down the street to the same delicious crepe place we had gone the day before. We both got lattés, and I got the same incredible dessert meal. We sat out on the patio and talked about what we planned to do once we got home. He whipped out his phone and started videoing me eating my crepe. I laughed as I stuffed a giant piece into my mouth for the video. He laughed and made a growling munching sound, which made me laugh with a mouth full of food.

"And you broke the knife! Look at this, disgusting," he said, filming the plate with the flimsy plastic knife I had most definitely snapped. In my defense, it would have snapped trying to cut through pudding.

"You only live once," I said into the camera.

"What?!" he exclaimed. We both were cracking up. Over the last four days it had become a running joke that I had now become the fat ass and he was in shape. Even as sexy as he was, he'd most definitely had a semi dad bod when we started dating, and I had been rocking my recently divorced body. To clarify, I was not at all fat at this point, but I definitely had put on a solid five pounds and was not giving two shits about what I was eating. I would worry about it when I got home. Apparently, I was putting most things into the "worry about it once you get home" category. Luckily, I was a confident woman and wasn't affected by the dozens of comments from Javier about how much I was eating or the fact that I now had slightly more to grab onto. Jabs like this and sarcasm were his weird way of flirting. Like I said, emotional capacity of a five-year-old. I mean, remember the kids on the playground who would poke you with a stick because they liked you? Yeah, there you go.

"So, what have you learned on this trip that doesn't involve me?" He chuckled as he asked. While I saw the humor in the question, I couldn't help but scoff at it. First of all, it's not like I doodled Javier's name on my notebook and then obsessed over the fact that he didn't ask me to prom. We had a really intense, full force, zero to one hundred whirlwind of a relationship that ended in really shocking heartbreak, all of which happened immediately after a really blindsiding divorce. So while many of my lessons were deep-rooted ones about myself, yeah, many of them stemmed from things that had to do with him. What, now for the first time you suddenly *don't* want to be the center of attention? Please. Besides, all of the processing I had done and realizations I had come to around him went *way* deeper into personal things that stemmed from *long* before the tornado known as Javier swept through my life.

"Yeah. A lot," I answered, deciding to keep that inner dialogue to myself.

"Like what?"

"How to be by myself and be okay with that. That I can handle literally anything that gets thrown at me and how freaking strong I really am. And I started to figure out how to love myself...still figuring that one out," I answered.

"That's amazing, Gabs. I'm really happy you decided to go," he said genuinely. So was I.

After we finished our coffees, we headed back to the apartment just as it started to pour again. We opened the window to listen to the rain and plopped down on the bed to relax. That night everyone was planning on having one last big dinner together at a restaurant that belonged to the family of one of their friends.

We lay on the bed, listening to the weather outside, my head resting on his stomach. I was ready for a nap.

"Will you pet my head?" I asked. Having my head pet is one of my favorite things in the world. I swear, if I'm ever rich enough, I will have someone who literally will just hang out and pet my head. It's the best.

"Like this?" he asked, as he started to stroke my hair. I nodded as I closed my eyes. This serene moment lasted for about ten minutes until the entire energetic vibe had clearly shifted. His hand started rubbing my head more sensually, and my hand somehow made its way to rubbing his thigh. Other areas were soon being rubbed, until we found ourselves ripping each other's clothes off at four in the afternoon. I'm notoriously not the...*quietest* person when it comes to the bedroom, and our new housemate was napping right next door. Our window was also open to the street. We did our best and ultimately failed at not making too much noise. What can I say, the romantic rain of Italy took over? Not really. We just didn't care.

When we finished, I snuck into the shower, hoping our neighbor wasn't awake and in the apartment to see me running from our room to the bathroom naked. Success. I showered, and we both got ready for our last family dinner in San Vito. It was bittersweet.

A long table had been set up for our group at Ristorante Giardino Corallo. Our group of fourteen sat around speaking in Spanish, Italian, Portuguese, and occasionally English. I had become used to not understanding chunks of conversations early on when Javier and his friends would speak in Spanish. It didn't really bother me. I liked hearing the different languages and the culture that emanated from them. I sat next to Vincenzo and Alvaro. I had become close with both of them, and I was so fond of the witty banter we had all created with each other. Course after course of amazing dishes came to the table, and everyone sipped on wine and enjoyed each other's company.

Javier and I said our goodbyes to those we wouldn't be seeing the next day before leaving, and then headed back to the apartment.

"Do you care if I put a meditation on?" he asked as we got into bed.

"Not at all," I answered.

As the meditation played, I lay there with my thoughts. Again I had failed to say no to intimacy. But this time with Javier felt different. Why had I chosen to cross that boundary with him when I knew it was going to hurt my heart in the long run? Onion. Superficial thought?

• Our sex is amazing and we're in freaking Italy.

Yes, superficial indeed. However, it was so incredibly different than my other poor decisions in other countries. The connection we had was undeniable, and we both felt it when we were making love. It didn't feel like I was trying to protect myself. In fact, I consciously knew I was doing the opposite. So, what's the authentic thought?

• I can't help it, I'm fucking in love with him.

Well to be fair, put any female in a romantic apartment in a small town in Italy with a man she's in love with and see what happens. It's not like I suddenly wasn't wildly attracted to him. It was just flat out unfair. But I knew there was something much deeper underneath all of this. Subconscious thought?

- I love him so much that I want him in any way I can have him. Even if he can't give me what I want or deserve.

Oh. Fuck. That was profound and painful all at the same time. I knew that, for whatever reason, the man that I thought I would be having a life with woke up one day unable to give me what I want and what I deserve. Yet I was still willing to give him this part of myself because it meant I could hold on to what I had experienced for that month and a half. And that huge realization I'd had in Mykonos? *I know that this will keep them and therefore I won't be abandoned.* I was literally playing out a perfect example of it. Because I knew I could have him in that way. It wasn't just that I needed to love him *less*...I needed to love myself *more*. It was definitely not healthy. And it definitely wasn't okay.

I tried to quiet my mind. As I'm sure you're aware by now, my mind is rarely quiet, and that night was no exception. I *really* did not want to go home. Part of me genuinely considered just saying "fuck it" and picking a next place to go, but I knew that the cost of getting a different flight home and traveling in another few cities was way out of my budget. I had already been away from home for a month. So, although the idea of it was more than tempting, I knew it wasn't really a viable option. That's the funny thing about reality. No matter how far you try and run from it, it's always still waiting there to smack you right in the fucking face.

Fuck
Endings

(Even though you need them to have the new beginnings.)

DAY THIRTY

Waking up that final day in San Vito felt like reality had shown up to pour cold water all over me. I couldn't believe I had been on this trip for thirty days. It seemed as if it had gone by in the blink of an eye, but yet was the longest journey I had ever been on. I lay there for a while, trying to force my brain into accepting the fact that I was, indeed, going to be flying back to the USA tomorrow.

Javier and I got all of our things packed up and cleaned the apartment before we headed out for one last breakfast at the café down the street. He had come to know so many of the people in town so well, and I had gotten to know a few of them too. We sat on the patio and drank our last latté in Sicily.

"God, I'm really going to miss this place," he said.

"I know you are," I responded. I could tell he had really fallen in love with the town and the culture there. He was at peace in this place.

We finished our coffees and headed over to the library where Alvaro worked. It was a small book store that was exactly what you would expect in such a quaint little town. Outside was a trellis with vines weaving through. It shared a street with other colorful structures, all filled with character. Alvaro greeted us and we all chatted while I looked around. I picked out three postcards to add to my now substantial collection from the places I had been. I had grown so fond of Alvaro. He had an energy about him that showed you what a good human he was. We headed outside to the street in front of the shop.

"We have to take a picture here," I said, looking at the surroundings.

"I'll take it for you guys," Alvaro said. Javier and I swung our giant backpacks on and stood in the middle of the street side by side as Alvaro snapped a photo of us on our last day. We threw our stuff in Alvaro's car and walked down by the beach we had gone to the day I had arrived. Gio and another one of the Italians had come to meet us to say their farewells and get one last lunch together.

Right by the restaurant, there was a couple with a stand selling handmade jewelry. Their pieces were absolutely gorgeous, and I knew I wanted something to remember the final five days of my trip. I talked with the girl for a few minutes and learned they had traveled all the way from France selling their jewelry. Everything was handmade, and they could even custom make things while you waited. I settled on a dark brass ring that curled at the top and the bottom. It fit on the top half of my finger. It was so unique, and I instantly loved it. I decided to get a matching one to take back for Jess. She had been such a huge support to me the past three months, from staying at my house with me the two weeks Daniel was away to talking to me the entire time on my Europe trip, allowing me to vent about the situation with Javier. I was so thankful to have her. The second thing I decided on was a custom necklace with a double gold chain, one holding the om symbol and the other a tiger's eye stone wrapped in gold wire. I had lost one of my four stones in Amsterdam, and it had been the stone meant for balancing emotions.

"Tiger's eye is good for balance and emotion," the girl said in a thick French accent. Honestly, am I even surprised at this point? Of course it is.

While my necklace was being made, we went to a nearby restaurant and enjoyed our lunch out in the sunshine. It was a beautiful final day after the rain had cleared the night before. Yes, I too would miss this place.

After paying for my necklace, which I was absolutely in love with, we headed back to Alvaro's car, which would be taking us to Palermo. Palermo is at the very tip of Sicily and was about an hour and a half drive from San Vito. I gazed out the window and watched the ocean go by as we drove. It really was a beautiful place. I took out my phone and posted the photo Javier and I had taken earlier. It would be the first photo of just the two of us I had posted since everything had fallen apart. I wondered what certain people would think when they saw it—Jess, Emma, his sister, his mother, my friends back home, and all the people I had met on this crazy trip that I knew were now following my journey to see how it ended. I posted it with the caption: "Because in the end it only made sense to end this crazy journey with the one who started it all." For better or worse, it did.

We pulled into the airport drop-off and said our goodbyes to Alvaro.

"It was so good to meet you, and to have you here, Gabrielle," he said as he hugged me.

"I'm so happy I came. I can't thank you enough for everything," I responded.

"You are welcome anytime. Even without this idiot," he laughed, nodding at Javier. I stepped away a few feet for them to say their goodbyes. I knew how much Alvaro's friendship meant to Javier. He had been one of the main reasons he had wanted to come in the first place.

We headed inside and got checked in for the short one-hour flight from Palermo to Rome. Javier had booked an Airbnb the night before, and we were planning on settling in and grabbing one last dinner in Italy.

When we landed at the airport in Rome, I turned my phone on and a message from Chris popped up.

Chris: Send me some weekends you're free in October/November.

I instantly got a huge smile on my face. Seriously, this kid impressed me. We found our bags, along with the bus that was supposed to take us to the area where we were staying that night. After a short fifteen-minute ride, we hopped off and walked to where we would be spending our last night.

The woman who owned the Airbnb greeted us with a warm smile, and she and Javier immediately began to speak in Spanish. I swear, he can literally become instant friends with any person on the planet. She showed us our room, which was perfect for our one night there. After we got settled in, we headed out to a nearby restaurant. It was our last meal in Italy. Our last meal in Rome. Our last meal of this *trip*.

We sat on the front patio at a table away from the busyness of the restaurant, which was still quite alive for 10:30 p.m. I felt so many emotions sitting there, and I knew we were going to have another one of our heavy talks.

"So...what do you think was the most impactful part of your trip?" I asked. He paused for a moment.

"Probably talking with you," he answered. I looked at him a bit surprised. I wasn't expecting that answer.

"What do you mean?"

"I feel like the talks we had really made me see how poorly I handled this and made me realize things in my own life that I have to fix and work on," he answered.

"Good." Finally, I was seeing him take some accountability for... *something*.

"I'm really glad you came to San Vito. Really glad," he added.

"Me too," I agreed with a small smile that quickly turned into emotion.

"What?" he asked, seeing that there was something going on with me.

"I just really don't want to go home," I said. I had become a broken record.

"It'll be okay. Everything with the divorce is going to work out and everything will be fine." He tried to comfort me. What he didn't seem to understand was that it was more than just the hell of a divorce I was walking back into. It was the fact I knew I would be walking away from him.

"This has been insanely difficult on me, Javier," I said, and he knew I had switched from the divorce situation back to the one we were in.

"I know. I'm so sorry. You haven't deserved any of this," he replied.

"I'm just trying to figure out how to flip the switch to being best friends," I admitted. "It's just such a weird situation."

"I know," he agreed.

"We're going to need to have really good communication for this to work."

"Yes, absolutely. I know, and I'll definitely be better at that," he responded.

"I mean...I can confidently say that I want to be your friend. I know we'll always be a part of each other's lives. For whatever reason, we became each other's person so quickly," I said, trying to talk myself through my emotions while explaining them to him at the same time.

"So quickly. You are so important to me. You really changed my life."

"I just can't confidently say I'm going to be fine when I find out you're dating someone," I admitted honestly.

"Yeah," he said looking down. We were both aware what a weird and difficult situation we were in.

"I need you to know that certain things are going to stop when we go home," I said.

"What do you mean?"

"Like...I'm fully aware that I've wanted to sleep with you every night in Sicily. I know I'm going to sleep with you tonight...But when we go home, that can't happen anymore," I said firmly.

"I know," he said, although I'm sure it wasn't ideally what he wanted to hear.

"You don't deserve to have that from me," I added. Not that he had deserved it in Italy either.

"I know."

We talked about how hard everything had been on his end during this trip—how he felt no one could understand what he was experiencing or going through. I mean, hell, I definitely didn't, and neither did his mom or sister. At one point, I made a sarcastic jab at the fact that he broke my heart.

"How long am I going to have to pay for all this?" he asked. I had been mildly joking when I made the comment, but this struck me.

"Longer than a few days?" I suggested. God, he was such a typical male, already wanting his mistakes to be forgiven and forgotten. Unfortunately, neither he nor I knew how long my healing process would be.

"Sorry, I know. I just...I feel so bad," he said.

"Look. I don't want you to feel like you're constantly paying for what happened. That's not what I want. I'm just hurting and it's going to take some time. To have a healthy friendship is going to take some work."

"I know. And I'm willing to do that."

"So am I," I said.

We sat there for two and a half hours talking. Many times I had tears come and I let them. It was so interesting to me how open I was with my emotions with Javier. Daniel would always make me feel like I couldn't cry. Even the last six months together when we were in therapy, he would say, "I hate it when she cries. It feels fake, it makes me irritated, and I just want to get away from her." Who says something like that? Would you rather me scream and fight you instead of showing you that I am hurting? How incredibly sad that the person I was married to was so immune to my tears and had literally made me feel afraid to cry. Javier never made me feel that way.

At one point, there was a lull in the conversation and I looked at him.

"What?" he asked, seeing the question in my face.

"Nothing," I decided.

"No, what?"

"You don't have to answer this if you don't want to...I just...you never told me how everything happened with your brother," I said. He immediately froze. I could see the tears start to make their way to his eyes. "You don't have to tell me," I said again.

"No, I want to. I need to finally say it out loud," he said as he took a deep shaking breath. After a few long moments, he told me. Tears streamed down his face, as they did mine. I reached across the table and grabbed his hand. He clutched it like, if he didn't hold on, his heart was going to burst. "I haven't told anyone that since it happened," he said. In that moment, I was so many things at once: heartbroken for him, wanting to make everything go away, worried about him, but most of all, so incredibly *proud*. I was proud that he had said it out loud, proud that he had taken a step, and proud that it was with me.

We closed down the restaurant, and then strolled back to the Airbnb. Our host was already asleep so we quietly got ready for bed. As I climbed into bed next to Javier, I knew this would be the last time we were ever going to be together in this way. I had told myself that once we went home all the intimacy had to stop. There was no way to have a friends-with-benefits relationship with someone you're in love with. Besides, we clearly know now that this had proven to be *anything* but casual. I put my head on his chest and silently thought about all this.

I reached over him to turn off the light that was on the nightstand. He grabbed my arm as I reached for it.

"Stop," he said, pulling me back down, "I want to see you."

We made love for the last time that night in Rome. It was a mixture of sensual connection and rough passion. There were times we were kissing deeply and looking into each other's eyes, and times he threw me up against the wall and pulled my hair. It was a flood of so many different emotions.

"Say my name," I exhaled.

"Gabrielle..." he responded.

It was intimate, animalistic, connected, and heartbreaking—all at the same time. Because I knew that after that night, I would not allow myself to give up a part of me just to hold on to him. It was time to love myself more than that. It was time to choose me.

Javier fell asleep within minutes, as he usually did. Again, I hate people with that type of talent. I would literally give anything to be able to shut my brain off and sleep that easily. Me? I didn't sleep. Not like, "Oh, I slept an hour or dozed off here and there." No, I didn't sleep at all. At 4 a.m., I gave up and picked up my phone. I had a text from Javier's mom.

Ana: How are you?

If you only knew...

Me: Javier and I had a really long important conversation at dinner tonight. So I feel like I've gotten as much closure as possible.

Have I? Or am I just kidding myself?

Ana: Sorry to hear the word "closure," deep down I was waiting for something different.

Yeah. You and me both.

Me: I hope you know when I say closure, I mean answers I needed from him to be able to try and switch my feelings from what they've been to friendship feelings. Not by any means has that actually happened. We talked a lot tonight about how it will be tricky to navigate things in the future. He does fully understand how he handled things the wrong way and owned up to a lot and apologized. Ultimately, I shouldn't have to jump through hoops for who I'm supposed to be with. Which I know you know. It's just time to let everything settle and whatever may be in the future will be.

There's that damn "in the future" thought. Ugh, go away.

Ana: You are so right. I hope you can move on without feeling down, not sure how to explain it. There is no fault from your part, you are worth it, you deserve 100 percent.

That was one thing I did know. None of this that had happened was my fault. All I did was jump in, head first, heart open.

272

Me: It has shaped me into a better woman, nonetheless. I told him tonight, if for nothing else, it made me realize what real love, and more importantly, selfless love feels like. It was all worth it just for that. Because I will never be able to settle after this.

That thought was empowering and terrifying all at the same time.

I lay there in bed with my thoughts, knowing my alarm would be going off in an hour. That last thought was so interesting to me. I wouldn't be able to settle after this. I had always been in relationships and, whenever they ended, I would always (in one way or another) know that someone and something else was on its way. This was the first time that I genuinely felt...*scared*. Scared that I may not find something that would measure up to what this had been for that month and a half. Scared that I would be comparing everyone to Javier, and everything to what I had been feeling. And ultimately, scared that I wasn't going to be okay.

The other thought that kept popping in was how everyone this entire trip had told me, "You just need to focus on yourself." Yeah, I get it on a surface level, but why did I feel like I was so incapable of doing something so simple? There was enough time before my alarm to make my way through one more Thought Onion in Rome. What's the superficial thought?

• I have to focus on myself.

Yes, clearly we've established that, Gabrielle. That's *all* everyone has been in total agreement with since this all went down in the first place. So, what's the authentic thought beyond that?

• I can't let myself get pulled back into this when I go home.

Interesting. We had made it pretty clear that we were going to be "best friends" (why do I want to roll my eyes every time I use that phrase?), so why was I worried about getting pulled back into *something*? What is the subconscious thought underneath it all?

- I have given up a part of myself to take care of him.

Bingo. Big-time fucking bingo. From the moment he called me, telling me about the grief he was feeling, I had been by his side, sitting with him while he cried, talking him through solutions, coming when he needed me, and backing off when he needed space. I had allowed him to keep me on this limbo roller coaster throughout this entire trip, all the while defending and protecting him and constantly worrying about if *he* was okay. When was I going to worry about the fact that *I* was not okay? I kept hearing his words in my head. "You are so important to me. You've changed my life. I can't not have you in my life." Had I even stopped to consider if I was capable of giving him everything he *now* wanted as a best friend without getting any of the things I signed up for in the first place? Or was I just *that* scared of losing him that I would put myself through more pain to keep this person in my life? My life had changed in the last three months. I mean *really* changed, and he was a huge part of that. I couldn't really picture not having him in my life. Because, through all the love, all the heartbreak, all the bullshit...he really had become my best friend. What a fucking predicament, Gabrielle.

* * * * *

DAY THIRTY-ONE

My alarm went off and we got ready to head out. After saying good-bye to the sweet lady who had hosted us for the night, we walked down to the bus that went to the airport. Once we checked in, we grabbed breakfast and killed time before our ten-hour flight, which would then be followed by a second five-hour flight.

"It's so crazy how everything happens for a reason," I said. I had always been a believer of that, but the last thirty days had been a huge reinforcement of that belief. To start, one of the biggest challenges of my entire life has been being able to be okay by myself—and this trip literally forced me to face that head on. Even the way that every location ended up unfolding. I started in London with Emma where

I felt safe and had the comfort of my friend. Then in Amsterdam I stepped a little further out of comfort, staying with a stranger but one who was maternal, lovely, and was a family friend of a friend. Finally, I stepped out fully on my own in my first hostel experience. You know what I learned? That no matter where I went, I was protected, taken care of, and *fully* okay by myself.

But it went even deeper than that. So many little things along the way directed me to everything I did and everyone I met. If I hadn't gone on the pub crawl in Amsterdam, I wouldn't have ever met Yeung. It was only because of our night out in the Red Light District that I was convinced to go to the random peep show where I met Jason. If I hadn't met Jason I would have never ended up in Mykonos with Marcus. Picking the specific hostel in Barcelona was the only reason I met the group of people I became so close with. That was where I had felt supported and empowered for the first time on my trip. That was where I met Chris, and that was where I first healed a little bit. If I had chosen the party hostel in Rome over the much more mellow one, I would not have processed everything, taken myself to dinners, gotten drunk by myself, and texted Javier what would ultimately be the driving force that got me to San Vito. If I hadn't ended up in San Vito, I wouldn't have gotten any type of answers. I wouldn't have been on the beach to hold him when he broke down on his brother's birthday. I wouldn't have ended this trip how it began. Every, single, decision led me to somewhere I needed to be, to someone I needed to meet, or taught me something I needed to learn.

Sitting in the airport, I didn't feel so small anymore. In fact, I felt a newfound strength and purpose. After all I had survived, all the fears I'd faced, and all I had learned about myself—I felt pretty freaking big. I felt a power in knowing that I was meant to be here. I mean, if 2017 didn't kill me, I must have quite a bit of important work left to do in this lifetime.

This entire journey had quite literally forced me to give up control—control of plans, control of Javier's sudden change of heart, control of what I *thought* life should look like. I had lived twenty-eight years in control, and this trip had reset my inner wiring. And you know what? I felt fucking *free*. The only control I really have is what

I choose to do and how I choose to react. As long as my heart is in alignment with those two things, everything else will fall into place as it should. I guess parts of *The Four Agreements* resonated with me more than I first thought.

What about loving myself? Well, this entire trip I had been searching for a *how* instead of going *inside*. After all, it is called loving *myself*. So, as I sat there in the airport with my newfound self, I asked...well...myself, *what do you need to be happy*? And just like that, without me even knowing it, I had begun to love myself. I didn't have a huge revelation or an "aha!" moment. I simply started to take care of who I should have been taking care of this whole time. Me.

As for my recurring abandonment wounds? They clearly had been ripped wide open by both Daniel and Javier. I had been dealing with this issue since I was a six-year-old girl who walked in to find her father dead on the floor. But, on this solo trip, after all the Thought Onions, what I learned was this: I'm never truly abandoned—because I will *never* fucking abandon myself.

Did I have *all* the answers going home? No. Did I feel 100 percent clear on where Javier and I stood or what the future held? Not particularly. Was I miraculously healed from all the bullshit beatdowns life had thrown at me over the past three months? Probably not. But you know what? I was a different fucking person. *For the better*. I had learned more about myself in three months than I had in twenty-eight years. I knew stepping on that plane that I would *never* let someone treat me less than I deserved—that I was stronger than I *ever* imagined—and that no matter what, I would *always* be okay.

The night before, while I wasn't sleeping, I had snapped a picture of the inside of my journal. It had the title of my book, my passport, the necklace and ring I had gotten in San Vito, the brass ring from London, my three stones, and a Polaroid of Javier and I that we had taken in Sicily. This would be the final picture I posted on this crazy journey. As we boarded the plane home, I posted it. It read:

> This trip has been one of the most emotional, incredible, fulfilling, and life-changing experiences of my life. In the last three and a half months, I was

hit with a divorce, love, heartbreak, fear, loss, and insurmountable uncertainty. I knew I had to decide to face things that I have run from my entire life and choose to embrace all the things that were happening 'to' me. While I have always been a huge believer that everything happens for a reason, and I could clearly see why it was all happening, I couldn't understand why the reasons hurt so badly. Sitting with my mother on September 3rd, she looked at me with tears in her eyes and said, 'You don't have to go, baby.' And I responded, 'Yes I do.' Mommy, you will forever be my person. The people I have been with and met on this journey will never really know what an imprint they've had on my life. Emma, for being the first person to open her arms when everything changed. Being able to start this terrifying leap with one of my best friends was so invaluable. Ineke for taking care of me like her daughter and giving me a sanctuary to begin to heal in. My Amsterdam crew. The Jersey girls, Cally, Yeung, and Travis. Timothée and Alice for giving me comfort in a city I didn't know. My Barcelona family. Quincy for being my first friend at Pars Tailor's. The Torontos for making me feel way cooler than I really am and checking up on me the rest of my trip. Mallory for being so open and beautiful to be around. Karly for being so strong and courageous, you inspired us all. Rhonda, for making me feel like Beyoncé and empowering me more than you know. Alejandro and Damian for being so fun and loving to all of us: Alejandro you will be forever in my heart. Jacob for becoming such a good friend...drunk convos and all. And Chris, for being the person who really helped me start to heal. You will never know how you affected my heart—in the best way. Jason, for turning from the carefree kid to the person who became my partner in crime...you are so much wiser than you think. The Vodka Soda Boys and their spontaneous fun that made Mykonos what it was. Marcus, for being so much more with me than you ever care to let people see. Sophia, and your mother, for never allowing me to feel lost or alone. And Javier, for not only being the catalyst to this entire journey... but for being someone who my soul will always love, and a friend I will have for life. And for all of you that have been following this insane journey, I hope you see that you can truly overcome anything and choose the life you deserve. Everything has changed, and yet I am more me than I have ever been...What. A fucking. Trip.

Epilogue

While I had begun to scratch the surface of the concept of loving myself, I can't tell you that I fully and truly realized how to do it on my grand European adventure. This monumental discovery came well after my return home, after more heartache, gallons of tears, and a shit-ton of soul searching. I now know fully and completely how to love myself. I do it every day, and I preach it to my friends, family, and anyone who will listen. It has changed my life, and I would like to share that with you all. So here it is.

Make yourself a cocktail. Really, Gabrielle? No, not the type where you'll have a hangover of regret the next day—a self-love cocktail. Just like the Thought Onion, this is a trick that I now live by. The self-love cocktail. Let me explain...

What makes you happy? What brings you joy? What are the things that *you can control* that contribute to your happiness? For me, it is eating right, going to the gym, meditating, creating, and dancing. Those things are what make my soul *happy*. So go ahead, right now, and make your own list.

Now that you have your ingredients, it's time to make your cocktail. Some days you will only be able to give yourself a few of your ingredients. It will be a stiffer drink—vodka and olives. Be compassionate with yourself; you have to start somewhere. For me it was eating right and going to the gym. I needed to commit to giving that to myself...*every, single, day*. After I had built my tolerance up, I moved on to a cocktail with a few more fun elements: a base of healthy eating and gym time with a splash of meditation. I forced myself to continually give myself these things that I knew made me feel good and happy. After a while, I was having the full-on fancy mixology cocktail. Two parts healthy eating, one part gym. A splash of meditation garnished with dancing, shaken and poured over a whole shit-ton of creating.

It seems so simple doesn't it? I kept saying "I don't know how to love myself," when all I had to do was *give the things that I love to myself.* The more you give your soul the things that make you happy, the better you will feel, and without even realizing it, *you are loving yourself.*

I now have a self-love cocktail every day. Is my life completely perfect and figured out? Hell no...didn't you just read what a shit show my world can be? But you know what? I love the freaking *hell* out of myself.

So there you have it. Write out your ingredients. Make a cocktail. *And drink that shit every single day.*

Acknowledgements

The biggest thank you to my mother for always being the one constant in my life—you are my hero. Kelly, for all your guidance. Nick and Michele for all your work and help. Sam, your continued support and belief mean so much to me. Randileigh, for your selfless and wonderful work. Paul, for being in my corner. Every single person that went on this crazy journey with me and has cheered me on ever since. My girlfriends who are always there to hear about everything and love me through it all. And Tay, for being my unicorn.

Quoted Material

Kevyn Aucoin
"Today I choose life. Every morning when I wake up I can choose joy, happiness, negativity, pain...To feel the freedom that comes from being able to continue to make mistakes and choices—today I choose to feel life, not to deny my humanity, but embrace it."

Alan Cohen
"It takes a lot of courage to release the familiar and seemingly secure, to embrace the new. But there is no real security in what is no longer meaningful. There is more security in the adventurous and exciting, for in movement there is life and in change there is power."

C.G. Jung
"Until you make the unconscious conscious, it will direct your life and you will call it fate."

A.R. Lucas
"If there's even a slight chance at getting something that will make you happy, risk it. Life's too short and happiness is too rare."